CHEVROLET CAMARO & Z-28 1973-1981

Compiled by
R.M. Clarke

ISBN 1 870642 309

Distributed by
Brooklands Book Distribution Ltd.
'Holmerise', Seven Hills Road,
Cobham, Surrey, England

Printed in Hong Kong

BROOKLANDS BOOKS

BROOKLANDS BOOKS SERIES

AC Ace & Aceca 1953-1983
AC Cobra 1962-1969
Alfa Romeo Alfasud 1972-1984
Alfa Romeo Alfetta Coupes GT.GTV.GTV6 1974-1987
Alfa Romeo Guilias Berlinettas
Alfa Romeo Giulia Berlinas 1962-1976
Alfa Romeo Giulia Coupés 1963-1976
Alfa Romeo Spider 1966-1987
Aston Martin Gold Portfolio 1972-1985
Austin Seven 1922-1982
Austin A30 & A35 1951-1962
Austin Healey 100 1952-1959
Austin Healey 3000 1959-1967
Austin Healey 100 & 3000 Collection No. 1
Austin Healey 'Frogeye' Sprite Collection No. 1
Austin Healey Sprite 1958-1971
Avanti 1962-1983
BMW Six Cylinder Coupés 1969-1975
BMW 1600 Collection No. 1
BMW 2002 1968-1976
Bristol Cars Gold Portfolio 1946-1985
Buick Automobiles 1947-1960
Buick Riviera 1963-1978
Cadillac Automobiles 1949-1959
Cadillac Automobiles 1960-1969
Cadillac Eldorado 1967-1978
Cadillac in the Sixties No. 1
Camaro 1966-1970
Chevrolet Camaro & Z-28 1973-1981
High Performance Camaros 1982-1988
Chevrolet Camaro Collection No. 1
Chevrolet 1955-1957
Chevrolet Impala & SS 1958-1971
Chevrolet & SS 1964-1972
Chevy II Nova & SS 1962-1973
Chrysler 300 1955-1970
Citroen Traction Avant 1934-1957
Citroen DS & ID 1955-1875
Citroen 2CV 1949-1982
Cobras & Replicas 1962-1983
Cortina 1600E & GT 1967-1970
Corvair 1959-1968
Daimler Dart & V-8 250 1959-1969
Datsun 240z 1970-1973
Datsun 280Z & ZX 1975-1983
De Tomaso Collection No. 1
Dodge Charger 1966-1974
Excalibur Collection No. 1
Ferrari Cars 1946-1956
Ferrari Cars 1962-1966
Ferrari Cars 1969-1973
Ferrari Dino 1965-1974
Ferrari Dino 308 1974-1979
Ferrari 308 & Mondial 1980-1984
Ferrari Collection No. 1
Fiat-Bertone X1/9 1973-1988
Fiat Pininfarina 124+2000 Spider 1968-1985
Ford Falcon 1960-1970
Ford Mustang 1964-1967
Ford Mustang 1967-1973
High Performance Mustangs 1982-1988
Ford RS Escort 1968-1980
Honda CRX 1983-1987
High Performance Escorts MkI 1968-1974
High Performance Escorts MkII 1975-1980
Hudson & Railton Cars 1936-1940
Jaguar Cars 1957-1961
Jaguar Cars 1961-1964
Jaguar Cars 1964-1968
Jaguar MK2 1959-1969
Jaguar E-Type 1961-1966
Jaguar E-Type 1966-1971
Jaguar E-Type V12 1971-1975
Jaguar XKE Collection No. 1
Jaguar XJ6 1968-1972
Jaguar XJ6 Series II 1973-1979
Jaguar XJ6 & XJ12 Series III 1979-1985
Jaguar XJ12 1972-1980
Jaguar XJS 1975-1980
Jensen Cars 1946-1967
Jensen Cars 1967-1979
Jensen Interceptor Gold Portfolio 1966-1986
Lamborghini Cars 1964-1970
Lamborghini Cars 1970-1975
Lamborghini Countach Collection No. 1
Lamborghini Countach & Urraco 1974-1980
Lamborghini Countach & Jalpa 1980-1985
Lancia Stratos 1972-1985
Land Rover 1948-1973
Land Rover Series II & IIa 1958-1971
Land Rover Series III 1971-1985
Lotus Cortina 1963-1970
Lotus Elan 1962-1973
Lotus Elan Collection No. 1
Lotus Elan Collection No. 2
Lotus Elite 1957-1964
Lotus Elite & Eclat 1974-1981
Lotus Turbo Esprit 1980-1986
Lotus Europa 1966-1975
Lotus Europa Collection No. 1
Lotus Seven 1957-1980
Lotus Seven Collection No. 1
Maserati 1965-1970
Maserati 1970-1975
Mazda RX-7 Collection No. 1
Mercedes 190 & 300SL 1954-1963
Mercedes 230/250/280SL 1963-1971
Mercedes 350/450SL & SLC 1971-1980
Mercedes Benz Cars 1949-1954
Mercedes Benz Cars 1954-1957
Mercedes Benz Cars 1957-1961
Mercedes Benz Competition Cars 1950-1957

Metropolitan 1954-1962
MG Cars 1929-1934
MG TC 1945-1949
MG TD 1949-1953
MG TF 1953-1955
MG Cars 1957-1959
MG Cars 1959-1962
MG Midget 1961-1980
MGA Collection No. 1
MGA Roadsters 1955-1962
MGB Roadsters 1962-1980
MGB GT 1965-1980
Mini Cooper 1961-1971
Morgan Cars 1960-1970
Morgan Cars 1969-1979
Morris Minor Collection No. 1
Old's Cutlass & 4-4-2 1964-1972
Oldsmobile Toronado 1966-1978
Opel GT 1968-1973
Pantera 1970-1973
Pantera & Mangusta 1969-1974
Plymouth Barracuda 1964-1974
Pontiac Fiero 1984-1988
Pontiac GTO 1964-1970
Pontiac Firebird 1967-1973
Pontiac Firebird and Trans-Am 1973-1981
High Performance Firebirds 1982-1988
Pontiac Tempest & GTO 1961-1965
Porsche Cars 1960-1964
Porsche Cars 1964-1968
Porsche Cars 1968-1972
Porsche Cars in the Sixties
Porsche Cars 1972-1975
Porsche 356 1952-1965
Porsche 911 Collection No. 1
Porsche 911 Collection No. 2
Porsche 911 1965-1969
Porsche 911 1970-1972
Porsche 911 1973-1977
Porsche 911 Carrera 1973-1977
Porsche 911 SC 1978-1983
Porsche 911 Turbo 1975-1984
Porsche 914 1969-1975
Porsche 914 Collection No. 1
Porsche 924 1975-1981
Porsche 928 Collection No. 1
Porsche 944 1981-1985
Porsche Turbo Collection No. 1
Reliant Scimitar 1964-1986
Rolls Royce Silver Cloud 1955-1965
Rolls Royce Silver Shadow 1965-1980
Range Rover 1970-1981
Rover P4 1949-1959
Rover P4 1955-1964
Rover 2000 + 2200 1963-1977
Rover 3500 1968-1977
Rover 3500 & Vitesse 1976-1986
Saab Sonett Collection No. 1
Saab Turbo 1976-1983
Singer Sports Cars 1933-1934
Studebaker Hawks & Larks 1956-1963
Sunbeam Alpine & Tiger 1959-1967
Thunderbird 1955-1957
Thunderbird 1958-1963
Thunderbird 1964-1976
Toyota MR2 1984-1988
Triumph 2000-2.5-2500 1963-1977
Triumph Spitfire 1962-1980
Triumph Spitfire Collection No. 1
Triumph Stag 1970-1980
Triumph Stag Collection No. 1
Triumph TR2 & TR3 1952-1960
Triumph TR4.TR5.TR250 1961-1968
Triumph TR6 1969-1976
Triumph TR6 Collection No. 1
Triumph TR7 & TR8 1975-1982
Triumph GT6 1966-1974
Triumph Vitesse & Herald 1959-1971
TVR Gold Portfolio 1959-1988
Volkswagen Cars 1936-1956
VW Beetle 1956-1977
VW Beetle Collection No. 1
VW Golf GTi 1976-1986
VW Karmann Ghia 1955-1982
VW Scirocco 1974-1981
VW Bus-Camper-Van 1954-1967
VW Bus-Camper-Van 1968-1979
Volvo 1800 1960-1973
Volvo 120 Series 1956-1970

BROOKLANDS MUSCLE CARS SERIES

American Motors Muscle Cars 1966-1970
Buick Muscle Cars 1965-1970
Camaro Muscle Cars 1966-1972
Capri Muscle Cars 1969-1983
Chevrolet Muscle Cars 1966-1972
Dodge Muscle Cars 1967-1970
Mercury Muscle Cars 1966-1971
Mini Muscle Cars 1961-1979
Mopar Muscle Cars 1964-1967
Mopar Muscle Cars 1968-1971
Mustang Muscle Cars 1967-1971
Shelby Mustang Muscle Cars 1965-1970
Oldsmobile Muscle Cars 1964-1970
Plymouth Muscle Cars 1966-1971
Pontiac Muscle Cars 1966-1972
Muscle Cars Compared 1966-1971
Muscle Cars Compared Book 2 1965-1971

BROOKLANDS ROAD & TRACK SERIES

Road & Track on Alfa Romeo 1949-1963

Road & Track on Alfa Romeo 1964-1970
Road & Track on Alfa Romeo 1971-1976
Road & Track on Alfa Romeo 1977-1984
Road & Track on Aston Martin 1962-1984
Road & Track on Auburn Cord & Duesenberg 1952-1984
Road & Track on Audi 1952-1980
Road & Track on Audi 1980-1986
Road & Track on Austin Healey 1953-1970
Road & Track on BMW Cars 1966-1974
Road & Track on BMW Cars 1975-1978
Road & Track on BMW Cars 1979-1983
Road & Track on Cobra, Shelby &
  Ford GT40 1962-1983
Road & Track on Corvette 1953-1967
Road & Track on Corvette 1968-1982
Road & Track on Corvette 1982-1986
Road & Track on Datsun Z 1970-1983
Road & Track on Ferrari 1950-1968
Road & Track on Ferrari 1968-1974
Road & Track on Ferrari 1975-1981
Road & Track on Ferrari 1981-1984
Road & Track on Fiat Sports Cars 1968-1987
Road & Track on Jaguar 1950-1960
Road & Track on Jaguar 1961-1968
Road & Track on Jaguar 1968-1974
Road & Track on Jaguar 1974-1982
Road & Track on Lamborghini 1964-1985
Road & Track on Lotus 1972-1981
Road & Track on Maserati 1952-1974
Road & Track on Maserati 1975-1983
Road & Track on Mazda RX7 1978-1986
Road & Track on Mercedes 1952-1962
Road & Track on Mercedes 1963-1970
Road & Track on Mercedes 1971-1979
Road & Track on Mercedes 1980-1987
Road & Track on MG Sports Cars 1949-1961
Road & Track on MG Sports Cars 1950-1980
Road & Track on Mustang 1964-1977
Road & Track on Peugeot 1955-1986
Road & Track on Pontiac 1960-1983
Road & Track on Porsche 1951-1967
Road & Track on Porsche 1968-1971
Road & Track on Porsche 1972-1975
Road & Track on Porsche 1975-1978
Road & Track on Porsche 1979-1982
Road & Track on Porsche 1982-1985
Road & Track on Rolls Royce & Bentley 1950-1965
Road & Track on Rolls Royce & Bentley 1966-1984
Road & Track on Saab 1955-1985
Road & Track on Toyota Sports & G T Cars 1966-1986
Road & Track on Triumph Sports Cars 1953-1967
Road & Track on Triumph Sports Cars 1967-1974
Road & Track on Triumph Sports Cars 1974-1982
Road & Track on Volkswagen 1951-1968
Road & Track on Volkswagen 1968-1978
Road & Track on Volkswagen 1978-1985
Road & Track on Volvo 1957-1974
Road & Track on Volvo 1975-1985

BROOKLANDS CAR AND DRIVER SERIES

Car and Driver on BMW 1955-1977
Car and Driver on BMW 1977-1985
Car and Driver on Cobra, Shelby & Ford GT40
  1963-1984
Car and Driver on Datsun Z 1600 & 2000
  1966-1984
Car and Driver on Corvette 1956-1967
Car and Driver on Corvette 1968-1977
Car and Driver on Corvette 1978-1982
Car and Driver on Ferrari 1955-1962
Car and Driver on Ferrari 1963-1975
Car and Driver on Ferrari 1976-1983
Car and Driver on Mopar 1956-1967
Car and Driver on Mopar 1968-1975
Car and Driver on Pontiac 1961-1975
Car and Driver on Porsche 1955-1962
Car and Driver on Porsche 1963-1970
Car and Driver on Porsche 1970-1976
Car and Driver on Porsche 1977-1981
Car and Driver on Porsche 1982-1986
Car and Driver on Saab 1956-1985
Car and Driver on Volvo 1955-1986

BROOKLANDS MOTOR & THOROUGHBRED & CLASSIC CAR SERIES

Motor & T & CC on Ferrari 1966-1976
Motor & T & CC on Ferrari 1976-1984
Motor & T & CC on Lotus 1979-1983
Motor & T & CC on Morris Minor 1948-1983

BROOKLANDS PRACTICAL CLASSICS SERIES

Practical Classics on Austin A 40 Restoration
Practical Classics on Henry Manney At Large & Abroad
Practical Classics on Land Rover Restoration
Practical Classics on Metalworking in Restoration
Practical Classics on Midget/Sprite Restoration
Practical Classics on Mini Cooper Restoration
Practical Classics on MGB Restoration
Practical Classics on Morris Minor Restoration
Practical Classics on Triumph Herald/Vitesse
Practical Classics on Triumph Spitfire Restoration
Practical Classics on VW Beetle Restoration
Practical Classics on 1930S Car Restoration

BROOKLANDS MILITARY VEHICLES SERIES

Allied Military Vehicles Collection No. 1
Allied Military Vehicles Collection No. 2
Dodge Military Vehicles Collection No. 1
Military Jeeps 1941-1945
Off Road Jeeps 1944-1971
V W Kubelwagen 1940-1975

BROOKLANDS BOOKS

CONTENTS

BROOKLANDS BOOKS

ACKNOWLEDGEMENTS

Brooklands Books are reference books and are produced for owners wishing to know more about their cars, for restorers as a guide to what their vehicle was capable of when it left the manufacturers and for historians who wish to plot the progress of a particular model.   The copyright of the information they contain belongs to the publishers of the original journals.   They understand the needs of enthusiasts and for many years have generously allowed their road tests and other articles to be made available once again in this form.

Some 10,000 stories can be located within our 300 titles. They cover in the main afford-able post-WWII vehicles that can be bought, enjoyed and cherished by ordinary people.

Brooklands have reported on the Camaro's progress from its earliest days firstly in Camaro 1966-1970 which we published in 1979 and then more recently in Camaro Collection No. 1 with different stories covering much of the same period.

Our third title on this popular pony-car Camaro Muscle Cars 1966-1972 dealt with the more powerful Super Sport and Z-28 versions which were much sought-after before the oil crisis of the early seventies, and are now in great demand again.

We turned our attention to the '80's models earlier this year and released High Per-formance Camaros 1982-1988 covering the Z-28s plus the IROC and Rally Sport Cars.

We now complete our 22 years of Camaro coverage with this book, which means that over a 120 stories are currently available for those that take an interest in this successful marque.

We know that Camaro devotees will wish to join with us in thanking the management of Autocar, Car and Driver, Hot Rod, Motor Manual, Motor Trend, Road & Track, R & T Specials, Road Test and Small Cars for their continued support.

R.M. Clarke

CAMARO TYPE LT Z-28

With a pricetag that's actually decreased, it's a blue chip investment in a world of inflation

• Hang on for a surprise, you automotive bargain hunters. We've found a car with a pricetag that has actually *dwindled* in the past two years. In a day when your butcher must check credit references before he'll fork over a pound of ground sirloin, that's indeed a noteworthy discovery. What's more, this warp in the pricing structure belongs to a car any enthusiast can embrace: a Z-28 Camaro.

How could it be, you ask. Has Chevrolet suddenly declared a fire sale on its sporty car? Maybe you suspect the Z-28's vibrant small-block V-8 has been replaced by a Blue Flame Six to shrink manufacturing costs. The truth is that Chevrolet for 1973 offers the same Z-28 we've known and loved, with but a thin slice cut from the torque curve to undermine its *machismo*. And due to some equipment shuffling as well as a new model in the lineup this year, you end up spending less money for essentially the same car.

As proof of our claim, we refer you to a 1971 Camaro Z-28, (*C/D*, May 1971). If you add up a few key packages in that car, it is possible to make a direct comparison of costs with a current Phase IV priced Z-28. Total the items listed below and you have $4430.35 in 1971 dollars, or $4066.75 in today's money. That means a difference of $365.00, or almost all you'll need to upgrade your car with air conditioning.

1971

Base Camaro V-8	$3011.00
power steering	115.90
custom interior	115.90
sport steering wheel	15.80
Rally sport	179.05
Z-28 package	786.75
4-speed transmission	205.95
	total $4430.35

1973

Base Camaro Type LT	$3267.70
(includes custom interior, power steering, sport steering wheel and instrumentation package)	
Rally sport	97.00
Z-28 package	502.05
4-speed transmission	200.00
	total $4066.75

And from whence does this windfall come? The biggest chunk is of course the seven per cent Federal Excise Tax, deleted from new car prices since the fall of 1971. That amounts to about $290, which is still money in your pocket. The remaining $74 you could consider a rebate from Chevro-

5

let for the 30 horsepower drained during the past two years from under the hood.

Even with such compensations, there is a message. Camaros have not escalated in price during the past two years. In light of several ten-per cent-at-a-whack increases tacked on to imported cars, the Z-28 rises to a very appealing position—just by holding a firm price. It has been a $4000+ car all along, while imported competition—240Zs and Porsche 914s to name two—have long since blasted out of the $3000 range and are fast approaching the 5-grand bracket.

A large part of the Camaro's price advantage is due to the Type LT model, new for 1973. It is nothing more complicated than a plain Camaro flushed out with a few of the most popular past options . . . but the package is cheaper than the individual items added together. "Type LT" emblems on the sides of the car distinguish this version of the Camaro, which according to Chevrolet is tuned to the needs of Luxury Touring. That means a deluxe interior as standard equipment, along with such essentials as power steering and an instrumentation package. The only genuinely new element of the whole LT package is more effective sound insulation.

While you're bending your banker's ear with the 1973 Camaro's economic advantages, be sure not to forget the Z-28 option. It also costs you less in these days of Nixonomics, largely because it's much cheaper to build. That is especially true in conjunction with the LT package which preempts every bit of the Z-28's exterior identification. You still get all the heavy-duty chassis items with the Z-28: power brakes, sport suspension, positraction rear axle and F60-15 tires on 7-inch wheels. But now the engine is no more than a pale reminder of the vigor once behind every Z-28 badge. You should not revere it as the semi-racer powerplant it was in the high compression days of 1970. The solid lifter cam has left our midst for '73, as well as the Holley four-barrel carburetor and aluminum high-rise intake manifold. That lowers the power peak by 10 hp since last year, and the redline by 500 rpm.

Surprisingly enough, you don't feel the change on the drag strip. This year's heavier Camaro test car was within 0.10 seconds in the quarter-mile of the 1971 version we tested. And engineers at Chevrolet say our findings are in line with their test results. There are substantial performance variances from car to car due to production tolerances, but the engineers claim the fastest 1973 cars are every bit as strong as the fastest 1971 versions.

In fact, it was with very serious misgivings that Chevrolet allowed the premium components to go by the boards on the Z-28, for fear that the car's hard-earned reputation as a muscular sprinter would be tarnished. But when it came time to tool up for 1973, the wave of exhaust gas recirculation had irrevocably swept over Detroit. That prompted new intake manifolds for every engine, and the bean counters said an emphatic NO to a special one for the Z-28. So engine developers were left with last year's bulletproof four-bolt main bearing 350 cu. in. block and low restriction, 9.0-to-one compression ratio cylinder heads. But to crown that Wheaties-style base, Chevrolet chose a feeble intake system: a cast iron manifold and Rochester Quadrajet carburetor from the L48 engine—a low performance 350 cu. in. four-barrel motor. The new parts are definitely a step down from the Z-28's old induction system, and its reputation in the eyes of street racers will ebb accordingly. But the Chevrolet engineers were more objective, and you can be sure that there were countless dyno runs before the new hydraulic cam was finalized. Reports from the engine lab say the results were indeed encouraging. The new Z-28 engine has suffered at the high end, but

there's more torque at low engine speeds, so quarter-mile performance still stands at 1971 levels—the low 15s. One side benefit is the fact that the Z-28's asking price is now considerably cheaper (appoximately $90.00 less for 1973).

Where you lose out is in throttle response. The lightning-fast reflexes of the old Z-28 are but a memory. If you rudely mash the throttle these days, you'll very likely get an awkward stumble before the revs climb. Once you pass that transition, however, things are fine. The Z-28 is still happy with high rpm, even more so than Pontiac's brute motor, the SD-455.

But with 455 inches in a Firebird, there is never a shortage of low-end torque. That's not the case in a Camaro, because for 1973 there are no longer any big block engines to choose from. The Z-28 is now at the top of the horsepower *and* the

6

cubic inch ladder as far as Camaros are concerned. So whatever you can do to make that limited supply of torque work harder for you, the better off you are.

One way is to choose the wide-ratio 4-speed transmission. Admittedly, it would be the last choice for road racing, but street operation is another matter. There you need the lower first gear to get the car rolling smoothly without slipping the clutch. The Z-28 engine is no longer peaky, and its torque curve is about a mile wide, so it does not insist on tightly spaced gear ratios. In fact, for around town flexibility, you can't beat the wide ratio gear box.

Nor will you want to casually skim over the air conditioning line on the order blank. This is the first year that option is available with the Z-28 engine. In the past, warranty engineers feared incompatibility between the air conditioning compressor and the Z-28's penchant for high rpm. But now hydraulic lifters put an upper limit on the revs, and the rear end ratio is limited to a 3.42 with AC, so life is easier on engine-driven components.

And life is also more comfortable for the passengers. Chevrolet knew they were losing Z-28 customers in the southwest because air conditioning was not available. We feel it is particularly desirable for any part of the country because the Camaro's standard ventilating system has definite shortcomings. It is of flow-through design, with circulation augmented by a 4-speed blower. But before the air arrives at the passenger compartment, it is mysteriously heated to an uncomfortable

ACCELERATION standing ¼ mile, seconds

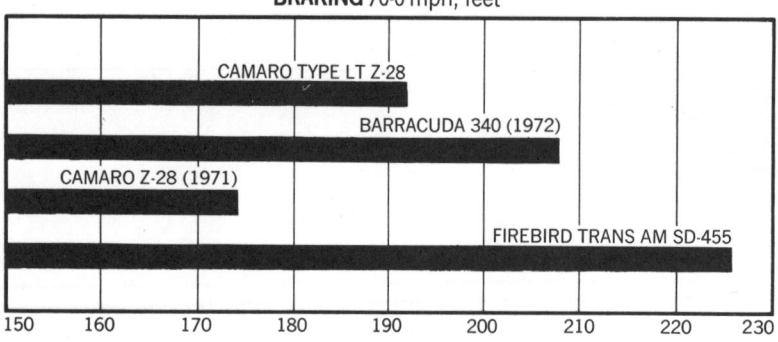

CAMARO TYPE LT Z-28	
BARRACUDA 340 (1972)	
CAMARO Z-28 (1971)	
FIREBIRD TRANS AM SD-455	

13 14 15 16 17 18 19 20 21

BRAKING 70-0 mph, feet

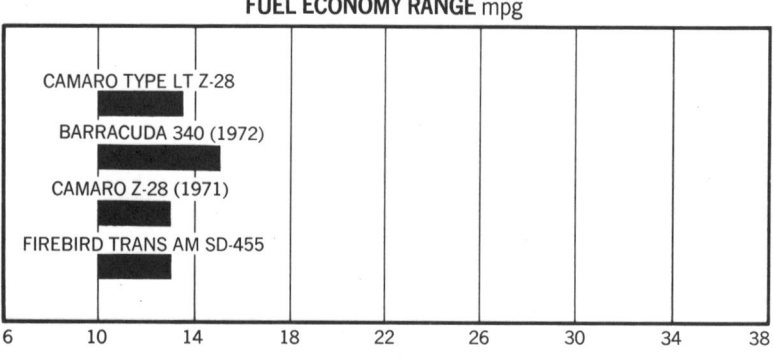

CAMARO TYPE LT Z-28	
BARRACUDA 340 (1972)	
CAMARO Z-28 (1971)	
FIREBIRD TRANS AM SD-455	

150 160 170 180 190 200 210 220 230

FUEL ECONOMY RANGE mpg

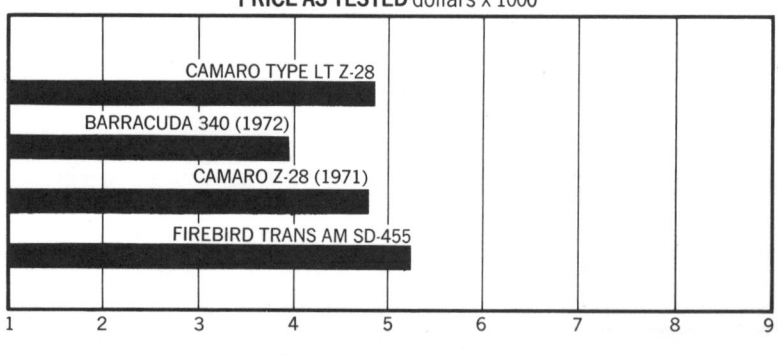

CAMARO TYPE LT Z-28	
BARRACUDA 340 (1972)	
CAMARO Z-28 (1971)	
FIREBIRD TRANS AM SD-455	

6 10 14 18 22 26 30 34 38

PRICE AS TESTED dollars x 1000

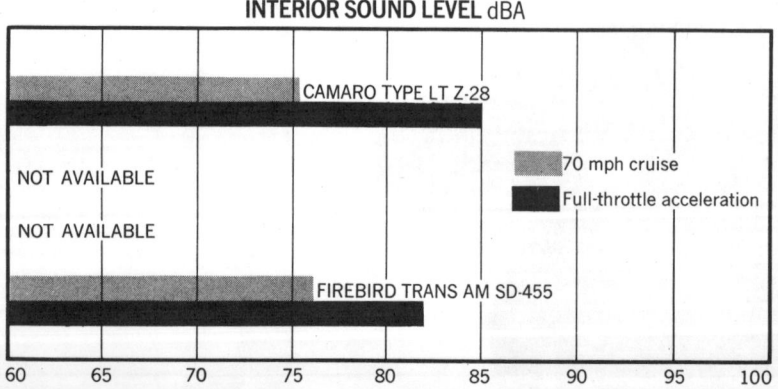

CAMARO TYPE LT Z-28	
BARRACUDA 340 (1972)	
CAMARO Z-28 (1971)	
FIREBIRD TRANS AM SD-455	

1 2 3 4 5 6 7 8 9

INTERIOR SOUND LEVEL dBA

CAMARO TYPE LT Z-28	
NOT AVAILABLE	
NOT AVAILABLE	
FIREBIRD TRANS AM SD-455	

■ 70 mph cruise
■ Full-throttle acceleration

60 65 70 75 80 85 90 95 100

CAMARO TYPE LT Z-28

Manufacturer: Chevrolet Motor Division
General Motors Corporation
Detroit, Michigan 48202

Vehicle type: Front engine, rear-wheel-drive, four-passenger, two-door coupe

Price as tested: $4855.25
(Manufacturer's suggested retail price, including all options listed below, dealer preparation and delivery charges, does not include state and local taxes, license or freight charges)

Options on test car: Base Camaro Type LT, $3267.70; Rally Sport, $97.00; Z-28 package, $502.05; 4-speed wide-ratio transmission, $200.00; air conditioning, $397.00; rear window defogger, $31.00; vanity mirror, $3.00; deluxe seat belts, $14.50; tinted glass, $39.00; light package, $15.00; AM/FM radio, $135.00; rear speaker, $15.00; adjustable seat back, $18.00; front and rear spoiler, $77.00; tilt steering wheel, $44.00

ENGINE
Type: V-8, water-cooled, cast iron block and heads, 5 main bearings
Bore x stroke . . . . 4.00 x 3.38 in, 101.6 x 88.4mm
Displacement . . . . 350 cu in, 5740cc
Compression ratio . . . . 9.0 to one
Carburetion . . . . 1 x 4-bbl, Rochester Quadrajet
Valve gear . . . Pushrod-operated overhead valves, hydraulic lifters
Power (SAE net) . . . . 245 bhp @ 5200 rpm
Torque (SAE net) . . . . 285 lbs-ft @ 4000 rpm
Specific power output . . . . 0.70 bhp/cu in, 42.7 bhp/liter
Max. recommended engine speed . . . . 6000 rpm

DRIVE TRAIN
Transmission . . . . 4-speed, all synchro
Final drive ratio . . . . 3.42 to one

Gear	Ratio	Mph/1000 rpm	Max. test speed
I	2.52	8.7	52 mph (6000 rpm)
II	1.88	11.6	70 mph (6000 rpm)
III	1.46	15.0	90 mph (6000 rpm)
IV	1.00	21.9	123 mph (5600 rpm)

DIMENSIONS AND CAPACITIES
Wheelbase . . . . 108.0 in
Track, F/R . . . . 61.3/60.0 in
Length . . . . 188.5 in
Width . . . . 74.4 in
Height . . . . 49.1 in
Ground clearance . . . . 4.2 in
Curb weight . . . . 3689 lbs
Weight distribution, F/R . . . . 57.3/42.7 %
Battery capacity . . . . 12 volts, 61 amp-hr
Alternator capacity . . . . 854 watts
Fuel capacity . . . . 18.0 gal
Oil capacity . . . . 5.0 qts
Water capacity . . . . 16.5 qts

SUSPENSION
F: Ind., unequal-length control arms, coil springs, anti-sway bar
R: Rigid axle, semi-eeeiptic leaf springs, anti-sway bar

STEERING
Type . . . . Recirculating ball, variable ratio, power assist
Turns lock-to-lock 2.8
Turning circle curb-to-curb . . . . 38.5 ft

BRAKES
F: . . . . 11.0-in vented disc, power assist
R: . . . . 9.5 x 2.0-in cast iron drum, power assist

WHEELS AND TIRES
Wheel size . . . . 7.0 x 15-in
Wheel type . . . . Styled, stamped steel, 5-bolt
Tire make and size . . . . Firestone, Wide 60 Oval, F60-15
Tire type . . . . Bias-belted, polyester and fiberglass cord
Test inflation pressures, F/R . . . . 28/28 psi
Tire load rating . . . . 1500 lbs per tire @ 32 psi

PERFORMANCE

Zero to	Seconds
30 mph	2.8
40 mph	3.9
50 mph	5.2
60 mph	6.7
70 mph	8.3
80 mph	10.4
90 mph	13.2
100 mph	17.8

Standing ¼-mile . . . . 15.2 sec @ 94.6 mph
Top speed (observed) . . . . 123 mph
70-0 mph . . . . 192 ft (0.85G)
Fuel mileage . . . . 10.0-13.5 mpg on regular fuel
Cruising range . . . . 180-240 mi

degree. So even on the highway where airflow is sufficient without the blower, you must either accept the noise of an open window or a warm air blast from the ventilators. Unless of course, you buy air conditioning, which is definitely the recommended procedure.

This year's Camaro interior is also more liveable due to a new adjustable seat back option for the driver's side. It is a simple two-position device, much like the one Vegas have had since 1970. At the very least, it offers a welcome alternative to last year's bolt upright angle. The second position is comfortably reclined, and it lets you steer without folding your arms in half at the elbow.

Still, the Camaro's interior is far from perfect in our eyes. The shift linkage is in serious need of attention to stop its buzzing. We'd prefer a body-mounted shifter as used in Vegas and Corvettes because it does not transmit powertrain vibrations to the interior. And the throttle should be closer to the brake pedal for heel-and-toe operation. You can manage now if you strain, but in a driver's car of the Z-28's ilk, it should be as natural as shifting gears.

Those are but minor irritations compared to the shortcomings of the instrument cluster. It's not a problem of inadequate information. There are two large diameter dials for the speedometer and tachometer, as well as four subordinate openings for fuel level, ammeter, water temperature and a clock. But the small gauges fail in their primary function—delivering information—for two reasons. First of all, they are miniaturized to the point of being illegible in spite of the fact that each is but a tiny island in a vast sea of test-tube walnut. And as if that were not enough, several gauges are cleverly positioned so that you need X-ray vision to take a reading—the Porsche-style four-spoke steering wheel stands rudely in your line of sight. In that respect, Chevrolet could take a lesson from the Firebird Trans Am. The Pontiac design is the epitome of function and good looks, while the Camaro's instrument layout is an ergonometric disaster.

One area in which Chevrolet engineers have not lapsed their attention is in sound insulation. There is a new noise deadener and insulator package standard with the Type LT and optional in other Camaros. It works in conjunction with the tight sealing system inherent to Camaros since 1970. The long door de-

sign leaves only two moveable pieces of glass that aren't permanently sealed. And they match up to fat, soft seals that are hollow in section so the window edge is completely engulfed in rubber as it closes. That insures freedom from noisy wind leaks at freeway speeds. The interior is in fact so tightly sealed that a relief valve is provided .

But there is still engine noise to contend with. The Z-28's low restriction exhaust system is largely unchanged since 1970, and it very effectively subdues the discharge end of the engine. That moves the audible center of activity under the hood, where the Z-28 breathes through a chrome-plated unsilenced air cleaner. It is at noisy odds with the new LT sound package. Apparently, Chevrolet preserves the lusty moan of inrushing air for those that need audible proof of Z-28 muscle under the hood. The proof amounts to 85.0 dBA during wide open throttle acceleration, a little noisier than the SD-455 Trans Am's 84.0 dBA sound level. At idle, the Z-28 engine also pierces your consciousness with 57.5 dBA of noise, in comparison to more reserved conveyances like the Datsun 240Z, which generates only 50.5 dBA at idle. In the Camaro, noise level is high because the idle speed has been set at a boisterous 900 rpm to help the Z-28 gain a seal of approval from the government .

Handling has always been the Z-28's strong suit, and it is still, even though you end up paying less for it in 1973. There has been only one minor change in that area this year. With power steering, the effort required at the wheel has been raised slightly by means of subtle modifications within the variable-ratio steering gear. The intent is to strengthen the tie between the driver's fingertips and the tire/road interface. We found the steering to be quick enough that it's not necessary to change your hand position on the wheel during rapid maneuvers. And the Z-28's steering precision translates every minute correction at the wheel into a definitive action at the road, so you can guide the car exactly where you want it. But on the highway, the Z-28 had only a numb inclination to travel in a straight line. There is nothing so disturbing as gross wandering, just a shortage of that locked-on-a-line feel you get in a Citroën SM or a Mercedes 450 SL. It has very little to do with the power steering, because it performs exactly as the manual gear in the on-center range.

Chevrolet engineers know that additional caster in the front suspension geometry would enhance directional stability. The Camaro is built with caster set between −2 and zero degrees, while this year's Monte Carlo has a +6 degrees to emulate Mercedes stability. But power steering is necessary to keep steering effort at manageable levels with a high caster suspension. Chevrolet considered it justifiable in the more expensive Monte Carlo, but not for the Camaro. So directional stability suffers because of a compromise Chevrolet feels necessary to accommodate the few Camaro buyers who reject power steering.

The convolutions of General Motors corporate policy have also shortchanged the Camaro in the choice of tires. You can buy steel belted radials on the Firebird this year, but not the Camaro. Camaros outsell Firebirds by over two to one, and the tire supply will not yet accommodate both lines. So high level decisions have delayed radials for Camaros until the 1974 model year when the radial designed by GM will debut.

The primary benefit with radial tires on the Firebird is a smoother ride. The bias-belted 60-series Firestones on the test Camaro are so stiff that road irregularities caused the interior to creak in protest. But there is no doubt that the bias-belted tire is better for handling. It generates higher cornering forces, and stays tight and responsive right up to the limit. There is initial understeer built into the Camaro—more than we found in the Trans Am, and more than we like. But you can easily negate that tendency with the throttle. The Z-28 is perfectly content to corner with the tail hung well out, while that is an awkward attitude in the Trans Am with radial tires.

But you don't have to rely on cornering ability alone to be satisfied with a Z-28 Camaro. You have a comfortable interior to coddle your body on those high speed trips across the country. Everything isn't perfect for the driver—especially the instruments—but the Z-28 is still a car with which you can have a passionate affair. Because few cars at any price offer the Camaro's refinement in going, stopping and turning abilities. And that refinement is housed in one of the most handsomely chiseled forms ever to roll out of Detroit. But the real clincher is price. Rated in terms of feeble 1973 currency, the latest Z-28 Camaro is strictly a blue chip investment. ●

RT/TEST REPORT

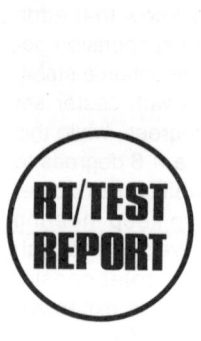

A Grand Touring Machine– Detroit Style

The Camaro Z-28 is definitely alive and surprisingly healthy.

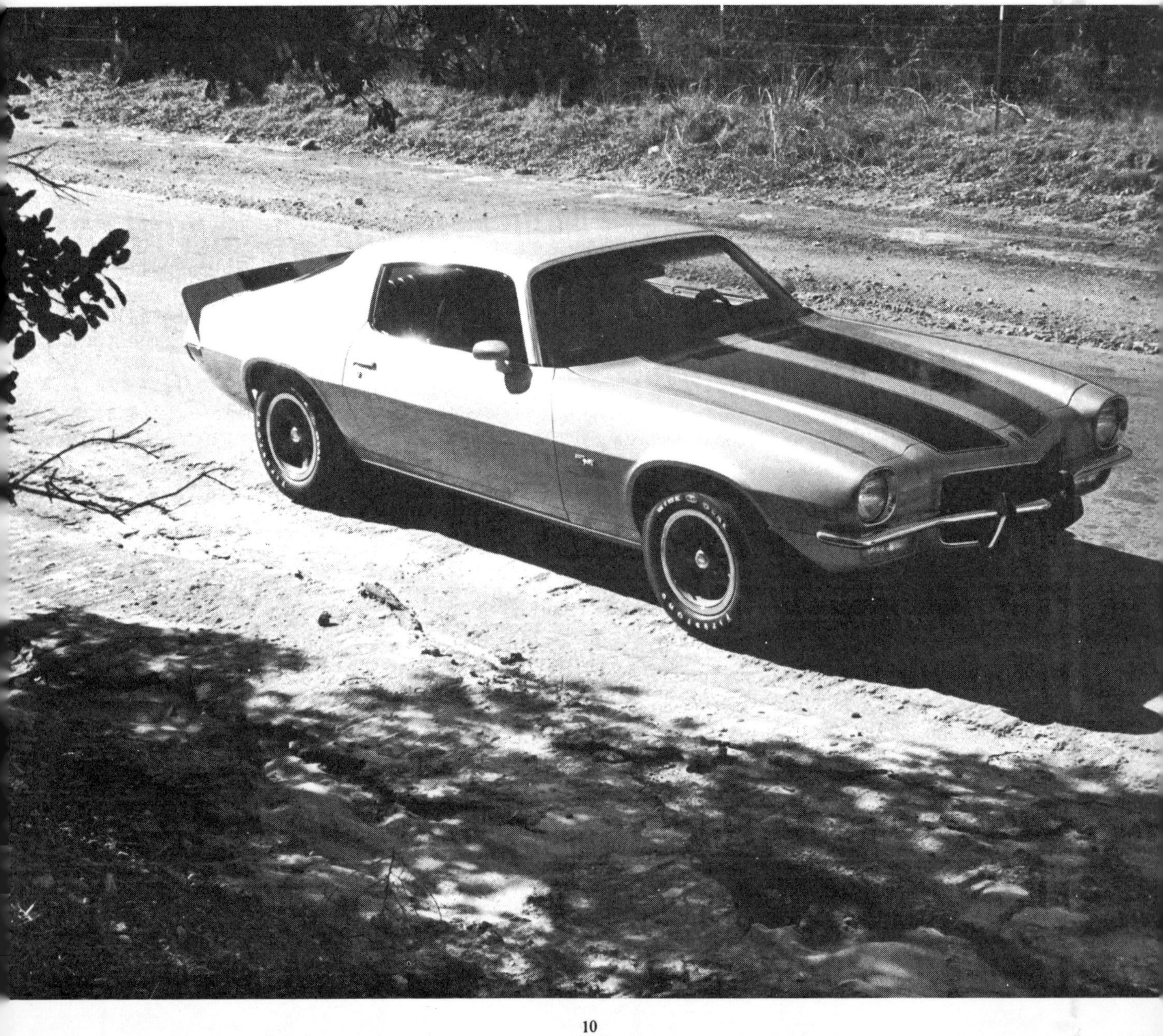

With automakers struggling frantically to meet state and federal regulations on safety, air pollution, and sundry other items, it is a wonder that Grand Touring Cars survive at all in the current line up out of Detroit. Next year the first of the "pony" cars, the Mustang, will have been on the market ten years, and the evolution of the style of car that takes its nickname "pony" from the original Mustang, has come nearly full circle. The wild engines are gone from the scene — the blistering acceleration that made the cars popular among street racers and drag types, and the enormous variety of performance options have passed into history. What remains, in the case of the Z-28, is the zoomy styling, the fine handling, and a far more civilized car.

The Chevrolet Camaro was hatched in 1966 and it was hailed by the press as an all new model. Alarmed by the galloping Mustang sales, Chevrolet introduced the Camaro on a bit of a crash

Rear spoiler is fiberglass and does more for the looks than the handling. The big road holding aid is the hefty rear sway bar, just visible under the car.

Attractive seats are also quite comfortable, rear seat room is minimal. Wrap around dash is pretty but extremely unhandy, cockpit head and leg room are ample for most any size driver.

Despite dire predictions, the Camaro and the Z-28 option live on in the seventies. Zoomy styling and all around good behavior have replaced the wild engines and options of yore, but the sales figures are going up once again.

program, but it was still two years behind the Mustang in reaching the showrooms. The majority of the components came from the Chevelle and Chevy II, and a full range of six cylinder and V-8 engines were on the list with the famed 327 at the top of the performance heap. The original Camaro came with the two speed automatic (Powerglide) or three or four speed manual transmission. The long option lists included all kinds of trim packages and a front disc brake option as well. The interior styling and some of the hardware were frankly reminiscent of the Corvair, and sales, against competition that included the new Cougar and Barracuda as well as

the Mustang, were not exactly a bonanza to dealers.

Before the year was out the Z-28 evolved in the performance minds and the production facilities of the engineering groups. The sports car racing set had a new series of road races for cars called Trans-Am sedans, and the Z-28 model of the Camaro was tailored just for this type of racing. It was homologated by the Chevrolet factory for international racing recognition under the FIA Group 2 regulations. The 1966 Z-28 had a light weight body, heavy duty suspension, power disc brakes, and a keen rear spoiler and racing stripes. The five liter engine (305 CID was maximum displacement) required for the racing class came from a destroked 327 V-8, and the size was down to 302 cubic inches . . . the engine was a screamer!

For the next few years there were only minimal changes in the Z-28 and the whole Camaro line. As all the domestic factories got deeper and deeper

into the performance game in the late sixties, the wild options available escalated accordingly. The road racers, for instance, needed better brakes, so the Z-28 model had an option of four wheel disc brakes with a retail price over 500 bucks. There were more scientifically designed rear spoilers, and front spoilers that serve as air dams in racing all went on the list for the road racers. The drag strip devotees were able to buy any engine including the hefty 396 or 427. The fire breathing 302 was further refined, and Trans-Am racing power plants exceeded 600 horsepower easily. The same five liter Chevy moved into open wheeled racing in Formula 5000, and to this day is the overwhelming choice of engine for Formula racers in the category in America, England, and Australia. However, the basic body and interior styling of all Camaros was relatively stable for the first four years of production.

All things must change, and when the 1970s dawned Detroit was already feeling the nudge of federal and state governments, all eager to get into the car manufacturing business. The yearly Camaro face lift was canceled and an all new body and engine line was introduced on the 1970 Camaro. A change in the Trans-Am racing rules that allowed the destroking of an existing engine to reach the five liter limit, was one of the major reasons for Chevy dropping the exciting 302 engine from production. In 1970 the base Camaro engine, as always, was the 250 cubic inch six, and the bottom of the line V-8 was the new 307 cubic inch, 200 horsepower number that bore no relationship to the spunky 302.

The most popular engine for the Z-28 performance package in the new model was the 350 cubic inch V-8 rated at 360 horsepower at 6,000 rpm. It sported an 11 to 1 compression ratio, and 8,000 rpm redline, and this nifty did the quarter mile in the mid 14s, zipping through the traps over 100 mph on street tires. In everyday use the Z-28 averaged around 13 mpg but burned the best fuel available. The Z-28 Camaro came with fancy fat tires, keen spoilers, and the new option of the smooth, GM turbo-hydramatic three speed automatic transmission.

Since 1970 a lot of changes have occurred in the Camaro, but few are immediately visible. Of course the whole concept of cars has been changed by legislation, and the "muscle" or "performance" cars has been somewhat doomed since the initiation of the divergent emission control gadgetry and the added weight and bulk of the safety items. Road Test does not quibble with the need for emission controls and better occupant protection in cars, but it is a fact that the weight and protrudence of things like funny bumpers, and the gas gulping habits and choked down performance of the newest engines are inhibiting to flat out go-power. We were curious about the mutation of the Z-28 into a properly street legal car today. We drove a 1973 Z-28, a properly legal car for 1973, around town and on a long, 600 mile highway trip. We were pleasantly surprised with the Camaro, and we feel it is more than worthy of wearing the Z-28 emblems in all areas but one, and that is exciting engine performance.

There are three different versions of the 350 V-8 engine optioned for the Camaro, and the top of the line is the Z-28 unit with a healthy 9 to 1 compression ratio, and a single four barrel carburetor; it adds up to a wild 245 (SAE net) horsepower at 5200 rpm. The engine revs quickly into the danger zone at 5500 rpm, and the current redline is down to six grand, although the tach reads to eight. The Z-28 special performance package, at $598.05 extra, includes this engine, that mates only to the four speed manual or the three speed automatic transmission. Further hints of performance come with the

footnote about air conditioning not being available when the close ratio, four speed tranny is ordered. The special Z-28 engine comes with finned aluminum rocker covers and bright accents, and there is increased cooling capacity, power brakes, dual exhausts, a black finished grille, sporty heavy duty suspension, heavy duty starter and clutch, and positraction. The front disc brakes are now standard throughout the line. The Z-28 emblems and decals are included, as is the twin, remote control, bullet shaped outside mirrors, the 15 x 7 inch spoke wheels that really look slick, the F-60 x 15 wide oval tires with white lettering, and a 3.73 rear axle ratio, unless the car has air conditioning, like our test unit. Then it is fitted with a 3.42 axle ratio. The extra suspension bits are a front and a rear stabilizer bar, and special front and rear shock absorbers.

The Z-28 on test had the full package of everything known to the salesman. We enjoyed the power steering and the turbo-hydromatic trans. Other extras encompassed the tinted glass, color keyed floor mats, hide away windshield wipers, a console glove box, the racing stripes, the front and rear spoilers, a three position steering wheel, heavy duty battery, AM/FM radio with a rear speaker, and the special instrumentation which gave us a tachometer, ammeter, temperature gauge, electric clock and additional interior lighting. The base price of the 1973 Camaro Sport Coupe in California is close to 2800 bucks, and we added nearly two grand in accessories for a grand total before taxes of $5,076.75. Not too bad when you consider the price of a Z-28 covered in *Road Test* three years ago was just a few hundred less in dollars.

There are few new touches in the Z-28, but what is new for 1973 is much appreciated. The good handling of the Camaro has been further enhanced by a new design on the rear stabilizer bar, and the new shock valving, as well as the 15 x 7 inch wheels. The test car was shod with the F 60-15 Firestone wide ovals, which are supposedly developed from the racing tire program. We believe it after feeling the tire perform in a wide range of conditions. The whole works adds up to actual handling improvement. Truly the Z-28 handles like a proper sports car, keeps a positive, near neutral feel going into and coming out of a hard corner. Even with the power boost, the steering wheel has a sporty firmness to the feedback, due partly to the use of a stiffer torsion bar actuator on the power assist unit. The big brakes with front discs and the power boost also have a very positive feel, and they are well balanced for daily use as well as panic situations. The Camaro we tested will stop in the 160 foot area from 60 mph with no strain and do it all with no fuss or bother. The braking stability is

helped mightily by the fat rubber, and, with the mid-winter torrential rains in the Los Angeles basin, we can honestly say the brakes and handling are nearly as good in the wet as they are in the dry. The wide oval tread design seems to plow through heavy weather as well as a radial, something different than most fatties, and it all adds greatly to the GT flavor of the Z-28.

The sleek, Italienesque looks of the Z-28 are relatively unchanged for 1973. There have been persistent rumors of Detroit dropping the pony car lines completely, but, the current sales figures on models from most makers are on the rise. The Camaro, and probably its brethren in other factories, will definitely live through a few more model years, if not longer. Although Camaro has had just one major body change during its life, subtle changes update the car each year. The current bucket seats, for example, are nicer and more comfortable than those available in 1970. The mandatory headrest is now integral with the seat, and not quite as high so one can actually look into the back seat. Still missing is a decent reclining mechanism for the seat's backs, but maybe next year . . . Seating in the rear is not very spacious, and is suitable for adults only in a pinch. But it is very handy for carrying the luggage that won't fit in the trunk. Our Z-28 did not have the space saver spare tire, so the small trunk area was half filled with the spare tire. Only small bags or soft luggage will fit in the trunk, so the grand touring is actually limited to two people.

Trunk space is really inadequate with the full size spare tire, and it would require a packing genius to carry complete trip luggage for more than two people in the Z-28 Camaro.

Driver accommodation is quite good with plenty of room for long legs and torsos. Despite the low look to the roof line there is good head room for tall folks in the front. The bucket seats are mounted right on the floor and are well positioned for most any size physique. Instrumentation and controls are packed into a semi-circle in front of the driver in

The Z-28 Camaro stops straight and sure in a panic stop, and it is one Detroit built GT with a proper brake/tire combination.

the current vogue, and it is well nigh impossible to view it all in a single glance. The sporty cross bars on the small diameter steering wheel and the driver's hands effectively block half of the dials and knobs from view. It just depends on the driver's height whether he sees the top or the bottom half. Heater and air conditioning controls are on the bottom edge of the dash near the right door, and it requires the braille system or a real "eyes off the road" look to adjust air flow and temperature. Accordingly the ash tray, the only one in the car, is mounted to the right of the steering wheel just forward of the driver's right knee, and it is unhandy for use, especially for a passenger. Styling rather than function obviously won the design battle on the dash panel of the Camaro.

The automatic transmission shift lever is placed on a center console with a good sized glove box between the seat backs. Although there is space for the shift pattern on the console, this bit of information is now revealed in a vertical slit window between the speedo and the tach, and it takes a bit of hunting to find it the first few times. The manual overrides on the trans work easily, but we found just a slight difference in on road performance between stirring the gearbox or letting it shift for itself. The dash mounted glove box is just that, being so tiny inside that it is nearly filled with the owner's manual and other information now supplied with all new cars. There are fair sized pockets in each of the

The Z-28 rides well on a variety of surfaces with a firm, but comfortable feel. Hidden windshield wipers really help the clean and sleek appearance.

wide, wide doors for in flight stowage of sun glasses, cigarettes, and similar trip goodies. The interior finish is well above standard, and the degree of detailing in the test car was real quality, putting the Z-28 in the true GT category.

With all its good looks and comfort, the Z-28 is still quite the performance car among the offerings for 1973. Gone is the bone jarring torque, and the wild rumbling sounds from under the hood, but gone also is the very harsh ride quality and stiff steering. The Z-28 is quiet at speed, and the only objectional noise comes when the single pane windows are open. Then the resulting roar

soon drives one to use the air conditioning instead of attempting to breathe fresh air. Steering has a firm feel, but good response to input, although six turns lock to lock is a bit of a bother. Roadholding is good over a wide range of road surfaces and conditions, but the tires do tend to catch in freeway grooves, similar to radial wander under the same road conditions, and the Z-28 tries to steer itself on rutted roads.

The major performance carp we have is the lack of acceleration and the sluggish shifting in normal driving. The 350 V-8 performs well despite all the smog plumbing, but like most new cars, it needs a warm up period before moving out of the driveway . . . just like cars did 30 years ago. Our test car did not gasp and stumble, but intermediate range throttle response was stodgy. Once up to speed the Z-28 steps down the highway smartly and will cruise without effort on top of the speed limit. With the fancy rear end ratio it runs up to redline quickly through the gears, a bit too quickly for the trans to catch up it seems. Full throttle holds the intermediate gears for a goodly distance, and the automatic shifts right on the danger zone of 5500 rpm. Still, on a lonely desert road we ventured up to an actual 100 mph, and the Z-28 still had more to give in top end speed. Passing torque on the highway comes on well too. With the shift lever in drive it took four seconds flat to move from 30 to 50 mph, and moving the lever into second gear knocked a mere two-tenths of a second off that time. Forty to sixty in drive took 4.9 seconds, and in second gear, 4 seconds flat. Unfortunately, the constant rain during the test period precluded a trip to the drag strip to get an actual quartermile time and speed on the newest Z-28.

Summing it all up, the Z-28 is alive and surprisingly healthy for 1973 and beyond. The fresh upward spurt in sales has provided the "ponies" with a new lease on life. Somewhere in Chevrolet there must be a group of engineers devoted to keeping the performance image for the Z-28, and whoever they are, they are getting the job done. The 1973 vintage Z-28 is a most civilized Grand Touring car from Detroit. We think it handles beautifully, goes very well, and most important to many, it stops quick and clean. Basically, the only thing missing is the initial squirt we expect from a Z-28, but the general run of customer will never miss that feature. We miss the more radical engines of yore for their positive punch and cantankerous noises, but we all must conform to ecology and safety under the law.

The neat and tidy dash is a big complaint too. It looks fine, but it is impossible to read and imparts a cramped feeling to the otherwise spacious cockpit. The rear seat is adequate for a 2 plus 2, and that is precisely what the Z-28 is. Fuel economy ranges between 11 and 13 miles per gallon, and the Camaro will really burn the mid-range 91 octane regular low lead fuel sold in California. It would be nice if the Camaro had a larger gas tank to give it Grand Touring highway range. Trips are interrupted about every 160 miles for a gas stop. Most of the poor fuel economy is related to the smog controls, and, although the tank read empty, we could never get more than 13 gallons in the tank. Apparently the gas tank vapor vent control takes up a good bit of room on the Camaro.

The Z-28 on test has a total price of over five grand plus tax and license. In that price range there are a number of choices for the performance minded buyer in both foreign and domestic sporty cars. For the driver who needs an occasional back seat, we think the Z-28 Camaro can hold its own in the price class, even if it seems a rather high tag for the full equipment. It is after all, the options that make the Z-28 the fine handling sports car that it is! *Jean Calvin*

CAMARO Z-28

SPECIFICATIONS AS TESTED

Engine	350 cu in. V-8, OHV, 4v
Bore & Stroke	4.00 x 3.48 ins.
Compression ratio	9.0:1
Horsepower	245 (SAE Net) at 5,200 rpm
Torque	280 (SAE Net) at 4,000 rpm
Transmission	3-speed, automatic
Steering	6 turns lock-to-lock
	38.5 ft curb-to-curb circle
Brakes	disc front, drum rear
Suspension	front, independent, coil springs, anti-sway bar rear, live axle, multiple leaf springs, anti-sway bar
Tires	F-60 x 15 Firestone wide oval

Dimensions (ins.):

Wheelbase	108.0	Rear track	60.4
Length	188.4	Ground clearance	5.4
Width	74.4	Height	49.1
Front track	61.7	Weight	3,349 lbs

Capacities:

Fuel	18 gals (approx)	Oil	4 qts
Coolant	18 qts	Trunk	7.3 cu ft (total)

PERFORMANCE AND MAINTENANCE

Acceleration:		Gears:
0-30 mph	3.8 secs,	1st
0-40 mph	5.0 secs,	1st
0-60 mph	10.0 secs,	1st, 2nd
0-70	11.5 secs,	1st-3rd
0-¼ mile		n/a
Ideal cruise		70-80 mph
Top speed (est)		110 mph
Stop from 60 mph		observed 160 ft
Factory Consumer information		196-201 ft
Average economy (city)		11-12 mpg
Average economy (country)		12-13 mpg
Fuel required		Regular
Oil change (mos/miles)		6/6,000
Lubrication (mos/miles)		6/6,000
Warranty (mos/miles)		12/12,000
Type tools required		SAE
U.S. Dealers		6,000 plus

BASE PRICE OF CAR

(Excludes state and local taxes, license, dealer preparation, and domestic transportation): $2,871.70

Plus desirable options:

$ 211.00	Destination
$ 39.00	Soft Ray tinted glass
$ 12.00	Color Keyed Floor Mats
$ 21.00	Hide Away windshield wipers
$ 397.00	4-season Air Conditioning
$ 77.00	Front & Rear Spoilers
$ 77.00	Sport Stripes
$ 297.00	Turbo-Hydramatic Trans
$ 44.00	Comfortilt Steering Wheel
$ 113.00	Power Steering
$ 15.00	Heavy duty battery
$ 82.00	Special Instrumentation
$ 135.00	AM/FM push button radio
$ 15.00	Rear Seat Speaker
$ 15.00	Calif. Assembly line Emission test
$ 598.05	Z-28 Performance Package
$5076.75	TOTAL

n/a—not available

CAMARO/CHALLENGER/FIREBIRD/JAVELIN
THE FEARSOME FOURSOME

By John Fuchs

CAMARO Z-28	JAVELIN	CHALLENGER	FIREBIRD
13.3 mpg	**15.2** mpg	**15.5** mpg	**19.2** mpg

Shortly before the end of the last century, a morbid rumor circulated through parts of America that Mark Twain, the brilliant humorist and novelist, had kicked the bucket. Twain, upon hearing the rumor, immediately dispatched a cable to the Associated Press. It read: "The Reports of my death have been greatly exaggerated."

Likewise, the automotive press— *Motor Trend* included—has been predicting in recent years that the American pony car, born during the carefree, pre-emission days of the early Sixties, was either seriously ill, dying or dead. The reason, of course, was the sales picture.

But each year at new-car time, the pony car comes galloping out of Detroit.

To the contrary, that blanket of uncertainty generated by the Energy Circus will very likely serve to resurrect the entire pony-car population—not as zoomy, pseudo-race cars, but as small, sporty sedans that are quite economical once you choke down the purchase price.

To provide a broad view of the field, we have mixed and matched our test cars. Each offers a hot-dog performance version with quick steering and handling suspension, and each offers several lesser models, tailored for those who simply drive about without requiring a checkered flag at the parking lot. Of the five cars that qualify for this category— Camaro, Firebird, Barracuda, Challenger and Javelin—we were able to obtain current examples of all but the Barracuda. We found that ponies are as enjoyable at a trot as they are at full gallop.

Starting at the top, in both performance and price, we have the 1974 Camaro Z-28—a quick, comfortable and fine handling example of the state of the art in performance cars. Its 350 cubic-inch four-barrel V-8, while no contest for the high performance 302 of earlier Zs, still managed to rip off quarter-mile times in the mid-15s at over 90 mph. Not too shabby for a '74 car.

Handling is another area where the Z excelled, and well it should since it had the biggest tires of the group (Firestone F60-15 belted Wide Ovals) and was the only car with a rear sway bar. There was little or no understeer with the Z's fairly stiff suspension, and judicious application of power was suf-

ficient to bring the back end around with ease. It could be cornered very quickly and very smoothly, but the power level is high enough and the excellent variable-ratio power steering is quick enough that it's not too difficult to get in over your head.

As always the Camaro interior was well-finished, tasteful and comfortable. The Z-car offers a surprising amount of room for adults in the rear. The small steering wheel is nice, the drivers' position is very good and the array of gauges is impressive…except that sunlight reflects off the faces too often due to their angle.

As a consequence of the stiff suspension and quick steering, however, ride quality was nothing to write home about. It's really quite harsh and choppy and the car seems to dart or stray during normal street or freeway driving. In fact, we'd really have to love the performance car feel and handling that this Z-28 provides in order to live with the super stiff ride. Ya pays yer money and ya takes yer choice. And speaking of money, our well-equipped Z is again no match for days of old since its sticker price is pretty close to $5300. For that kind of money you get a Camaro Type LT Coupe with an automatic trans, air conditioning, power windows, console, tinted glass, neat front and rear spoilers ($77), and bold, eye-catching, cop-baiting Z-28 wide stripes (also $77), and of course the Z-28 package ($513.45) that includes the big V-8 engine, brakes, suspension and tires. It's a lot of money, but the Z is still a lot of car.

While the Pontiac Firebird is the Camaro's fraternal twin—they share the same basic body—these two cars are as different as night and day. The Bird had the big 400 cubic-inch engine, but with a two-barrel carb, and it had the soft boulevard suspension that gets left in the dust on a handling course. While quarter-mile times were almost two seconds and 10 miles an hour off the Z, the Firebird's power level was more than sufficient due to good low-end torque of a big-inch motor. And besides that, the 'Bird got an amazing 19.2 miles per gallon around our mileage course. That kind of number is impressive, especially with a 400 cubic-inch engine in a car

that weighs over 3800 pounds, but it bears out the findings of our big-car gas mileage elsewhere in this issue that not only Hondas stretch gasoline.

As mentioned, the suspension won't win any racing trophies, but the handling is more than adequate, the steering is quite nice and the ride IS something to write home about. It's comfortable without being too soft, and still provides the good "feel" that have made sporty cars so popular. Like the Camaro, the interior is tasteful and fairly roomy, though the Firebird is much quieter and more of a luxury-car feeling. The instrument panel, however, is too bare. We'd be much happier with a more complete array of gauges in place of the idiot lights. It's nice to know what's going on under the hood, before you have to park it for repairs. bring the back end around. On the other

Among our other gripes about the Firebird is the fact that the male end of the seat belt has nasty habit of flopping over as you get out of the car, then the door gets slammed on it, and then the aluminum sill plate gets chewed up. Our test car had only a couple thousand miles on it but the sill plate already needed replacement.

Though we were unable to get a Barracuda, it's virtually identical to the Challenger, and that car was the surprise of the test. Our Dodge was equipped with the small 318 cubic-inch V-8 with a two-barrel, and an automatic transmission, yet it sucked the doors off the bigger-engined Firebird and was only a little over a second slower than the Z. In the passing speed tests, the Challenger was less than .2-second slower than the Z-28. All that with 32 less cubes and two less barrels.

The Challenger has handling comparable to it's power, meaning that it was better than most but not up to the Camaro. Understeer is evident and the engine is not quite strong enough to hand, the ride is far less bumpy than the

Camaro's, since the suspension isn't nearly as stiff nor the steering as quick. Again it retains that special sporty-car feel while including a certain amount of softness for the benefit of the passengers.

While the interior of the Challenger was definitely adequate, it was the least attractive of the group. It is stark and angular, and there seems to be a blatant use of crassly finished plastic everywhere. The driver's seat is very low and the belt-line is very high, which combines to give you the distinct impression that you're sitting in a hole. The low driver's position also doesn't help the relationship between the seat and the steering wheel. Remember of course that this is the oldest of the current sporty-car bodies, having been introduced as a 1970 model, and the design both inside and out is becoming dated. It's still a good car since, like all Chrysler products, the mechanical components and the engineering are superb, but the rest of the package is in need of a major redesign.

Last but by no means least is the AMC Javelin, again as in the past the most balanced entry in the test. It had the smallest engine of the lot, a 304 cubic-inch two-barrel V-8, and hence was the slowest, but the power level is still adequate for anything except trying to chase a Z-28 along Mulholland Drive. Sadly, however, the 15.2-mpg figure obtained on our mileage loop was just under the Challenger's 15.5, far less than the Firebird's 19.2, and barely better than the Z-28's 13.3. We had expected better, and we'd certainly be interested in trying a Javelin with the big 258-inch six-cylinder, since we feel that the performance wouldn't suffer too much and the mileage should improve markedly.

Handling of the Javelin was again more than adequate, helped in part by the Goodyear radial ply FR78-14 tires, and it could get around a corner as well as the similarly suspended Firebird. The

CONTINUED ON PAGE 37

SPECIFICATIONS	CHALLENGER	JAVELIN	CAMARO	FIREBIRD
Engine:	OHV V-8	OHV V-8	OHV V-8	OHV V-8
Bore & Stroke — ins.	3.91x3.31	3.75x3.44	4.00x3.48	4.12x3.75
Displacement — cu. in.	318	304	350	400
HP @ RPM	150 @ 4000	150 @ 4200	245 @ 5200	175 @ 3600
Torque: lbs.-ft. @ rpm	255 @ 2200	245 @ 2400	280 @ 4000	315 @ 2000
Compression Ratio	8.6:1	8.4:1	9.0:1	8.0:1
Carburetion	1-2V	1-2V	1-4V	1-2V
Transmission	3-speed auto.	3-speed auto.	3-speed auto.	3-speed auto.
Final Drive Ratio	2.76:1	3.15	3.73:1	3.08:1
Steering Type	Recirc. Ball	Recirc. Ball	Recirc. Ball	Recirc. Ball
Steering Ratio	18.74:1	Variable 16.0:1 to 12.0:1	Variable 16.0:1 to 13.0:1	Variable NA
Turning Diameter (curb-to-curb-ft.)	39.19'	39.8'	38.5'	NA
Wheel Turns (lock-to-lock)	3.5	3.3	2.41'	NA
Tire Size	FR-70x14	FR-78x14	F-60x15	F-78x14
Brakes	Disc/Drum	Disc/Drum	Disc/Drum	Disc/Drum
Front Suspension	Independent Torsion Bars	Independent w/Coils	Independent w/Coils	Independent w/Coils
Rear Suspension	Rigid Semi-Eliptic Leaf	Rigid Semi-Eliptic Leaf	Rigid Semi-Eliptic Leaf	Rigid Semi-Eliptic Leaf
Width — in.	77.4"	75.36"	74.4"	73.4"
Front Track — in.	60.2"	58.52"	61.6"	61.9"
Rear Track — in.	60.7"	60.00"	60.3"	61.1"
Wheelbase — in.	110.0"	110.0"	108.0"	108.0"
Overall length — in.	198.6"	195.25"	195.4"	196.0"
Height — in.	50.9"	51.33"	49.2"	50.3"
Curb Weight — lbs.	3520 lbs.	3435 lbs.	3840 lbs.	3845 lbs.
Fuel Capacity — gals.	18-gal.	16-gal.	21-gal.	21.5-gal.
Oil Capacity — qts.	4-qts.	4-qts.	4-qts.	4-qts.
Storage Capacity — cu. ft.	9.6	10.54	NA	NA

PERFORMANCE	CHALLENGER	JAVELIN	CAMARO Z-28	FIREBIRD
Acceleration 0-30 mph	3.20	3.70	3.10	3.48
0-50 mph	7.30	7.95	5.85	7.00
0-60 mph	9.60	11.20	8.10	10.35
0-75				
Standing Start 1/4-mile Mph	80.21	83.05	90.54	82.11
Elapsed time	16.870	17.299	15.415	17.052
Passing speeds 40-60 mph	4.52	6.20	4.38	4.70
50-70 mph	5.09	7.15	4.90	5.70
Stopping distance From 30 mph	29' 5"	26' 0"	31' 10"	30' 0"
From 60 mph	135' 8"	135' 0"	123' 8"	139' 7"
Gas mileage range				
Speedometer error Electric speedometer	27.08 37.05 46.32 56.17 65.0	29.29 38.36 47.34 58.40 66.32	30.29 40.26 50.99 61.26 71.42	30.12 38.89 48.70 57.98 67.92
Car speedometer	30 40 50 60 70	30 40 50 60 70	30 40 50 60 70	30 40 50 60 70

* Speeds in gears are at shift points (limited by the length of track) and do not represent maximum speeds.

A new look.

Same fine feel.

Front discs standard.

Sport Coupe

With Camaro, you can be practical.
Or go bananas.

Z28

Type LT interior.

Deck stripes.

Sport mirrors.

Special Z28 wheels.

If you can restrain yourself when it comes time to order the extras, you can move into a handsome 1974 Camaro Sport Coupe for less money than you might imagine.

That's one approach. Approach "A" we'll call it.

There's also Approach "Z". The renowned Camaro Z28 package. All the basic good things plus a 350 V8 with 4-barrel, a dual exhaust system, special sport suspension, Positraction rear axle, sport mirrors, F60-15 white-lettered tires and more. If you *really* want to go bananas you can add spoilers and those bold new Z28 hood and deck stripes.

(There's a third approach, comfortably in between: Camaro Type LT with its sumptuous interior and other elegant touches.)

Camaro. The way it looks is the way it goes.

Chevrolet

18

PROJECT MILEAGEMAKER

HRM takes a brand-new Camaro LT Z/28 out into the real world of expensive gasoline to find out just what works and what doesn't in the maze of miracle mileage mods

Well, here we are in the middle of summer, July 1974, and the infamous Energy Crisis that caused every motorist in the country so much trouble earlier in the year is, in most localities, little more than a faint memory. The pipelines are full, there are supertankers full of crude oil coming our way from all directions, and there are no more block-long lines at service stations in metropolitan areas.

If you have been reading the last few issues of Hot Rod, you know that we have been very concerned about the Energy Crisis and its effects on the automotive enthusiast and his machinery. In these past few months while the E.C. was in its critical stages, we have tried to bring you every single piece of gas-saving information we could, based on history, engineering and the experiences of our staffers with their own machinery. If you've read, absorbed and tried any or all of the tips we've been passing along, you are getting more miles to the gallon than you were before, or you must have done something wrong somewhere.

The point is this: The Energy Crisis with a capital E and a capital C is over. But we at HRM feel that we owe it to ourselves and to our readers to continue to probe the whole subject of fuel consumption as a matter of course with all future projects, to make fuel economy tips a regular part of the magazine's editorial coverage, and to keep close track of fuel consumption of all road test cars.

But before all of that comes to pass, we are going to go directly into a brand-new combination project with a brand-new car to test out most, if not all, of the information we have been sending your way about driving habits and equipment changes that affect gas mileage. We are hopeful that four major areas, including drivability, fuel economy, drag strip performance and emissions levels, can be improved by the time the short-range project is over.

What, you say, are we going to use as raw material for this penetrating project? Well, from a wide-open field of choices, we selected one of the most popular combinations going, the 1974 Camaro LT coupe with Z/28 equipment. We could have selected a four-door sedan just as easily, but we know that the LT/Z package has been a consistently popular performance car since the day it was introduced, detuning over the years notwithstanding. It's a ponycar, certainly, but it is a challenging one to work with, especially in the area of driving habits, because any one of us on the HRM staff who slides into the left seat is going to want to make it do what it does best all the time. So it is a challenge from the driving aspect for sure. Second, the LT coupe that we ordered out is by no means a stripped-down version. We'll get into specific equipment shortly, but we want you to know out front that it was loaded up with options for a bunch of sound reasons. There would be little challenge involved in making a stripped-down model with the standard Camaro powerplant get excellent mileage. It wouldn't have to weigh very much, there would be little drain on the engine from power accessories, and it probably would be an okay car to drive right on through the summer, as we plan to do with the Camaro we now have. But instead of taking that route, we got the complete Z/28 performance package and a bunch of heavy, power-robbing accessories to bring the car into an average situation so that more readers could get more benefit out of following the project through to its final stages, whatever they may be. The engine will be responsive, the package will carry sufficient weight to be challenging, and the car will be very easy to live with because of the creature comforts it now has (remember, we have to drive it daily between stops for modification and checking in the L.A. basin, where the summertime temperatures get up over 110 degrees every once in a while and stay above 90 for days at a time).

The rundown on the car is as follows: The basic LT Camaro coupe has been fitted with the complete Z/28 package of suspension, wheels, tires, and trim, air conditioning, AM/FM stereo radio, power steering, power disc/drum brakes, power windows, rear defogger, vanity mirror, adjustable driver's seat back, color-keyed floor mats, a center console, wide-ratio four-speed manual transmission, dual horns, auxiliary lighting package, style trim group, spoilers front and rear, body side moldings, deluxe lap belts and tinted glass. The basic car lists out at $3505.70, and our project car came to $5388.15, including the required California emissions package and test, but not including destination charges. No question about it, she's a loaded piece.

The plan over the next few months is going to be one of careful baselining in all areas, including emissions, gas mileage and drag strip performance, followed by a systematic replacement of key components like the induction and exhaust systems, ignition work and some special pieces for the induction systems, both stock and modified, to improve mixture distribution and particle size. We'll be changing tire types around, and we may get into some experimentation with special lubricants and other antifriction methods. We'll be devising a "mileage loop" within Los Angeles County that will include freeway, city streets, mountainous sections at fairly high elevations, sea level sections and so on, so that we can throw out as many variables as possible for greatest accuracy. After each set of modifications is made, we'll be checking mileage, emissions, power output and drag strip performance; and we'll try very hard to run around the mileage loop at a time of day when the least resistance will be encountered. If we have to abort a mileage run because of a total traffic jam, we will. We want very much to see what really can be done, and to be able to tell you for sure which steps and pieces really work and relate that information to cost per mile per gallons gained. Got that? Good. We'll be back in August with a whole gang of baseline information about Project Mileagemaker, and we promise plenty of informative, entertaining and maybe even provocative installments in the months to come. ■■

PROJECT MILEAGEMAKER

PART TWO

Mileage and performance—can you have both? You'll find the answer to that question in what we've been doing to our Z/28 project car

Text & photos by C.J. Baker ■ Last month we outlined our plans for equipping our Z/28 Camaro project car with after-market mileage and performance pieces. Our overall goal is to find and test those products that will improve gas mileage without hurting the performance, drivability or emission characteristics of this car. If anything, we hope we'll be able to show improvements in these characteristics, along with increasing gas mileage.

For the last few months we've been advocating the use of such aftermarket parts to better gas mileage. Now, this is it, the proof of the pudding, the naked truth about what does or doesn't work.

Before we could begin our test program, a suitable test course had to be selected. Such suggestions as Las Vegas and back immediately came forth, but the people in charge of staff expense accounts vetoed that. It really wouldn't have been practical anyway. Our course had to include virtually every kind of driving commonly encountered. After a great deal of thought and consideration, a 58.3-mile course was chosen. It begins at a gas station (one that is willing to put up with our fussiness about personally filling the tank to an exact point time after time as this project goes on) near the middle of the San Fernando Valley, the northern part of Los Angeles. The course then proceeds for nearly 19 miles over easy-flowing freeways. Average speed here is a consistent 55 mph. After leaving the freeway, the course then traverses slightly less than ten miles through the winding low mountains in Malibu Canyon. Speed varies between 35 and 50 mph in this section as the road winds down to the Pacific coast.

Next, the course follows the ocean shore along the Pacific Coast Highway for about ten miles. Average speed here is about 45 mph and there are occasional stoplights. This section of the course takes us to Santa Monica, where the route turns east on Wilshire Boulevard for about five miles. This stretch is loaded with stoplights and stop-and-go traffic.

The last leg of the trip is back on the freeway through the Sepulveda Pass to return to the San Fernando Valley and back to the same filling station for a careful refilling of the gas tank to the exact same level. The same gas pump is always used and the Camaro is parked in the same spot each time it is filled.

With the course laid out, it was then determined that the Z/28 should be fitted with some sort of driving indicator to

help make the acceleration rates and driving style as consistent as possible each time the car was taken around the course. We could have used a vacuum gauge or even a fuel flow meter for this, but instead we elected to install a new piece of equipment, called an Electronic Power Indicator (EPI). We came across this device while ordering our Multiple Spark Discharge (MSD) ignition system for this project from Autotronic Controls Corporation, 6908 Commerce, El Paso, Texas 79915.

Actually this EPI is just a spin-off from the Dynamic Dynamometer Model 701, which we reported on in the April '74 HRM. What this unit does is to compute the power-to-weight ratio being experienced by the car at all times. It does this by monitoring changes in vehicle velocity, with respect to time, from a single sensor on the speedometer cable. All of this gets to be pretty heady stuff, but in effect it basically determines whether the vehicle is being accelerated or decelerated in an efficient manner at any given instant. And rather than giving the driver a gauge to indicate this readout, which like a vacuum gauge would require close attention, a simple three-light indicator panel is used. When the car is being driven within an economical power-to-weight range, a green light illuminates. If the power-to-weight ratio is increased beyond a preset point, a yellow light illuminates, followed by a red light if still more power is applied. It's an excellent driving aid, and it's quite simple to keep tabs on your driving by watching the indicator lights out of the corner of your eye. Of course the unit does have a couple of drawbacks on manual transmission cars, since it has no way of knowing whether the driver is in the most economical gear for the road and traffic conditions. And it doesn't know if you're going up or down a hill, which also changes the vehicle's power requirements. But overall, it's a great driving aid, especially for automatic transmission cars that always select the best gear for road conditions based on manifold vacuum.

With the EPI installed (it took about a half hour to put in), all runs were made keeping the Camaro "in the green," using the same driver and the same vehicle warm-up procedure prior to each test. Mileage drives were also done during periods of low traffic congestion to eliminate running into any bumper-to-bumper back-ups that would abort the run.

We began by establishing a baseline for our loaded '74 Camaro Type LT Z/28. The car was carefully tuned to OEM specs and emission levels. So tuned, it recorded a mileage

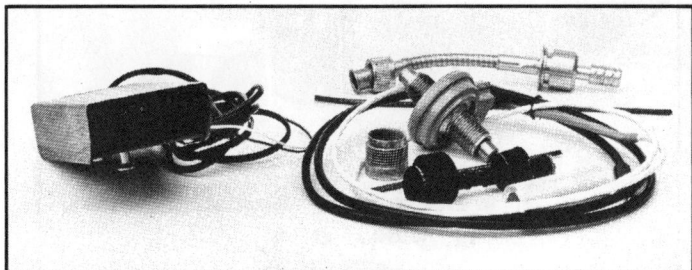

ABOVE—The Autotronic Electronic Power Indicator is very compact. It comes with an assortment of speedometer cable adapters to hook up the input sensor. BELOW—The three-light indicator panel can be located anywhere that is convenient, such as under the dash as shown here.

RIGHT— Shown here is the high-buck MSD-404B ignition setup with the special high-output coil. This unit works with either points or magnetic pickup distributors. ABOVE– This is the MSD-2 multiple-discharge spark ignition system. It is compatible with stock coils, point-type distributors and most electronic tachs.

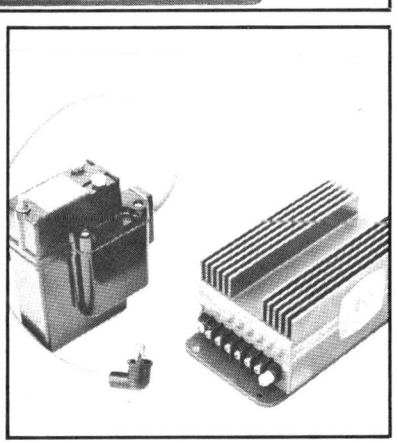

figure of 16.9 mpg—not too shabby for a late-model emissions engine. Of course we obtained this mileage figure while driving carefully and paying close attention to gas consumption, but still, during everyday normal driving, the car got in excess of 14 mpg. It just goes to show what good-mileage driving techniques and a tune-up can achieve. Also, our Z/28 has a four-speed, which helps gas mileage. Motor Trend, our less-performance-oriented sister publication, tested a similar '74 Z/28 with an automatic transmission and found it to be getting 13.3 mpg in everyday driving.

Then, just for fun, we drove the car around the course again with both the air conditioning and the headlights on to see what that would do to our 16.9-mpg figure. The result was worse than expected as mileage fell to 13.7 mpg. It almost sounds like Catch 22—don't drive at night and don't drive during the day, when you need air conditioning. Of course you have to drive sometime, so just keep in mind what that creature comfort can cost you.

Next, we took the car to Irwindale Raceway to see how it performed. The clocks recorded the bad news, as the best we could do was 16.12 seconds at 88.66 mph. Certainly this was not the Z/28 of days gone by.

With these baseline figures recorded, two things became apparent: one, there was plenty of room for performance improvement; two, mileage gains were going to take some work, since it was good going in. Now we were ready to start changing things.

The first piece of equipment tested was the Autotronics MSD-2 ignition system. This is a multiple-spark system that fires the spark 20 to 40 times each firing cycle instead of just once. The result is a spark over 15 to 20 degrees of crankshaft rotation to improve probability of igniting the lean mixtures.

The unit we tested is one of two MSD versions offered by Autotronics. One is designed to work with the stock coil and point-type distributor. This is the MSD-2 that we tested. It sells for just under $70. The second version, the MSD-404B is designed as the ultimate setup for high-output engines. It will work with either points or magnetic impulse distributors. The price of this unit is a stiff $160. A special high-output coil is also recommended for this version.

The installation instructions for the MSD-2 indicated that increasing the spark plug gap to .055-inch might further improve gas mileage with their unit, so we tested it with both the stock .035-inch gap and the .055-inch gap. With the stock .035-inch gap, the mileage improved to 17.4 mpg. Opening the gap to .055-inch showed no improvement.

The next item to be tested was a Carter Thermo-Quad carburetor. After consulting with the Carter folks about our goals with this project, they recommended the T.Q. 6318 SA carb. This is a spread-bore carb that is used on late-model MoPar 340/360 engines. It is rated at 800 cfm. Since the Z/28 has

BELOW—The MSD-2 ignition (foreground) is quick and simple to install. It could easily be swapped from one car to the next at trading time.

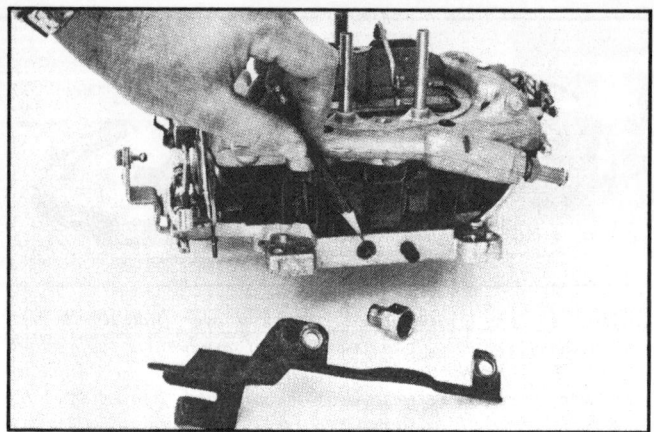

Carter suggested we try this T.Q. 6318 SA 800-cfm carb. It's the standard carb on small-block MoPars. Their suggestion was valid, as both mileage and performance were improved.

This vacuum port had to be enlarged to 7/16-inch and tapped to accept the Chevrolet power brake line fitting. It's not a difficult task.

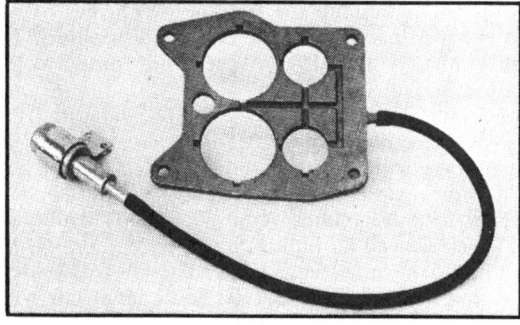

ABOVE LEFT—Because of interference with the stock EGR valve, this dashpot had to be removed. A slight bog results when the throttle is first punched. ABOVE—Installed, the T.Q. looks right at home, as it has fittings for the necessary hoses and an idle solenoid, as did the stock Q'Jet carb. LEFT—This is the portion of the Echlin retro-fit emission kit that was installed. It showed a slight mileage improvement.

a Quadrajet spread-bore carb as standard equipment, the swap wasn't too difficult, although there were a few problems. A vacuum port at the rear of the Carter carb must be drilled to 7/16-inch diameter and tapped for ¼-inch pipe thread to accept the power brake vacuum line fitting. It was also necessary to remove a dashpot that prevents the secondary air valve from opening too quickly. This had to be removed to clear the stock EGR valve on the Chevrolet manifold. Unfortunately, with the dashpot removed, the engine bogs when the throttle is nailed suddenly, but not as badly as you might think. Overall, performance is improved. The dashpot could probably be reconnected if someone gave it some thought and made a bracket. It is also necessary to fabricate some new linkage arrangement to connect the automatic choke.

The dashpot and choke problems didn't concern us too much, since the secondaries aren't used during the mileage test and the engine is fully warmed prior to the test so the choke plays no significant part either. Besides, we knew we'd be changing to a different manifold in the future that would eliminate the problems.

Anyway, the carb was installed and tuned to idle and emission levels equivalent to the stock carb. A mileage test was then made and mileage improved once again to 18.2 mpg. Now

that we had our mileage gain, it was back to the drag strip to see what happened to performance. More good news. The e.t. dropped to 15.88 seconds and mph went up to 89.82. That's still not too exciting, but at least we were on the right track. And remember, the car was bogging and still getting this kind of performance.

The last piece of equipment that we'll cover this month is the Echlin Ultrasonic NOx emission kit. We had heard claims that this emission retro-fit kit could actually show mileage gains. This kit is designed for 1966 through 1970 cars to limit the amount of NOx in the vehicle exhaust; hence it really wasn't designed for our '74 Camaro, which already has NOx controls on it. Consequently, we didn't perform all of the distributor and carburetor adjustments recommended in the instructions, for fear of upsetting the car's factory calibrations. Instead, the ultrasonic spacer plate and the signal generator (sometimes referred to as the "dog whistle") were all that was used. After this was in place, we toured the mileage course again and recorded an 18.5-mpg reading, which seems to indicate that the device does indeed show a slight improvement.

Next month we'll begin more serious modifications, such as manifolding changes and radial tires, just to mention a few. So check again next month for more of the good news. ■■

PROJECT MILEAGEMAKER

PART LAST

Over 21 miles per gallon—that's what we were able to squeeze from our '74 Z/28 Camaro. Here's how we did it

Text & photos by C.J. Baker ■ You will recall that by the end of last month's segment of this mileage project, we had managed to boost the miles-per-gallon figure for our '74 Type LT Z/28 Camaro to a very respectable 18.5 over our predetermined mileage course, while simultaneously bettering quarter-mile drag strip performance by .24-second. This month we'll conclude this project by evaluating still more aftermarket equipment in our search for better mileage without hurting performance and without degrading the emissions characteristics of the Big Z.

The equipment already installed on the car from last month's test included a Carter Thermo-Quad 6318 SA 800-cfm carb, an Autotronics MSD-2 ignition system and the ultrasonic portion of the Echlin NOx emission retro-fit kit. Since the first item to be tested this month was Offenhauser No. 6008 Dual-Port Aluminum intake manifold, which is slightly taller than the stock OEM cast-iron manifold, the Echlin ultrasonic spacer plate was removed from beneath the carburetor to eliminate any possible air-cleaner-to-hood clearance problems. Removal of this spacer plate dropped our Camaro's mileage back to 18.2 mpg before swapping manifolds, a loss of .3 mpg.

The hardest thing about installing the Offy Dual-Port manifold was trying to work around the spaghetti-like maze of hoses that connect the various emission devices and the air condi-

tioner on this car. But even with all of these obstacles, the installation, which included EGR adapter plumbing, was completed in one evening. The only difficulty we encountered was with the upper radiator hose inlet neck. Since Offy produces this manifold to fit any 283-through-400-cubic-inch small-block Chevrolet engine, and since Chevy has relocated the inlet neck position a time or two since 1957, our '74 inlet neck didn't point exactly where it should have, but it was still usable. If you're particular about this sort of thing, Chevrolet does have quite an assortment of various necks, and one of them is bound to be just right.

With the manifold installed, we returned the car to Offenhauser's chassis dyno facility to check both the Rochester Quadrajet and the Carter Thermo-Quad carburetors on the Dual-Port manifold to verify that they were tuned for optimum efficiency and the proper emission limits. To accomplish this, Ollie Morris, Offenhauser's chief research engineer, ran the car through the Federal driving cycle while monitoring the exhaust gases for CO, CO_2, HC and NOx levels.

With the carburetors tuned to the induction system, it was back to the mileage loop. Atop the Dual-Port the Quadrajet produced 18.2 mpg (as compared to a best of 17.4 mpg for this carb on the OEM manifold), and the Thermo-Quad recorded 19.1 mpg. This verified that the manifold was indeed good

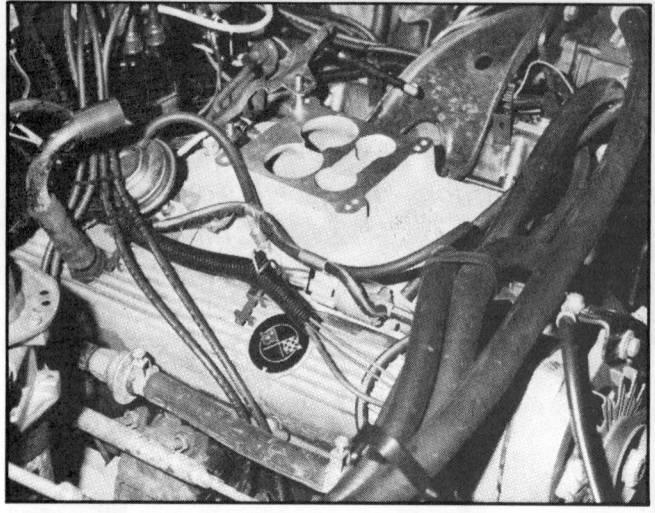

ABOVE—An Offenhauser Dual-Port aluminum intake manifold was installed in place of the stock cast-iron manifold. The Dual-Port, which was a spread-bore version, was fitted with all of the stock emission devices such as TCS and EGR to keep everything within the letter of the law.

ABOVE—The 1⅝-inch-diameter primary tube headers were fabricated and installed by Hedman. To further smooth the exhaust pulses and thereby improve low-end torque while simultaneously reducing exhaust noise, a 2-inch-diameter "H" pipe was welded in immediately behind the bellhousing.

ABOVE—After installation of the manifold, the Z/28 was run on Offenhauser's chassis dyno to dial both the Quadrajet and the Thermo-Quad carburetors into the more efficient induction system. BELOW—Here Ollie Morris, Offenhauser's chief research engineer, puts the Camaro through the federal driving cycle while checking exhaust emissions. RIGHT—The exhaust content was accurately analyzed and recorded on Offenhauser's sophisticated equipment.

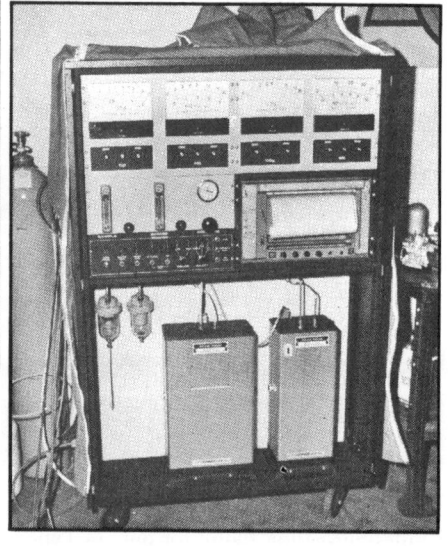

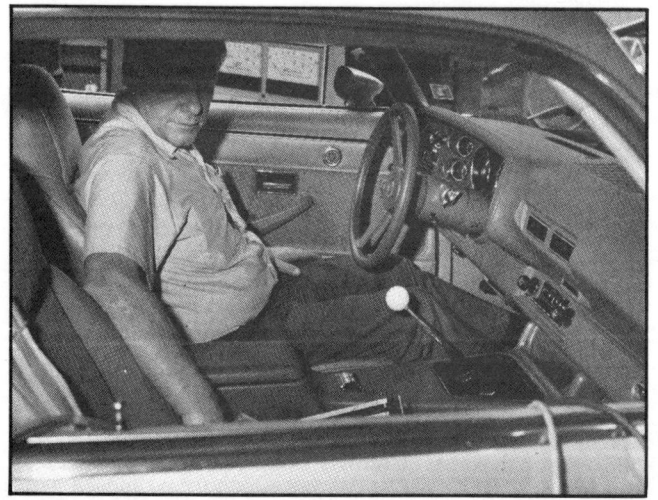

for a five-percent mileage increase on our test car, regardless of which carburetor was used.

Having found this mileage gain, it was now time for another drag strip check to see what was happening to performance. We were anticipating an improvement in quarter-mile times, since the car was noticeably more responsive in the lower rpm ranges with the installation of the Dual-Port. Our anticipations were confirmed as the Z/28 ran 15.65 at 89.50 mph. This represented over .2-second reduction in elapsed time but also about .3 less mph. Since the e.t. was better and the mph relatively unchanged, chances are that the secondary side of the carburetor was a little bit lean and that further improvements could be made by richening up a bit.

Our next modification was the installation of headers. For this phase of our test we took the car to Hedman Hedders, where they installed a set of their 1⅝-inch-diameter tubes. These headers were fitted with a mini-manifold for the air injector reactor fittings on our Z/28 so that all emission equipment could be kept operable. Additionally, Hedman fitted the headers with an "H" pipe between the collectors just behind the bellhousing. The purpose of this "H" pipe is to smooth

LEFT—This popular mileage device, the Hydro-Catalyst, was tested, but we could detect no improvement in gas mileage. However, we weren't able to test the device for the 1500 miles the manufacturer claims may be necessary before significant gains are seen. See text. MIDDLE—Our Z/28 came with a set of F60-15 bias-belted ply tires. For comparison we tested a set of GR70-15 Goodyear GT Radials mounted on American's newest wheels, the Vectors. Switching to radials showed a worthwhile gain. RIGHT—The radial tires were both taller and narrower than the bias-belted tires, which, along with the type of construction, helped improve mileage. Note: The radial tires hadn't been run on the car yet when these pictures were taken. That's why the molding flashing is still on the tire shown on the left.*

the exhaust pulses, improve low speed torque and reduce noise. It is a good addition to any set of street headers.

With the headers installed, we returned once again to the mileage loop. To our suprise, the headers showed no improvement in mileage on our test car. This was perplexing, since we've seen mileage improvements on countless test cars when headers were installed. Thinking the headers were upsetting the carburetor jetting, we tried an assortment of jetting and metering rod combinations, but our efforts were unsuccessful. After careful thought, our conclusion is that the rpm range that the Z/28 was operated at during the mileage tests (maximum of 2500 rpm) probably wasn't high enough for the headers to show any real improvement. At this low speed, the stock manifolds were apparently able to handle the exhaust flow without excessive power loss. Second, the Z/28 was still equipped with the stock cross-flow muffler, which is quite restrictive. It is quite possible that the muffler is the biggest restriction in the exhaust system and freeing up the exhaust manifolds didn't help the total system. Had low-restriction mufflers, such as the Corvair Spyder mufflers, been used, the results would undoubtedly have been more impressive.

On the drag strip, however, it was quite another story, as the headers really started to work. Quarter-mile times dropped to 15.48 seconds, with trap speeds just over 92 mph. This supports our theory that the headers work in the upper rpm ranges.

As we had been proceeding with this project, we had heard claims of special low-friction motor oils and lubricants that reportedly offered substantial mileage improvements. At first these claims sounded exaggerated, but we decided to give the products a fair chance and see what happened. To get the full story on why these oils are supposed to improve mileage, we contacted one of the prime firms engaged in producing special oils, Ten K Plus Products. We were told that their lubricants undergo much more extensive refining to remove additional tars and abrasives that the major oil refinders find impractical to remove. However, smaller refiners can take the time and expense to go through these additional purification steps, even though the oil necessarily must sell for two to three times the price of oil that has received only normal refining. This all sounded good, but we still weren't convinced, so we asked the Ten K Plus people to flush the existing oil out of our Z/28 and fill it with their motor oil. They also replaced the lubricant in the manual transmission. To our amazement, the mileage on our Z/28 jumped to 20.3 mpg, an increase of 1.2 miles per gallon. But before you run down to the store to buy some of this oil, be advised that Ten K Plus is still in the middle of establishing their distribution network and the product won't be generally available for another four or five months. If you're really interested, you can write to Ten K Plus Products, 27957

Cabot Road, Laguna Miguel, California 92677, for specific information as to when their lubricants can be purchased.

Next on our list of mileagemakers to try was radial tires. Our Camaro came equipped with a set of F60-15 bias-belted tires. These are good-looking tires with plenty of width and good traction, but the wider the tire, the more rolling resistance it offers. Therefore, we contacted Goodyear and arranged to test a set of their latest Exten GR70-15 Customgard GT Radials. Like the bias-belted tires, the radials were raised-white-letter versions. Unlike the bias-belted tires, the radials offered a narrower tread face and they were a little taller (1½ inches). The Z/28 is equipped with 3.42:1 gears, so installing these taller radials had the same effect as lowering the rearend gear ratio to 3.31:1. This, along with the lower rolling resistance of the radial ply construction of the tires, boosted our Camaro's gas mileage to a peak of 21.4 mpg. Obviously, the type of tire can make quite a difference.

To make the installation and removal of these radial tires more convenient, we seized upon this opportunity to improve the appearance of our Camaro by mounting the radials on a set of really nice-looking aluminum wheels. The wheels we chose are American Racing's newest Vector versions. These wheels really dressed up the car, as you can see in the lead photograph of this feature.

Before terminating this project, we decided to try one other popular device for improving gas mileage. It's called the Hydro-Catalyst. The device consists of a spacer plate which is installed beneath the carburetor. The spacer plate is fitted with two cuplike screens under the primary throttle bores. Each of these screens is actually a double layer of two dissimilar metals which reportedly impart a catalytic action to the fuel passing through the screens. After installing the device, we were unable to detect any improvement in gas mileage, although the manufacturer's instructions warned that no significant improvement might be noted until the device had been on the vehicle for 1500 miles to allow the catalytic action to properly clean the combustion chambers. Unfortunately we were unable to test the device for that period of time, but our sister magazine, Motor Trend, is contemplating such an extensive test of the device.

If we had additional time, there are several other things we would have liked to try, such as one of the aftermarket mileage camshafts, a vapor injector and a different rearend gear ratio. However, as it was, we were able to improve the gas mileage on this already economical vehicle by over 26 percent while bettering quarter-mile time by over .6-second and more than three mph.

The technology and equipment is available if you're willing to look for it and pay the price. Who says you can't have your cake and eat it too? ■■

THE LINES HAVE BEEN EXTENDED TO FORM AN ATTRACTIVE NOSE.

The short-spoke cast steel wheels, tinted glass and side moulding with padded vinyl inserts. The seats are the deep bucket type providing good all around support especially in long distance touring. Legroom is short for the rear seat passengers (common with many domestics these days). More than four passengers would prove to be uncomfortable, we found. The big plus for the Camaro is its handling—not harsh, but firm and with a good feel of the road. Body lean is held down to an acceptable minimum.

By **MIKE UNO** ■ Enter the '74 Camaro LT. What kind of car is it??? Well, let's get right to the point and clear the air from the beginning by telling you that it's hardly "basic transportation." It's quite a bit beyond that actually, and yet, it's not something that could be called outlandish or extravagant by anyone, save the most penny-conscious miser. What it is is one of the best all around mid-price range automobiles built in the United States today. Granted that American cars aren't exactly the cream of the world's crop anymore, but if you want something that is relatively roomy and quite comfortable, looks exceedingly good, is reliable, feels safe, performs well and is reasonably economical, and you don't feel like shelling out the price of some hand-tailored import, or you're quite simply enamored of the domestic breeds, then perhaps this is just the kind of automobile you'd care to own.

The first thing that comes to mind when thinking about what sets the Camaro apart from its domestic cohorts is that it is, to our way of thinking, the most tastefully styled of the '74's. First of all, the Camaro, along with the very similarly styled Firebird, is about the only automobile that displays an

imaginative approach to blending in the Federally-mandated impact-absorbing front and rear bumpers. Rather than have the bumpers appear as some sort of "ramming prows" that have been merely tacked onto the car, the Chevrolet designers have managed to extend the already clean lines of the Camaro into a very subtle and attractive nose. At the rear of the car, the bumper has been affixed so as to appear a logical extension of the Camaro's gently sloping rearward lines. There are no unsightly bulges or protrusions. The result is a car that appears very long and low relative to its overall size, presenting a very sleek silhouette, and giving all the aesthetic pleasure that any aerodynamic form does.

While the car is for the most part identical to the '73 version, the faintly more converging curvatures and gently swooping nose, plus the visibly less abrupt tail section gives the car the overall appearance of being less chopped off than previous models. There are no sudden flat spots or blunt areas to mar the overall effect of the cars appearance. In short, it is externally a very good looking car.

Our particular test car came in bronze, accompanied by the "Saddle" interior with matching seatbelts (the matching

CAMARO LT

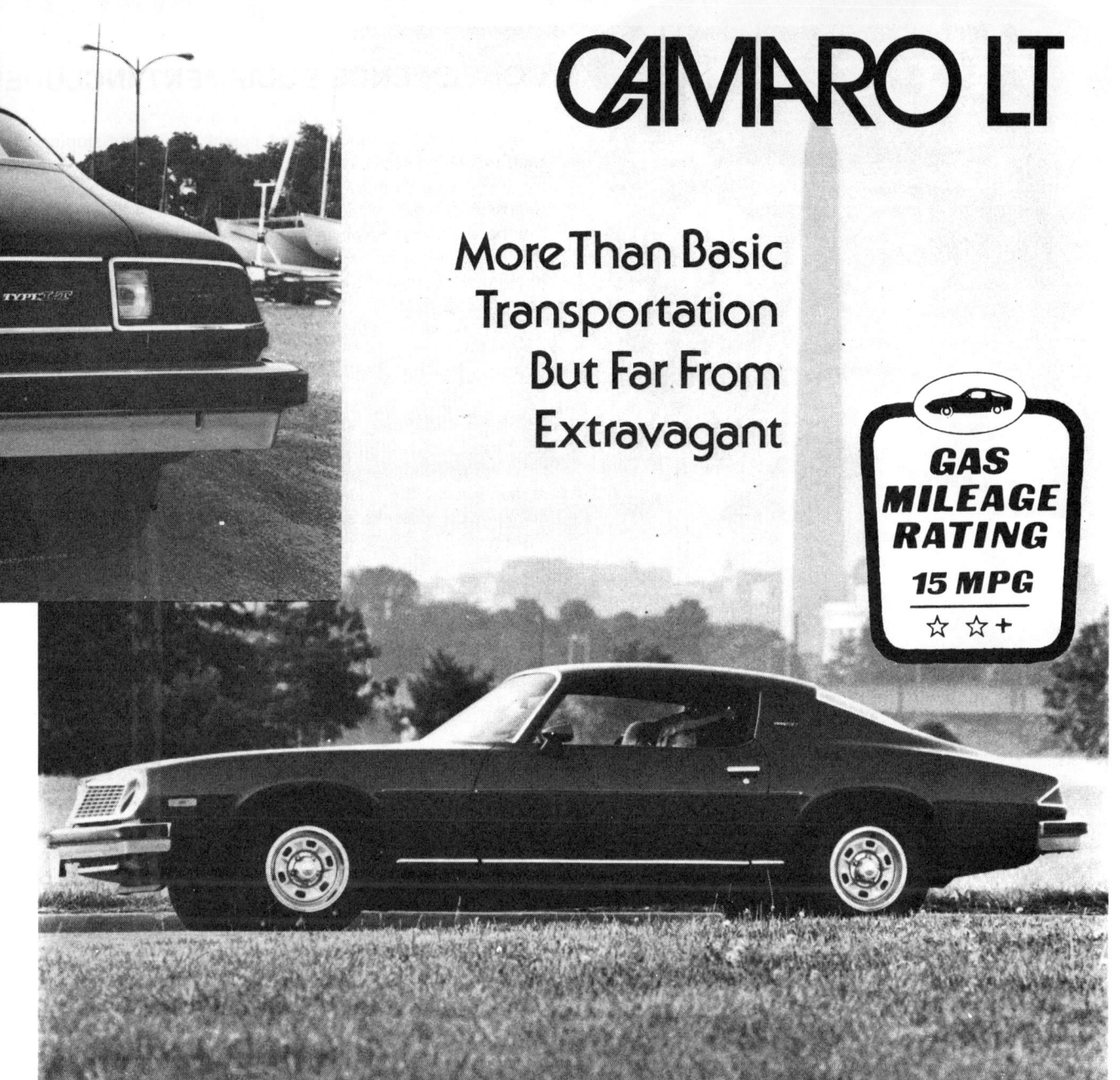

**More Than Basic
Transportation
But Far From
Extravagant**

**GAS
MILEAGE
RATING
15 MPG
☆ ☆ +**

seatbelts are optional, since the standard belt and harness arrangement in all Camaro's is black, regardless of the color of the interior). Also standard with the LT are the highly attractive short-spoke cast steel wheels with chromed steel rim inserts, tinted glass, sport mirrors, hideaway windshield wipers and side moulding with padded vinyl inserts. The side mouldings are very definitely an asset, as they prevent your doors from obtaining unwanted dings and chips in the paint job from hasty, careless door openers who always seem to inhabit crowded parking lots, and always right next to your car. As well, they serve this purpose unobtrusively, heightening the appearance of the car by breaking up the expanse of the cars side, and adding to the longitudinal suggestion of the car's lines.

Inside, the Camaro presents an interior commensurately attractive and comfortable with its rich external appearance. The seats are very deep bucket-types giving good lateral support, and even more importantly to those who have occasion to commute long distances, they also give very good lower lumbar and buttocks support. The Camaro's seats are among the few that we have ever found to be endurable for

extended long-distance driving. In standard form, they come in all vinyl and are colored so as to match the rest of the interior, but as a slight extra cost option, they are available with brushed cloth inserts giving an appearance not unlike velour.

The dashboard and instrument panel (featuring a simulated hardwood paneling insert) are solidly constructed and in keeping with the rest of the car, are very clean and subtle in their attractiveness. Our only complaint with the instruments was that in keeping with what seems like an American tradition, a clock has taken precedence over an oil pressure gauge. Perhaps this is minor as it will probably never become critical in most cases, but it is worth noting that an oil pressure gauge will tell you in an instant what is going on inside your engine's oiling system, whereas an "idiot light" will only tell you that it totally failed five minutes ago, giving you no clue to impending disorders that would befall the motor.

One word of warning regarding the interior, lest you expect too much. As with most cars produced these days save the very largest models, the Camaro is short on rear seat leg

• CONVENIENCE EQUIPMENT INCLUDES

room. Add to this the low roof height due to the sloping routine, and you can easily see that the Camaro is not the car for a growing family. Seating more than four is a near impossibility, and if the four are all six-footers, then even four becomes very much an improbable number, not because they won't all fit but because the two in the back will in all likelihood complain after a very short while that they just aren't comfortable.

The powerplant in the LT Camaro is the tried and true 350 cubic inch V-8 engine bearing the designation L-65 (except in California, where the L-65 is not available). This is the standard engine in the LT, and comes with a two-barrel Rochester carburetor, single exhaust with a crossover pipe (all pipe 2" o.d. tubing), hydraulic lifter camshaft, and an 8.5:1 compression ratio which makes it compatible with low- or non-leaded fuel. The combination is rated at 145 net horsepower, with the engine reaching peak power at only 3800 rpm. The torque rating of the engine is 250 lbs.-ft. at 2200 rpm, meaning that maximum pulling power is well within the normal useable rpm range.

Crowded engine compartment houses the 350 cubic inch V-8 engine which uses low-lead or unleaded gasoline. Powerplant is equipped with a two-barrel carburetor and delivers 149 net horsepower. The dash and instrument panel feature a simulated hardwood panel insert, is solidly constructed. Our man behind the wheel complained that the clock took precedence over an oil pressure gauge. Standard transmission with the engine is a 3-speed manual unit featuring a 2.54:1 first gear ratio, 1.50:1 2nd and 1.00:1 3rd. Rear bumper treatment is good with attractive tail lights.

The standard transmission with the engine is a 3-speed manual unit featuring a 2.54:1 first gear ratio, a 1.50:1 second gear ratio and of course a 1.00:1 third gear ratio. Our particular test car came equipped with the optional Turbo Hydramatic 3-speed automatic transmission, carrying gear ratios of 2.52:1 in first and 1.52:1 in second. Available as an extra cost option is the 4-speed manual transmission having ratios of 2.54:1 in first gear, 1.80:1 in second, 1.44:1 in third and 1.00:1 in fourth. The shift lever location in all cases is on the floor.

With either of the manual transmissions, the only rear axle ratio available with the LT is the 3.08:1 unit. With the automatic trans, the standard ratio is the 2.73:1 unit, with a 3.42:1 unit available as a trailer towing option.

Fuel economy, while not on a par to the compacts available, is certainly within an acceptable range. During open road driving with constant speeds in the 50-55 mph range, our two-barrel carbureted car managed mileage figures as high as 18.3 miles per gallon with the engine not really in peak tune. Coupled with the Camaro's 21-gallon fuel tank capacity, up almost 3 gallons from last year, this gives a cruising range of about 370-380 miles. In city traffic, the mileage figure dropped down considerably, varying anywhere from about 12½ to almost 15 miles per gallon, depending upon conditions.

It may be true that this is not the best of mileage, but one should remember that in order to have the advantages and comforts of a car the size of our 3700 pound Camaro, one must have available sufficient power, and that takes gasoline. The L-65 engine does a fair job of hauling the car around, having adequate torque to handle all types of driving easily. Engines not being what they once were, though, the L-65 is perhaps lacking in responsiveness and acceleration, meaning that in critical passing situations, we found it to leave something to be desired.

For those that desire a little more snap in their cars, two optional engines are available in the LT line, the LM-1 for California and the L-48 for the rest of the country. Both of these power-plants also displace 350 cubic inches, and as with the L-65, have 8.5:1 compression ratios.

What sets these engines apart from the standard power-plant is that they both come equipped with Rochester Quadra Jet four-barrel carburetors. The California engine is rated at 160 net horsepower at 3800 rpm and 250 lbs.-ft. of torque at 2500 rpm, having a single exhaust system. The L-48 engine is rated at 184 horsepower at 4000 rpm and 270 lbs.-ft. of torque at 2600 rpm, having a dual exhaust system flowing into a single low-restriction muffler.

It is worth noting that all engines of this type can be converted over to the new Delco "High Energy Ignition" system, which is standard equipment on all Z-28 Camaro's built after May 1, 1974 (the Z-28 is the high performance option in the Camaro/LT line). This new ignition system features a distributor with a self-contained spark producing capacity, rather than having to rely on a separate coil to produce electrical charge as in a conventional distributor. As well, the HEI system does away with the ignition breaker points which are characteristic of conventional designs.

The advantages of the new system are twofold. Since the HEI eliminates most of the moving parts that wear and require adjustment in a conventional ignition system, it requires less maintenance than a conventional breaker-type system. Secondly, since the HEI produces a hotter and more accurately timed spark of longer duration than conventionally produced sparks, it provides more complete and efficient combustion of the fuel mixture, resulting in noticeably better fuel economy and cleaner exhaust. As well, it can continue to fire worn spark plugs beyond what a conventional system is capable of. As a result, the HEI owner can expect longer service life from a given set of spark plugs before cleaning or replacement is needed. All this amounts to the fact that it is

CONTINUED ON PAGE 32

Chevrolet Camaro LT

SURVIVAL OF THE FITTEST—
CAMARO AND FIREBIRD

One of the great fascinations of the world of automobiles is that it functions on a miniature parallel with the entire nation. The laws of supply and demand are usually in effect for long periods of time before any results appear. When they finally do take effect, the reactions are swift and overwhelming.

Watergate was the bursting dam of political pressure and interaction. The wave of price reductions and rebates is the natural result of buyer resistance.

The world of Pony cars underwent a similar cataclysmic housecleaning, predating the political and economic upheavals by a year. Mustang created the class in 1964, giving rise to a host of imitators. In a classic misreading of market signs, each Pony car was hastily dispatched down the road to its own demise. Mustang waxed fat and lazy, only recently shedding its husk to return to the original concept. Barracuda and Challenger selected the performance image, falling by the wayside when performance ceased to sell. Cougar ballooned into obesity and left the fold for the realm of luxury. Javelin drove in wandering circles never really finding any definition or intended direction of movement.

The only survivors are the Camaro and the Firebird. They too were flirting with self-induced strangulation from overpricing when the rest of their motoring mates made overpricing a way of life.

Camaro and Firebird have survived for a number of reasons. They are small cars in an era of demand for small cars. They are versatile enough to be operated economically when economy is mandatory. They ride smoothly enough to satisfy the domesticated urbanite, they handle sprightly enough to slake the lust for excitement for the young man on the move regardless of his age or the duration of his movement. They are overpriced, but this is an age of overpricing. Their saving grace is quality.

At first glance the two machines appear to be virtually identical twins. This is a deceiving illusion. The only common exterior sheet metal panels are the roof and the rear deck area. Hood, doors, and fenders, front and rear, are individual. Even the front sub-frames and radiator mounts are sublty unique to each car.

Both machines offer a very smooth, though firm ride. Both machines have excellent street handling. The well refined suspensions are mounted on front sub-frames to perform the dual function of isolating road vibration from the occupants as well as improving rigidity of suspension mounting points. Front coil springs, five-leaf rear springs, stabilizer bars and shock rates are all computer selected to match the weight of the specific engine.

Both cars are equipped with GM's new High Energy Ignition system, cold air intake, and catalytic converters. Firebird is powered by the 400-cubic-inch 4V engine while Camaro mounts the 350-4V. Although the Firebird outperformed the Camaro in acceleration, the edge in cubic inches is very nearly offset by the quite low 7.6:1 compression ratio of the Pontiac 400 as compared with the 8.5:1 ratio of the Chevy 350.

Although the difference in ride is subtle, the Camaro is smoother than the Firebird. Conversely, the Firebird handles better than the Camaro. A firmer Firebird suspension plus wider tires, GR7-15 to FR78-14, account for the difference.

Illogically, the Camaro stopped in less distance than the Firebird. With the wider tires and 35 pounds less weight, on the Firebird, it should have been reversed.

Inside, the Firebird has an excellent instrument panel. Pontiac consistently creates the better designed domestic instrument layouts. Tachometer and speed meter are large and centrally placed. Oil pressure, water temp, fuel and voltmeter are all visible.

The contoured bucket seats are firm, reasonably comfortable with good retention, but have no rake adjustment.

Pontiac Firebird Trans Am

Unforgivable. Our blue Trans-Am had a white vinyl interior which we think is an excellent combination.

Rearward visibility is very good, thanks to the long needed wrap-around rear window. Dual outside mirrors are necessary, but our test car did not have a remote control for the right mirror. This is a mandatory option.

Although the heater and air conditioner work quite well, the natural ventilation was unimpressive. The auto trans shifter is well located and is the correct size.

The rear seat, one of the selling points and reasons for the creation of the Pony car, is really vestigal in nature, suitable only for children or short riding adults. It is really just a convenience. But it is a convenience.

Camaro, while similarly configures inside, has its own distinct personality. The cloth and velour covered buckets are equally as comfortable as the Firebird's, but have, in addition, a two-position rake adjustment. Not what we really want, but a step along the way.

Door controls are a bit more conveniently located in the Camaro. Both cars have good open spoke steering wheels. We like the smaller diameter wheel in the Firebird.

The dash panel in the Camaro is a joy to behold. A neatly curved recess with a bird's-eye maple applique which is very nicely executed. There are a full set of gauges, almost, which are readily visible, almost. In spite of a very nice layout, Chevrolet persists, to the point of obstinacy, to place at least two of the engine instruments directly behind the hands on the steering wheel.

The heater and air conditioner work as well as the Firebirds, but the vent position passes more outside air.

Shifter handle is nicely located with an easy to use thumb detent, but we don't like the remote dash located shift position indicator. That is personal preference. It has advantages.

Like the T/A, there is no remote control for the right hand mirror.

The big surprise was the lower section of the dash panel. Very shoddy, with an ill-fitting glove box door and a ratty looking ashtray. Most unlike GM fit and finish.

Camaro suffers from cold engine stumble and a little hesitation at very low rpm. A situation allegedly cured by use of the catalytic converter. Warmed up and running at over 2000 rpm, response is smooth and almost brisk.

Both cars exhibit excellent tracking on both city streets and freeways with rain grooves in them. Since both have different size steel-belted radials, the dead straight tracking puts the lie to the excuse often used by other manufacturers that front end wander is caused by radial tires and/or grooves in the pavement.

Both cars have positive feel in their variable ratio power steering and quick response. Camaro has a faster ratio than Firebird.

Both cars have a good solid feeling, low center of gravity, excellent visibility considering the styling, and good responsive handling characteristics.

One of the nicer features of both is a complete absence of ratchet hangup when dragging out the seat belts.

In spite of prices nudging $6000, which we consider to be too high, the customer is assured of quality in the basic product.

It is true that both Chevy and GM are cutting corners and trying to sneak a few things through, but all of the short cuts are visible, such as the Camaro lower dash, to the scrutinous eye. Simply check your car over carefully before you accept it.

You can be assured, at least at this point, that ride, handling, and engine response will be satisfactory. Quality of the running gear can be counted on. The Camaro had the LT options and the Firebird was the Trans-Am. Camaro does have a firmer suspension option if you desire.

Which is best? Too many variables to determine. We liked the Firebird's overall combination of ride, handling and response.

Camaro's recessed instrument panel, walnut applique finish and open-spoked wheels are pluses that offset partial obscuration of engine instruments by hands.

Firebird's engine-turned dash panel has the engine instruments out to the side for visibility. Controls are well within reach.

CONTINUED FROM PAGE 29

worth considering installing one of the HEI units in a Camaro should you purchase one.

Perhaps the pleasantest aspect of the Camaro's performance that we observed during our testing was the handling characteristics. Without being harsh, the ride was very firm and sure. Although the suspension in the LT is not up to par with high performance set ups, it at all times gave a very good feel of the road. The suspension features coil front springs and multiple-leaf rear springs, with spring rates that have been compu-

ter selected according to vehicle weights, including the weight of optional equipment. This gives the suspension the proper stiffness to keep body lean during cornering within acceptable limits. In addition, direct double action shock absorbers are mounted at all four corners, giving good road shock recovery and stability under most any circumstances you are likely to encounter. Finally, the LT, being equipped with a V-8 engine, is fitted with anti-sway bars front and rear, and front item having a hefty 15/16'' diameter and the rear having a 9/16'' diameter. Hence, the car is capable of keeping a level attitude, even during fairly hard cornering, with only a slight tendency towards understeer (front end plowing) unless the car is really pushed.

The standard power steering makes driving the car a snap. The Camaro steers easily, and the standard E78 x 14 Goodyear Power Cushion Polyglas tires respond quickly to directional changes, as well as complementing the suspension by giving good lateral adhesion. The overall result is that you feel very much in control of the car at all times, knowing full well that you are driving it, and not the converse.

Stopping is also one of the Camaro's stronger points. Chevrolet engineers have seen fit to make front disc brakes standard equipment on all Camaros. As well, all V-8 equipped Camaro's come with the front brakes power-assisted, so naturally these were on our LT. During our testing, we found the Camaro capable of repeated lock-up stops without brake fade setting in.

The availability of convenience equipment in the Camaro is on a par with most other automobiles, including such niceties as air conditioning, tilting and/or telescoping steering wheel, luggage compartment, underhood and courtesy lamps, and rear window defogger (mechanical, not electrical) just to name a few. We might make mention that we found the AM/FM stereo radio option to provide unusually good separation and sound fidelity.

And that, in a nutshell, is what the '74 Camaro LT is like. The price, being in the $4500-$5500 range, is not inordinately expensive. It is a dependable car that delivers satisfactory performance (as satisfactory as can be expected in these days of smog motors) with the added attractiveness of being downright comfortable. It is moderately sized, being neither too big nor too small, and is awfully nice to look at. It's not just an ordinary car—it's something more, for the person who wants a little more. ●

SPECIFICATIONS	TRANS-AM			CAMARO		
Engine	OHV V-8			OHV V-8		
Bore & Stroke-ins.	4.12 x 3.75			4.00 x 3.48		
Displacement-cu. in./c.c.	400/6400			350/5600		
HP @ RPM	185 @ 3600			155 @ 3800		
Torque (lbs.-ft. @ RPM)	NA			250 @ 2400		
Compression Ratio	7.6:1			8.5:1		
Carburetion	4V			4V		
Transmission	3-Speed Automatic			3-Speed Automatic		
Rear Axle Ratio	3.08:1			3.08:1		
Steering Type	Recirculating Ball			Recirculating Ball		
Steering Ratio	16.5:1 to 14.3:1			15.03:1 to 10.61:1		
Turning Circle-ft.	38.9			38.5		
Wheel Turns (lock-to-lock)	2.41			2.41		
Tires	Goodrich Steel Belted Radial GR 70-15			Firestone Steel Belted Radial FR 78-14		
Brakes	Disc/Drum			Disc/Drum		
Front Suspension	Coils/Shocks/Stabilizer			Coils/Shocks/Stabilizer		
Rear Suspension	Leaves/Shocks/Stabilizer			Leaves/Shocks/Stabilizer		
Body/Frame Construction	Integral w/Sub-Frame			Integral w/Sub-Frame		
Wheelbase — in./mm	108.1/2702.5			108.0/2700		
Overall Length — in./mm	196.0/4900			195.4/4885		
Width — in./mm	73.0/1825			74.4/1860		
Front Track — in./mm	61.2/1530			61.6/1540		
Rear Track — in./mm	60.3/1507.5			60.3/1507.5		
Height — in./mm	49.6/1240			49.1/1227.5		
Weight as Tested — lbs.	3850			3885		
Storage Capacity cu. ft.	6.4			7.2		
Fuel Capacity — gals./liters	20.2/80.8			21.0/84		
Oil Capacity — qts./liters	5.0/20			4.0/16		
Base Price	$4740.10			$4070.05		
Price as Tested	$5960			$5878.78		
Performance						
Acceleration						
0 — 30 mph	3.8			4.0		
0 — 40 mph	5.4			5.9		
0 — 50 mph	7.4			8.0		
0 — 60 mph	9.8			11.0		
Standing Start ¼-mile						
Elapsed Time (sec.)	16.75			17.43		
Speed (mph)	84.98			79.64		
Passing Speeds						
40 — 60 mph	4.9			5.7		
50 — 70 mph	6.1			6.9		
Stopping Distance (ft.)						
30 — 0 mph	27'8''			26'3''		
60 — 0 mph	134'8''			122'4''		
Fuel Mileage	16.59			16.5		
Speedometer Error						
Indicated Speed	40	50	60	40	50	60
True Speed	39.16	48.62	58.32	38.62	48.07	58.02

One More Time: Camaro Rally Sport

BY STEPHAN WILKINSON

Growing old gracefully isn't all bad.

• The Camaro is, if nothing else, a survivor. There are those who'd have had it go out smoking, wanting it to die with its boots on, but the Camaro has learned to compromise and instead of fading away has become an old soldier. The chunky, square-shouldered, tight-muscled *macho* appeal that made the original Camaro a favorite of a whole generation of high-schoolers has become a smoother, looser line—more flash than class—and the heavily rouged Rally Sport is only a

halfhearted hint of the blood-bailing Z28 of yore. Yet . . . and yet the Camaro keeps on keepin' on.

For good reason, really. It is still a relatively honest, handsome car, and it's still a competent car. Not exhilarating, not pulse-pounding, not super-bad, just "competent." The car handles like . . . well, maybe not a thoroughbred but a sight better than your ordinary horse. One also gets the feeling about the Camaro that even with the most basic, most easily

understandable handling modifications, you or I could turn this stone into Mighty Joe Young. Better shocks and stiffer anti-sway bars from the GM parts shelf or the after market, stickier tires; the car is an excellent platform—balanced and predictable in its handling—for cottage industry to improve upon.

The aging Camaro is the car that continues to make the Monza, enthusiastic little upstart that it is, look foolish. Or at least its price makes the Monza's "luxury subcompact" sticker seem enough of a corporate aberration that over twice as many coupe buyers have chosen the Camaro (base price $3685 with the 350-cubic inch V-8) as have opted for the V-8 Monza 2+2, which lists for $4151. Similarly equipped with typical popular options, the Camaro comes out about $300 more expensive than a Monza. Chevrolet decided there was gold to be mined in the small-car hills ("If those frightened ninnies want small cars, make them pay for it . . ."), so they priced the Monza accordingly—and watched many of the buyers that it attracted into their showrooms depart in Camaros. Bigger engine, slightly bigger interior and trunk, moderately better performance for approximately the same price. Not a difficult choice to make, unless you are in love with fuel economy; only there does the Monza have a substantial edge.

Chevrolet now builds a Rally Sport Camaro—a 1975½ model that began coming off the line last spring—with lots of black paint and stick-on striping. And little else, for the car we tested didn't have such recommended options as the stiffer "F-41" sports suspension, special steering gear with a stiffer

internal torsion bar that allows it to impart more road feel, and stickier E60-15 non-radial tires on larger Trans Am wheels. But boy, did it have flat-black paint. Whoever started this paint-the-hood-black craze must have seen *Twelve O'Clock High* too many times. But the hype apparently works. Though it hardly serves the kind of anti-dazzle function it used to fill on aircraft, the paint gets more than its share of glances on the highway and attracts gas-station attendants the way a Carrera's foot-high gold lettering never will.

It's a strange color to paint any sunward facing surface on a car, since black (especially nonreflective black) absorbs heat almost as nicely as glass does. Perhaps this is why Chevrolet painted the roof a semi-gloss black. Unfortunately, the slight difference in paint quality is about the second thing the guys at the gas station notice about the car: "Bitchin' paint job, man . . . really fine, ya know . . . but hey, looka the

The car that carried a generation of high-schoolers to heights of ecstasy has shed its studs and leathers for fancy threads.

PHOTOGRAPHY: GENE BUTERA

ACCELERATION standing ¼ mile, seconds

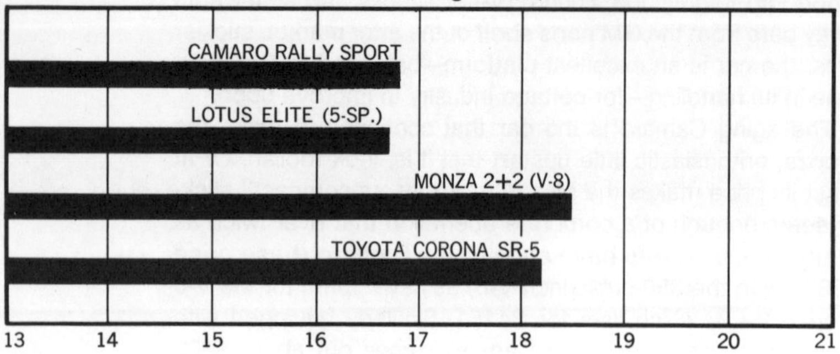

CAMARO RALLY SPORT
LOTUS ELITE (5-SP.)
MONZA 2+2 (V-8)
TOYOTA CORONA SR-5

13　14　15　16　17　18　19　20　21

BRAKING 70-0 mph, feet

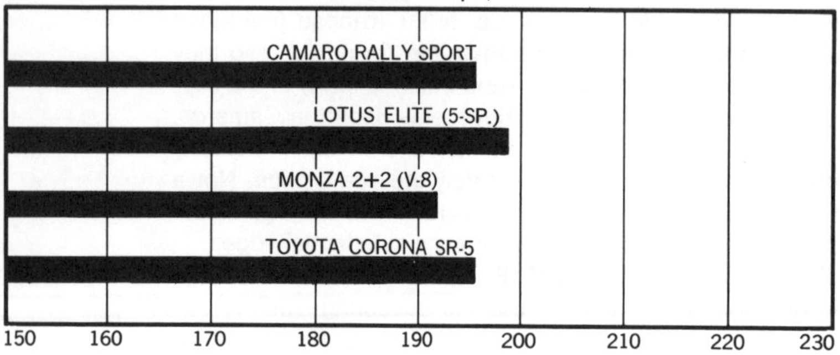

CAMARO RALLY SPORT
LOTUS ELITE (5-SP.)
MONZA 2+2 (V-8)
TOYOTA CORONA SR-5

150　160　170　180　190　200　210　220　230

FUEL ECONOMY C/D mileage cycle, mpg

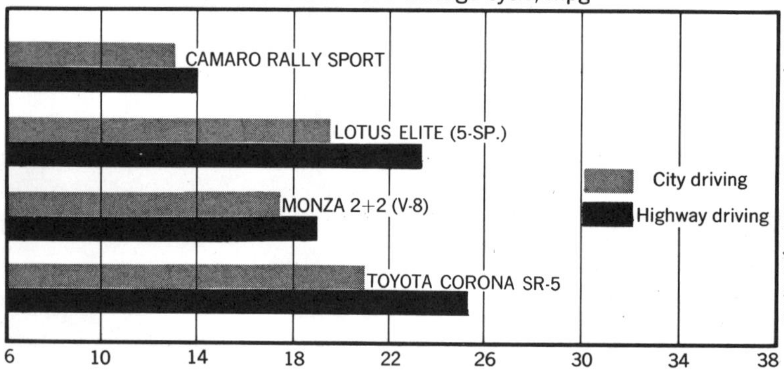

CAMARO RALLY SPORT
LOTUS ELITE (5-SP.)
MONZA 2+2 (V-8)
TOYOTA CORONA SR-5

City driving
Highway driving

6　10　14　18　22　26　30　34　38

PRICE AS TESTED dollars x 1000

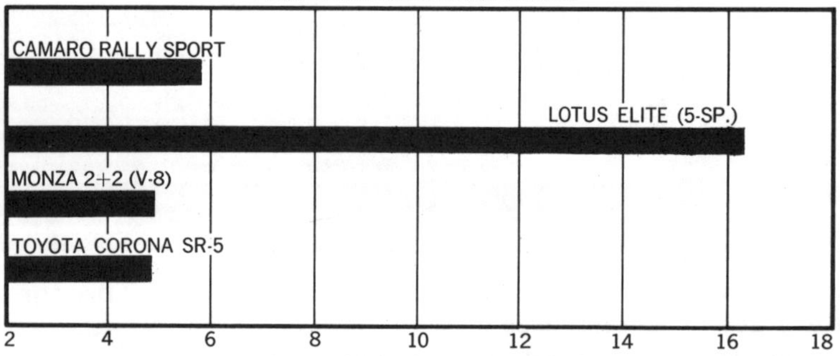

CAMARO RALLY SPORT
LOTUS ELITE (5-SP.)
MONZA 2+2 (V-8)
TOYOTA CORONA SR-5

2　4　6　8　10　12　14　16　18

INTERIOR SOUND LEVEL dBA

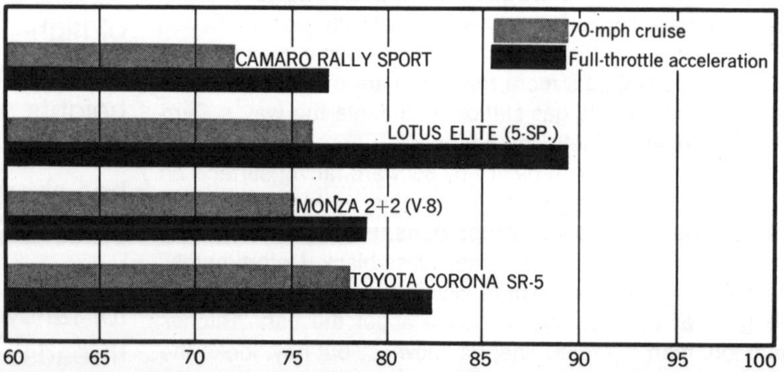

CAMARO RALLY SPORT
LOTUS ELITE (5-SP.)
MONZA 2+2 (V-8)
TOYOTA CORONA SR-5

70-mph cruise
Full-throttle acceleration

60　65　70　75　80　85　90　95　100

CHEVROLET CAMARO RALLY SPORT

Manufacturer: Chevrolet Motor Division
General Motors Corp.
Warren, Michigan 48090

Vehicle type: front-engine, rear-wheel-drive, 2-door coupe

Price as tested: $5873.78
(Manufacturer's suggested retail price, including all options listed below, dealer preparation and delivery charges, does not include state and local taxes, license or freight charges)

Options on test car: base Camaro Type LT, $4057.05; Rally Sport equipment, $16.00; 350 engine, $54.00; Turbo-Hydra-matic transmission, $235.00; air conditioning, $490.00; Positraction, $49.00; radial tuned suspension, $35.00; front and rear spoilers, $77.00; white letter radial tires, $46.00; AM/FM radio, $135.00; rear speaker, $19.00; console, $68.00; rear window defogger, $41.00; visor vanity mirror, $3.00; floor mats, $14.00; power windows, $91.00; power door locks, $56.00; tinted glass, $45.00 adjustable driver's seatback, $18.00; custom seatbelts, $16.00; tilt steering wheel, $49.00; space-saver tire,–$1.27; dual horns, $4.00; auxiliary lighting, $20.00; style trim group, $55.00; destination charges, $33.00

ENGINE
Type: V-8, water-cooled, cast iron block/heads, 5 main bearings
Bore x stroke ....4.00 x 3.48 in, 101.6 x 88.4 mm
Displacement ....350 cu in, 5730 cc
Compression ratio ....8.5 to one
Carburetion ....1 x 4-bbl Rochester Quadrajet
Valve gear ...pushrod-operated overhead valves, hydraulic lifters
Power (SAE net) ....155 bhp @ 3800 rpm
Torque (SAE net) ....250 lbs-ft @ 2400 rpm
Max. recommended engine speed ....5000 rpm

DRIVE TRAIN
Transmission ....3-speed, automatic
Final drive ratio ....3.08 to one

Gear	Ratio	Mph/1000 rpm	Max. test speed
I	2.48	9.9	54 mph (5000 rpm)
II	1.48	16.5	83 mph (5000 rpm)
III	1.00	24.4	116 mph (4750 rpm)

DIMENSIONS AND CAPACITIES
Wheelbase ....108.0 in
Track, F/R ....61.6/60.3 in
Length ....195.4 in
Width ....74.4 in
Height ....49.2 in
Curb weight......................................3970 lbs
Weight distribution, F/R.......................57.0/43.0%
Fuel capacity ....21 gal

SUSPENSION
F: ...ind., unequal-length control arms, coil springs, anti-sway bar
R: ....rigid axle, semi-elliptic leaf springs, anti-sway bar

STEERING
Type ....recirculating ball, power assisted
Turns lock-to-lock....................................2.4
Turning circle curb-to-curb ....38.5 ft

BRAKES
F: ....11.0-in dia vented rotor, power assisted
R: ....2.0 x 9.5-in cast iron drum, power assisted

WHEELS AND TIRES
Wheel size ....7.0 x 14-in
Tire make and size ......Goodyear Steel Belted Radial, FR78-14
Test inflation pressures, F/R ....24/24 psi

PERFORMANCE
Zero to	Seconds
30 mph	3.6
40 mph	5.0
50 mph	6.4
60 mph	8.5
70 mph	11.2
80 mph	15.9
90 mph	24.1
100 mph	27.5

Standing ¼-mile ....16.8 sec @ 81.5 mph
Top speed (observed) ....116 mph
70-0 mph ....196 ft (0.84 G)
Fuel economy, C/D mileage cycle........13.5 mpg, city driving
14.0 mpg, highway driving

roof's a different kinda paint, man . . ."

Though your basic Rally Sport is entirely a decor exercise—Power by Paint—the car wears its colors well, in part because the color design is reasonably tasteful and partly because the styling extremists have been kept away from the Camaro's basic form. There's nothing far-out on the car, little to mar its smooth lines, no signboards or extra emblems or bogus vents/scoops/spoilers. The sole sheetmetal change for 1975 on all Camaros is the wraparound rear window, and visibility all around is quite good despite the wide rear pillars. It does take awhile to get used to that Camaro quality of feeling you're sitting deep "in" the car, though, due to its high beltline and low roofline.

The view inside the car, however, is as bad as outside visibility is good. All four of the peripheral gauges on the panel, outboard of the tach and speedometer, are obscured either by the steering-wheel rim or one of its spokes. (But it does have a real horn button, right in the center—a benefit that becomes more meaningful in direct proportion to how many padded hubs you have vainly stroked, pounded and massaged, and how many headlights you have flashed and torrents of windshield-washer fluid you have loosed, in frantic attempts to find trick horn actuators.)

The Camaro's days as a street racer are only a memory now, and with the 350-cu. in. two- and four-barrel V-8s the only engines available besides the six, the car has settled into senescence as a boulevardier who no longer has any in-tention of getting his new suit messed up in a one-on-one scuffle. A good thing, too, for the four-barrel Rally Sport with the three-speed automatic eked out 16.8 seconds in the quarter with a trap speed of 81.5 mph. (The Monza 2+2 with the 262 V-8 and automatic does the job in 18.5 seconds/75.4 mph.) The car has a moderately high (3.08) rear-end ratio, doubtless in aid of fuel economy; if acceleration is your paramount concern, best you at least specify the four-speed manual transmission available only with the 350 four-barrel engine.

What remains the Camaro's strong suit is the one thing legislation is hard pressed to take away from it: handling. The longer you drive a Camaro, the happier you become in it; the car seems to shrink around you until its moves become surprisingly predictable. There is little body roll during moderately enthusiastic cornering or sharp transients from lane to lane, and the steering seems precise (though nowhere near as tactile and pleasant as the unit on the big-brother Firebird).

When pushed to the limit on the skid-pad, however, understeer arrives in embarrassing quantity: The Rally Sport limps around munching its outside front tire, which folds under like an rubber eraser. It doesn't help matters that the standard-equipment tire is a tall, soft FR78, with which a good ride is apparently a more important consideration than handling. During clockwise trips, the inside rear wheel lifts free of the ground, settles and grabs and lifts again, complicating matters by imparting a rocking-horse motion to the car as it al-ternately pushes and pauses to catch its breath. The optional ($66 in the Rally Sport, $112 on other Camaros) "gym-khana suspension," including stiffer anti-sway bars front and rear, would seem an eminently worthwhile deal.

The rear suspension bottoms with a clunk if the car gets light on a bump, but in order to provide extra axle rebound room, it's either that or give up even more of what must already be the smallest trunk on any coupe south of the Corvette. It's not bad for small weekender parcels strewn here and there, but there's little real room for more than one moderate-size suitcase. (Perhaps Chevrolet Division will one day give the Camaro a new career with a hatchback, which would make something meaningful out of the almost-useless back seats by converting them into easily accessible cargo area.)

It's hard to forthrightly say the Camaro's brakes are *good*, since the linings fade rapidly and require surprisingly high pedal pressure, but they do have one value beyond compare: They are well biased, and you'll be hard put to produce the kind of rears-only lockup that gets you looking sideways at things. Before fade sets in, you can haul the Rally Sport down from 70 in a competitive 196 feet.

So consider the Camaro, that graceful survivor. It's still around, and they still seem to love it in the showrooms, even though it's not the star it used to be. But like the light, agile flathead Fords of the mid-1930s, the Camaro is such a strong combination of handling, style and simplicity that it'll probably be around for a long time to come. •

CONTINUED FROM PAGE 16

Javelin has a particularly smooth and quiet ride without sacrificing the sporty car feel that's become part of the image of these cars.

Interior was perhaps the best of the lot, with a well-appointed and laid-out dash panel, soft comfortable seats, and a good driving position. The only thing we didn't like about the Javelin s interior was the fit, or lack of it, of some of the pieces on the instrument panel. Both our Javelin and another '74 model that we drove during the course of the test suffered from excessive air leaks and high wind noise at the leading edge of the front windows, but the AMC folks told us that this was only a problem with a small number of cars. AMC's quality has improved greatly thanks to their excellent Buyer Protection Plan, but it's still not perfect.

Another minor complaint about the Javelin was that the console-mounted transmission has no detent between drive and second gear, so it's easy to put the lever in second and think it's in drive. All the other cars have a detent there, so we think AMC could as well.

Aside from those nagging complaints, the Javelin had the best combination of ride, handling, available power and interior comfort and convenience—in our opinion Picking a winner is tough The inequities of engine sizes and suspension packages make a strict ranking highly subjective, and with that qualifier in mind, we'd grab the Javelin first and the Z-28 second. The latter two still are terrific alternatives

The only thing we can say for certain is that these cars have become expensive over the years. All of our test cars are priced above $4000 and we think you'd be hard pressed to get anything but a super-stripped econo-special for much less than that. And without trying to flog a dead dog, we also like to mention again, as we have in past road tests, that none of these so-called *Grand Touring* cars has a fully adjustable seat available, making the descriptive title somewhat thinner in impact. We'd like to see fully adjustable seats as standard equipment on all American cars. After all, if the Opel Manta can have one, why can't the American sporty cars?

Well, since we *didn't* title this story the Last Roundup, it just might be the kiss of death for ponycars. But we don't think so. We always felt that these good-looking, fine-handling machines had their own niche in the American automotive scene and perhaps the recent dramatic upsurge in ponycar sales has borne this out. After driving the current batch we can safely say that the ponycar is very much alive and every indication we get from Detroit, especially with the current trend away from the big car, is that the reports of its death are greatly exaggerated.

A Camaro With Track Shoes

BY PATRICK BEDARD

When better Camaros are built, Mark Donohue will build them.

• First some background: During his year-long hiatus from racing, Mark Donohue's position as head of Penske Racing required him to get next to 15 Camaros in order to prepare them for the International Race of Champions. By the time that project was finished, he knew as much as the factory about what makes these Chevy coupes run.

So much for his days in the office. When he is not working, one thing that makes Donohue breathe hard is boats—narrow-hulled open-ocean racers with enough horsepower to foam the Atlantic seaboard with one pass. These are serious boats, and you do not find them at your local yacht store. Instead, you have them made. Don Aronow of Miami builds a particularly lean and stable design known as a Cigarette, and with a pair of 500-hp engines, a Cigarette will part any wave you can throw at it. Aronow, it turns out, was looking for something out of the ordinary in a motor car, so a trade-out was arranged: Car racer trades car for boat from boat racer—a best-of-both-worlds kind of deal.

Only thing was, when the word got out that Donohue was building signature

model Camaros, an unexpectedly large number of sensible citizens wanted them too. And they were prepared to trade *money*. Which has Donohue teetering on the brink of a 10- or 20-car run of IROC GTs plus a number of kits for the do-it-to-yourself crowd.

Slog with us now across a flooded parking lot near Kennedy Airport on a drizzling spring night. Our hero has returned from the Grand Prix wars to drive the finished prototype, which has been built and prepared to his specifications and driven down to the city by Bill Mitchell, a clean-cut young engineer/racer in the Donohue mold. There is some apprehension because Donohue has driven the original, first-draft version and found it lacking. But this car has all of the fixes. Will Mark sign it off?

The silver Camaro is a drab gray-green under the mercury lights. Donohue eyes it critically. The gray pin stripes and the wheel-opening accents are more conservative than he had anticipated. But the 9.5-inch wide IROC Mini-lites fill out the rear wheel wells to his satisfaction. The XWX Michelins look aggressive enough. The chin spoiler is a

shortened version of the one used on the IROC Camaros with one driving light and one fog light tunneled in where you expect to find brake ducts. That gets a high rating, and the stock parking light modified to serve as a cold-air inlet to the carburetor is a hit. He is coming around. The chrome windshield clips and rear window straps look suitably racy. Mark Donohue the stylist, Gucci loafers soaked through to his Regency Street socks, stands back, grins and buys the whole package right there in a soggy car park in Queens.

But Mark Donohue the driver is reserving judgment. There is a labyrinth of deserted roads around the airport with enough kinks and humps to be a poor man's Nurburgring. He wants to see if the Camaro works like it looks.

Right away, even from my passenger seat, it's clear that this is no ordinary Camaro. It has the stiff-legged ride of an Italian GT car. No pitching. It hits the bumps, the suspension rebounds, then recovers immediately. The sensation befuddles one's internal computer: There you are looking past a Camaro dashboard through a Camaro windshield over a Camaro hood . . . with Maserati ride motions filtering up through the seat. Can this be?

The shocks are a bit more severe than he'd like—not enough low-speed leak, but not bad either. He tries the air horns, changing them from soft to loud with a switch on the console. A grin. Yet another switch flashes the lights in the manner of the flat-out Porsches on the autobahn. All systems operating. He gives the fat-rimmed wheel a flick to the left and lets go. The Camaro instantly centers itself. To the right. Same thing. He wrenches it into a hard lane change. Perfect composure. Again, this time through a huge puddle. The car slices through, sending a shower of water onto the windshield. "This car is great. I can't make it slide." He is delighted.

We tour the course in a series of bursts and lurches until we arrive at a traffic circle. Immediately he sees its possibilities as a skid pad. It's bumpy and slick with rain. Around to the left, stabbing the gas, toeing the brake, diving through shallow lakes with the tail out. The Camaro darts and dips like a wire-guided missile. He is euphoric. Off on a tangent road at full throttle, 75 mph through the spray past a cautious Thunderbird, firm on the brake, cut to the right, hard into the parking lot. "It's fantastic," he says. "We go with this."

Actually driving the IROC GT is even more of a revelation. It centers itself on the road as if possessed by some aerospace guidance system, straight down the freeway unless you tell it to do otherwise. And when you dial in a steering input, it doesn't wait around. In truth, it feels a bit overqualified for cruising—a kind of .357 magnum for knocking over beer cans. Normal motoring is just too easy for this car.

The amazing thing is that the handling feels very much like the Ferraris and Maseratis that faithful enthusiasts hold in such untouchable esteem. Stock Camaros have always been capable cars; but even so, their nerves are deadened by an injection of the isolation that Detroit considers so essential. They are competent but at the same time remote and uncommunicative.

The IROC GT talks to you. It's switched on all the time, feeling the road and giving you the latest reports.

The transformation is expensive but uncomplicated, and if anything, it shows how similar all cars—Italian and American—are under the skin. Because Donohue has not reinforced his Camaro with a hidden roll cage or provided new suspension geometry; he has merely strengthened the communication links. The flaccid GM radials have been replaced with Michelin XWXs—the same tires used on Ferraris. The 205/70 front tires on 7.0-inch wide wheels are matched to 215/70 rears on 9.5-inch rims. Then, to extract more work from the big rear rubber, the standard rear anti-sway bar has been replaced with one of larger diameter. The rest of the conversion includes stiffer shocks, front suspension lowered just over an inch and the alignment reset for more caster and negative camber. Presto, a Camaro that behaves like a Ferrari. And there is every reason to suspect that the reverse surgery performed on a Ferrari would make it act like a Camaro, which should reassure a domestic auto industry that never wanted to believe in Italian magic anyway.

Of course, to Donohue, none of this is magic. It's just the way cars work. After 15 years of modifying dozens of cars to make them better than everybody else's best shot on the race track, there aren't many secrets left. Still, it's not much fun being an expert if you can't share it. So Donohue is trying his hand at production cars: "I want to do a limited number for people who will appreciate them."

The IROC GT is his idea of a road car, a kind of latter-day Shelby Mustang. It reflects Donohue's typically thorough approach: chassis improvements for handling and braking; special bucket seats and padded steering wheel for comfort; and hood pins, windshield clips and spoilers for appearance. And, yes, maybe he can make a few bucks on it too if the idea catches on. The car (about $9500, depending upon factory options) and the kits (up to $3000, depending on the components selected) will be sold through his own outlet—Racemark Southeast, 2549 Park Lane, Hallandale, Florida 33009.

But there is more to it than money. Ferdinand Porsche started with Volkswagens, Colin Chapman reworked Austins, Enzo Ferrari massaged Fiats. All of that was years ago; maybe there is still room in the automotive world for a man with a vision. •

WHEN CHEVROLET joined the ponycar fracas in the 1967 model year, its offering, the Camaro, came in two different body styles, coupe or convertible, and with a choice of seven engines and nine transmissions allowing for 19 different powertrain combinations. There were also optional choices of visible or disappearing headlamps, paint stripes, vinyl roof coverings, interior and exterior trim packages, and wheel/tire alternatives. The danger facing a prospective buyer in those days was that he or she might select from the long list a combination of elements that made for a perfectly awful car! Times have changed, obviously, and the 1976 Camaro lineup is composed of either the Standard or Type LT coupe (the convertible disappeared in 1970), three engines and three transmissions. There is also a Camaro RS but its distinguishing characteristics are flat-black paint treatment and fancy rally wheels.

The Standard's base engine in all 50 states is the 250-cu-in. inline 6-cylinder which develops 105 horsepower at 3800 rpm. This is coupled to a 3-speed manual gearbox or to the optional 3-speed Turbo Hydra-Matic automatic transmission. The Type LT base engine is the 305-cu-in. V-8 (optional in the standard), also mated to the 3-speed manual gearbox and with the automatic optional. There is also a 350-cu-in. V-8. This puts out 165 hp at 3800 rpm compared to 140 hp for the 305, is optional in both Camaro models and can be ordered with either a 4-speed manual transmission or the automatic. Having said all that, we should hasten to add that *none* of the manual transmissions can be purchased in California.

Our test car for this report was a California-version Type LT with a lengthy option list that brought the as-tested price up to $6290. Included were such items as the 350 V-8 engine ($85), Turbo Hydra-Matic transmission ($260), air conditioning ($450), power windows ($99), AM/FM radio ($137), style trim group ($58) and California emission certification which is not really optional but costs the purchaser $50 anyway.

The 1976 Camaro is a considerably heavier car than the original Camaro of nine years ago (4020 vs 2900 lb) and one gets

CHEVROLET CAMARO

A comfortable and pleasant-to-drive American GT car

ROAD & TRACK
R&T
ROAD TEST

the distinct impression that this is representative of the different attitude about the car by the manufacturer. Performance and crisp handling characteristics have both given way to a car that accents comfort and perhaps refinement. It's an exceptionally good GT car for long-distance touring for two people (the rear seats are marked by low cushions and lack of leg room and are not comfortable for adults on anything more than short jaunts) and for the routine, day-to-day driving needs we all face. At the same time, however, it's quite large in exterior dimensions compared to most imported GT cars and utilizes the available space rather poorly. The usable trunk space figure of 6.5 cu ft given in the data panel is evidence that there simply is not much room for luggage or parcels.

Recognizing its shortcomings, the Camaro is nevertheless one of the best American cars we've driven. The independent front suspension and live rear axle combine to give a ride that is reasonably well controlled and only slightly jerky over surface irregularities. The handling is also acceptable with less body roll than most American cars and a predictable degree of understeer. A trip over rough, uneven surfaces will demonstrate the need for

more suspension travel and, of course, the solid rear axle will begin to hop if the car is pushed hard around corners when the pavement is not quite smooth.

Our acceleration testing made it clear that emission controls have taken much of the zip out of the Camaro as we managed a 0–60 mph time of 10.1 seconds compared to 8.8 sec for a 1970 version of the car with the 350 V-8. But, as we said earlier, performance is no longer the name of the game. In terms of driveability, the 350 V-8 proved to be as smooth as we could ask with no signs of lean surge, stumbling or cold or hot starting problems. It's long been evident that American manufacturers have the answers when it comes to building V-8 engines with useful torque and ample performance and the Camaro carries that tradition forward despite retarded ignition timing, air pumps, catalytic converters, and so on.

One of our complaints with the Camaro throughout its history has been that the brakes do not match the performance and

weight of the car. The front brakes are 11.0-in. vented discs but the rear brakes are still of the drum type. This combination does provide excellent control during panic stopping and the pedal effort, though power assisted, is about right to our way of thinking. Our criticism centers around the amount of fade that can be induced during repeated hard braking. In the everyday needs of traffic, however, the brakes are admirable.

The interior of our test car was marked by luxury and tasteful design and finish. The seats do not provide as much lateral support as we would like and the lack of seatback angle adjustment is disappointing, but overall we have little but praise for the ergonomics of the car. The air conditioning system could easily keep the car interior frosty on even the warmest day and the vent system, which is integrated with the air conditioning, works fairly well. The driving position is very comfortable and the tilt-away steering wheel is a nice option that makes getting in and out of the car much easier. The steering, by the way, is power-assisted on all Camaros and it is quick and relatively natural feeling although there is insufficient feedback from the front wheels.

By way of summing up, we feel the Camaro is a very good car. It's esthetically pleasing to look at, comfortable to drive, has acceptable ride and handling characteristics, ample if no longer startling performance, and a reasonable price tag in today's market. Exchanging the factory disc brake pads and drum brake linings for harder materials would probably cure our most serious criticism, the amount of brake fade, and the result would be a car that does everything well. We'd be hard pressed to name many other $6000 GT cars that could match the Camaro in terms of affirmative characteristics.

CHEVROLET CAMARO

PRICE
List price, FOB Detroit $4320
Price as tested, west coast $6290

GENERAL
Curb weight, lb 4020
Test weight 4370
Weight distribution (with driver),
  front/rear, % 54/46
Wheelbase, in 108.0
Track, front/rear 61.6/60.3
Length 195.4
Width 74.4
Height 49.2
Ground clearance 5.0
Overhang, front/rear 42.0/45.4
Usable trunk space, cu ft 6.5
Fuel capacity, U.S. gal 21

ENGINE
Type .... ohv V-8
Bore x stroke, mm ......101.6 x 88.4
  Equivalent in ....4.00 x 3.48
Displacement, cc/cu in 350/5736
Compression ratio 8.5:1
Bhp @ rpm, net .... 165 @ 3800
  Equivalent mph......................97
Torque @ rpm, lb-ft .. 260 @ 2400
Carburetion .... 1 Rochester (4V)
Fuel requirement .... unleaded

DRIVETRAIN
Transmission: automatic; torque converter with 3-sp planetary gearbox
Gear ratios: 3rd (1.00) 3.08:1
  2nd (1.52) 4.68:1
  1st (2.52) 7.76:1
  1st (2.52 x 2.0)................15.52:1
Final drive ratio.....................3.08:1

CHASSIS & BODY
Layout ....front engine rear drive
Body/frame .... unit steel
Brake system: 11.0-in. vented discs front, 9.5 x 2.0-in. drum rear
Brake swept area, sq in 326
Wheels .... styled steel, 14 x 7
Tires................................ FR78-14
Steering type: power-assisted recirc ball
Overall ratio.....variable, 15.0-10.6:1

Turns, lock-to-lock 2.4
Turning circle, ft 38.5
Front suspension: independent w/ unequal A-arms, coil springs, tube shocks, anti-roll bar
Rear suspension: live axle on leaf springs, tube shocks, anti-roll bar

INSTRUMENTATION
Instruments: speedometer, odometer, fuel level, clock

ROAD TEST RESULTS

ACCELERATION
Time to distance, sec:
  Standing ¼-mi, sec.............. 17.9
  Speed at end, mph.................80
Time to speed, sec:
  0–30 mph 3.9
  0–50 mph 8.0
  0–60 mph 10.1
  0–70 mph 13.5
  0–80 mph 17.6
  0–90 mph 22.7

SPEED IN GEARS
3rd gear (4200 rpm).................107
2nd (4700) 79
1st (4700) 47

FUEL ECONOMY
Normal driving, mpg 15
Cruising range (1-gal. res).........300

HANDLING
Speed on 100-ft radius, mph..32.4
Lateral acceleration, g 0.702

BRAKES
Minimum stopping distances, ft:
  From 60 mph 161
  From 80 mph 300
Overall brake rating .... good

SPEEDOMETER ERROR
30 mph indicated is actually 29
50 mph 49
60 mph 60
70 mph 70
80 mph 80
90 mph 89
Odometer, 10.0 mi 10.0

THE RESURRECTION OF Z

By Jim McCraw

"THE BEST CHEVROLET EVER BUILT"
—THE Z/28 CAMARO—IS BACK, STRONGER,
QUICKER AND FASTER THAN WHEN IT LEFT IN 1974,
WITH 15-SECOND, 90-MPH QUARTER-MILES AND
HANDLING THAT BORDERS ON THE INCREDIBLE!

Back in April, 1975, HRM brought you the bad news that the Z/28 Camaro had been discontinued, due to a combination of emissions and noise problems that would have slowed the '75 model down to a level not worthy of the name Z/28. After agonizing deliberations, the engineers and marketers decided to let the car die rather than produce a '75 version that would amount to a sheep in wolf's clothing.

But now, in April, 1977, HRM brings you the good news. The Z/28 Camaro lives! For a couple of years, the Chevrolet people had to produce Type LTs and Rally Sports and stand by while Pontiac sold more and more Trans Am Firebirds. The Trans Am offered superb handling, good acceleration with its big-block 400 and 455 engines, and the look of performance, characterized by its shaker hood scoop, brake scoops, decals, wide wheels and tires, and low stance. When the special black-and-gold version and later the T-top Trans Am were introduced, Chevrolet started sifting through the ashes to bring back the Z/28 for '77½, before it was too late.

You'll see in our photographs that the brand-new Z/28 is definitely *not* heavy on cosmetics. Production cars will have one name badge in the grille, one on each front fender, and one more Z/28 decal at the center of the rear spoiler, with tiny badges in the centers of the wheels, and one more tiny one centered on the steering wheel, with a distinctive reverse teardrop applique on the hood, and that'll be it. There'll be none of the screaming 14-inch-tall decals from the '74 model. Chevrolet engineers told us that the goal was a very high performance automobile that would sell itself on the basis of handling, responsiveness and acceleration not available in a Chevrolet in two and a half years, and *not* on the basis of stripes and scoops and the like. As

for '78, well, that may be another story altogether in the rivalry between Chevrolet and Pontiac, so let's get right into what the all-new Z/28 Camaro is all about.

ENGINE

Contrary to what you might expect, the '77½ Z/28 does not have a powerplant all its own, and neither did it borrow from the Corvette L48 or the optional L82. Rather, all Z/28 Camaros will come with the plain-vanilla 350-cubic-inch LM1 base engine that powers almost all Chevrolet cars. The LM1 engine boasts cast crankshaft, cast pistons, forged rods, 8.5:1 compression ratio, and a single Rochester Quadrajet carburetor with 1.38-inch primary and 2.25-inch secondary barrels with a standard air cleaner and over-the-radiator-support snorkel snout arrangement. The LM1 engine is rated at 170 horsepower in all other 49-state Camaros, but at 160 horsepower in Z/28s. In California, the engine is rated the same—160 horsepower—whether in a Z/28 or not. All 1977½ California Z/28s will be automatics, with buyer's choice available in the 49 states. For Z/28 applications, the engine is fitted with a special air-conditioning compressor pulley. The pulley is larger in diameter than stock. Also on Z/28 cars, the exhaust system is changed. A variety of dual exhaust system pipe diameters, including sections of 2-, 2.25- and 2.50-inch, are used with a single catalytic converter housing, splitting back into dual exhausts past the converter and using *no* mufflers at all. Two specially matched resonators are employed to keep the Z/28 noise-legal, but they are by no means silent. The Z/28's exhaust note is quite literally some of the most beautiful music we've heard in about three years, from idle right on up past redline.

Make no mistake: This engine is definitely *not* the original 302, nor is it the LT-1 350, but it sounds terrific, it's a lot stingier with gasoline than either of the aforementioned power-

plants, and it's cleaner and easier on the atmosphere. The engines in our fleet of two different Z/28 production cars (very early production cars, but production cars) responded very well, all things considered, but flat ran out of power and rpm at 5000 on good days, and at lesser rpm on bad days. This may have been due in part to a restrictive air intake system engineered for noise rather than power output, and an open-element air cleaner assembly from any earlier Z-model will not only improve performance but add greatly to the overall feel of the car. Throughout our test period, neither engine missed a beat or used any appreciable amount of fluid except gasoline, except during the process of "finding" the redline at the drag strip. Once we found the engines' limits, we stayed under them and avoided further confrontations. The most important thing is that the engines worked well enough in combination with the rest of the package to net the quickest and fastest stock-vehicle quarter-mile times we've seen around here in years, the 4-speed car hitting 15.35 at 91.00 miles per hour after a handful of quarter-mile break-ins!

DRIVELINE

The key to the combination is the way the base LM1 engine is geared to the car. From its big 11-inch clutch and pressure plate assembly, the LM1 engine spins the familiar Borg-Warner T-10 transmission, with ratios of 2.64 in first, 1.75 in second, 1.34 in third and direct in fourth. The power band of the engine is suited to these ratios pretty well, considering that the alternatives would have been the 2.43 Corvette gearbox, or the optional 2.85 unit, the former too tall and the latter too short and violent. Coupled to the slick, dependable B-W transmission is a General Motors Inland home-brewed shifter that's been refined and improved with longer levers, a new coupler and a new shift pattern for reverse, which now requires a lifting motion

43

RESURRECTION OF Z

and rearward stick movement to engage. Again, one of the slickest shifters we've experienced in a U.S.-made car in years (granting that there are *lots* of imports with better transmissions and shifters around). Believe it or not, we had three drivers on hand at Irwindale and made uncounted runs with the 4-speed car without a missed shift from any of us. Believe us, that is unusual, and we proved beyond a doubt that the clutch/trans combo in the new Z can take it.

The low-ratio 4-speed, 11-inch HD clutch, and the new shifter are still only part of the story. The power path goes back from there to a Positraction rearend assembly housing what we think are astoundingly low-ratio gears in this day and time. When it has become commonplace

The interior is one area where the Z is virtually like any other Camaro on the road, since you can order the Z/28 group of add-ons on a base Camaro or on the more luxurious Type LT. Our 4-speed car had a prototype 3-spoke steering wheel with a padded rim, but that was not a part of the final Z/28 group at the time. Exterior markings will be few and small for the '77½ version.

to see 5500-pound, 5-litre-engined wagons with 2.41 rears and passing distances measured in miles, along comes the Z/28 like a breath of fresh air packing 3.73 gears that do remarkable things for acceleration and feel. The automatic Z/28s will use their own gearset, a 3.42 that is proportionately low, too, in light of what's being offered. The automatic chosen for use in all Z/28 Camaros is the Turbo-Hydramatic 350, using a smaller 11.75-inch torque converter assembly and ratios of 2.52, 1.52 and direct. The Chevrolet specification charts call this one the M38 automatic, or the CBC. This transmission is calibrated to make the 1-2 upshift at 4900 rpm, and the 2-3 shift at 4700 rpm when used fully automatic, but can be manually overridden. The 7-inch slotted steel wheels, painted

body color on all Z/28 cars, are fitted with either Firestone or Goodyear GR70-15 steel radial tires, which come under the headline of drivetrain equipment but are an integral part of the suspension package as well. (Chevy engineers strongly advise against changing Z/28 tire sizes.) Production Z/28 wheels will have their own center caps, which were not available on our two test cars. Similarly, the little caps at the steering wheel center will also have special Z/28 markings in later production cars, while our steering wheels were blanks.

One other very important part of the total Z/28 package is the "must-order" inclusion of the RPO J50 power-assisted disc/drum braking system, with 11-inch discs and 9½x2-inch rear drums. These brakes, combined with the Goodyear Custom Steelgard radial tires, did a superb job on both cars, with no noise, no fuss and no sideways attitudes.

STEERING & SUSPENSION

Absolutely the heart and soul of the car is its completely redone suspension and steering system, and we're here to tell you that the car is a complete ball to drive. The group of engineers who helped Chevrolet win the Motor Trend Car of the Year Award for 1977 with the Caprice went directly from that project into the final refinements on the Z/28, basing the suspension on the very refined F41 package. The front stabil-

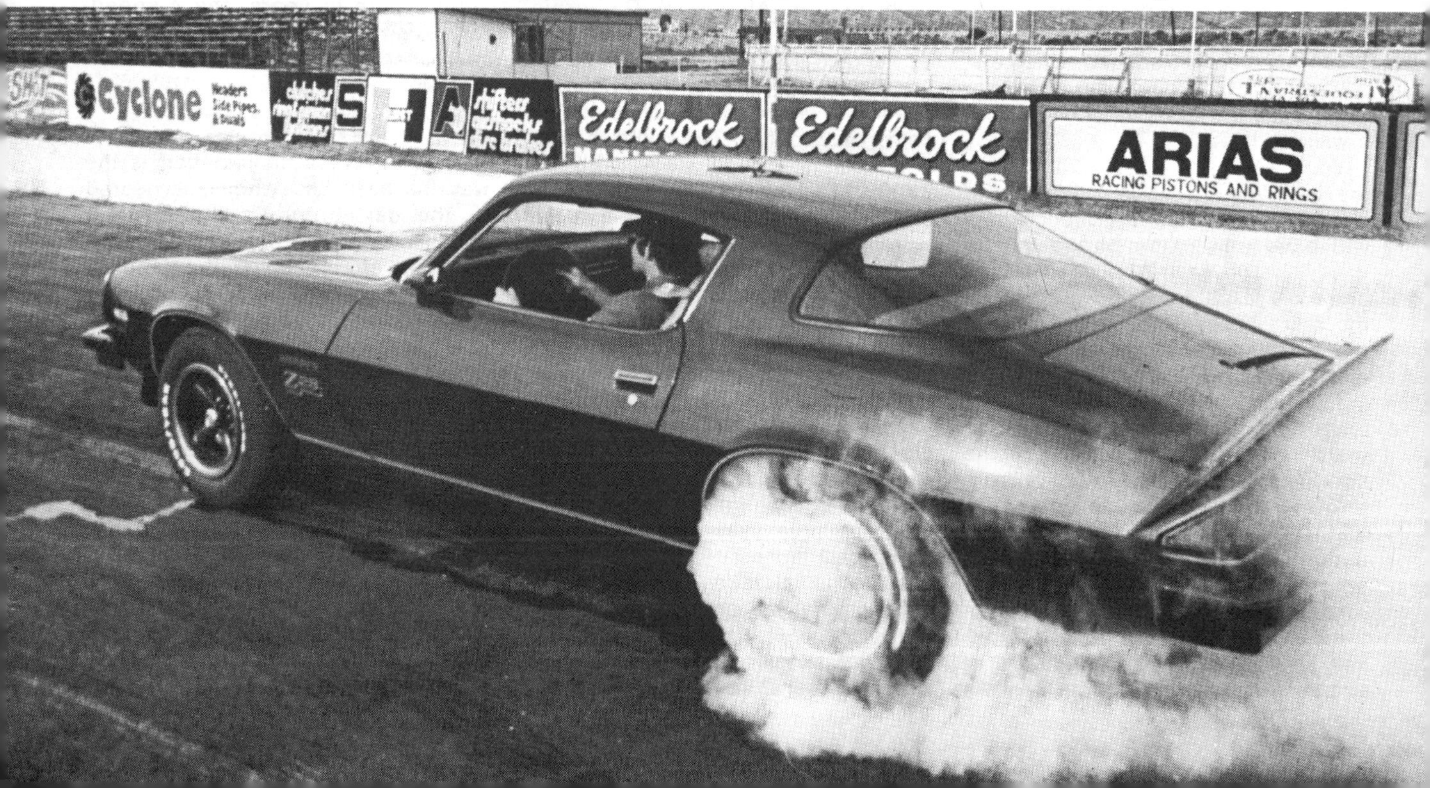

RESURRECTION OF Z

izer bar diameter was increased from 1.00 inch to 1.200 inches. Spring rates for the front coil springs were increased from 300 pounds per inch to 365 pounds per inch. The 56-inch rear leaf spring rates were beefed from about 95 pounds to nearly 130 pounds per inch, and the shock absorber calibrations from the F41 suspension package were carried over into the Z/28 package. The diameter of the rear stabilizer bar was *decreased* from .687-inch to .550-inch. The amount of jounce travel front and rear has been revised, and in the rear, new shackles with harder durometer bushings are used. All Z/28 Camaros will come with power steering and a straight-ratio steering gear setup sporting a fast 14:1 ratio overall, increased from 16:1 in the base '77 Camaro and coincidentally in the '74 Z-car. As we noted earlier, Chevrolet will use body-colored 15x7 slotted steel wheels and GR70 steel radials from only two manufacturers, Firestone and Goodyear, after field-testing virtually every tire of this size made or imported into the United States. All Z/28s will use the Space-Saver spare tire and CO_2 inflator cartridge.

APPEARANCE

While we've given you the rundown on what under-the-skin pieces and systems will make the Z/28 what it is, we haven't told you much about the appearance package, which Chevrolet admits is basically simple and straightforward. All Zs will get black semi-gloss paint on grilles, nameplates, taillight bezels, rear-end panels, license plate openings, headlamp bezels, parking lamp bezels and openings, rocker panels, wheelhouses, and front and rear moldings, with body-color bumpers, body-color mirrors, and body-color spoilers and wheels. Decals will be limited to a handful and combined with color-matched tri-stripe tapes running up and over the lower portions of the fenders and rocker panels. A complete list of Z/28 exterior and interior paint and upholstery colors was unavailable at press time, but you can bet they won't be dull. On the inside, the only items to distinguish the Z/28 will be the wheel-center identification badge, possibly a three-spoke polished-aluminum leather-covered padded steering wheel, and the RPO U14 special instrumentation package. The Z/28 Camaro is, after all, not a complete automobile, but rather it is a package of components and options and special items. You can

HOT ROD MAGAZINE'S ROAD TEST SPECIFICATIONS
1977½ Camaro Z/28

PRICE:

Base Price	$5170.60
Price as Tested	NA

GENERAL SPECIFICATIONS:

Curb Weight	3820 pounds
Wheelbase	108 inches
Track, Front/Rear	61.6/60.3 inches
Length	195.4 inches
Width	74.4 inches
Height	49.7 inches

CHASSIS/BODY:

Frame	Steel monocoque with subframes
Brake System	11.0-inch front disc with 9.5-inch drums rear, power-assisted
Wheels	15x7 steel-slotted
Tires	Goodyear G70-15 radial
Steering Type	Power recirculating ball type, 14:1 ratio
Turns, lock to lock	2.4
Suspension, Front/Rear	Independent SLA with coil springs, stabilizer bars, hydraulic shocks, rear leaf springs with stabilizer bar and hydraulic shocks

ENGINE/DRIVETRAIN:

Type	90° OHV V8
Bore and Stroke	4.00x3.48 inches
Displacement	350 cubic inches
Compression Ratio	8.5:1
Bhp @ rpm, net	160 @ 3800 rpm
Torque @ rpm	260 @ 2400 rpm
Carburetion	Single Rochester Quadrajet
Fuel Requirement	Unleaded, 91-octane
Drivetrain	Borg-Warner 2.64 4-speed or Turbo-Hydramatic
Gear Ratios	2.64, 1.75, 1.34, 1.1 or 2.52, 1.52, 1:1

PERFORMANCE DATA:

Standing Quarter-Mile	15.35 @ 91.00 mph (M), 16.17 @ 84.19 mph (A)
Top Speed (observed)	110 mph
Fuel Economy	13.95 mpg aggregate
Brakes, stopping distance	60-0 mph, 167 feet

ACCOMMODATION:

Seating Capacity, persons	4
Leg Room, Front/Rear	43.9/28.4 inches
Head Room, Front/Rear	37.2/36.0 inches
Shoulder, Front/Rear	56.7/54.4 inches
Hip Room, Front/Rear	56.2/45.8 inches

OVERALL COMMENTS:

(On a scale of 1-10, 5 is average)

Exterior Finish	7
Interior Finish	6
Interior Noise Level	7
Behavior in Traffic	8
Handling	9
Brakes	8
All-around Vision	6
Luggage Space	4
Rear Passenger Comfort	4
Driver Comfort	8
Dashboard Readability/Accessibility	7

have a Z/28 package installed on a base car with no other options, or you can add the Z/28 group to an already decked-out Type LT luxury car with sound options and power accessories.

PERFORMANCE

What you see on these pages is three different cars, the white fiberglass model car framed by all of the separate Z/28 components, and two real cars, one 4-speed and one automatic, one with Z/28 exterior markings, one without. The marked car was the automatic, and the plain car was the 4-speed. The automatic Z had the AM/tape radio and the base interior. The 4-speed car had the Type LT appearance package, and AM/FM stereo, along with tilt wheel and some of the other inexpensive convenience option packages. Both had identical steering and suspension systems, and both were painted and finished in metallic brown with tan interiors, one base, the other Type LT luxury. In terms of calibrations, the automatic was a "California" car, and the 4-speed was a legal 49-state model without the California emissions package. And both were sensational performers.

In high-speed steady-state handling maneuvers, where the differences between manual and automatic are canceled out, the Z/28s were unbelievably well-balanced, flat, and almost completely neutral. During off-road 105-mph lane changes in both cars, the feeling was that every single component in the steering and suspension was united and cohesive in responding to steering inputs. Everything happens right now, and only to the extent of inputs. Nothing more and nothing less. Steering feel in the wheel and the seat of the pants is excellent, and overall the feeling of this new Z/28 is one of lightness and extreme agility, with less of the brutishness and heavy feel. In a skid-pad test using a 200-foot-diameter circle of flat asphalt, the 4-speed car generated a cornering force of .74G, but out on the real straights and highways, which don't just go around in circles, the Z feels like it's pulling a lot more than .74G. The car will inspire a great deal of confidence almost immediately, and of course, the more one drives it, the better it feels, to the point where you begin to believe it can do anything, perform any maneuver it's told to perform. Had any lately?

On the drag strip, we made eight passes with the 4-speed car using

CONTINUED ON PAGE 79

COMPARISON TEST:

Camaro Z/28 Vs. Firebird Trans-Am

Good ideas never die: Pony cars and performance are together again.

• Five years ago, all the smarties, including those occupying positions of responsibility on this staff, told you that those manifestations of the great performance binge of the 1960s known as Pony cars were as surely doomed to the automotive tar pits as ragtops and side-mounted spares. No one believed these predictions more than the Detroit moguls who read the omens of inflation, energy shortages and the ravings of consumerist loonies as sure death for all performance automobiles in general and Pony cars in particular. Ruthlessly they offed the Barracuda, Challenger and Javelin from the corporate menus while altering the Cougar and Mustang to a point where they were to high-performance motoring what Longines Symphonette represents to the New York Philharmonic Orchestra.

Suddenly they were gone or transmogrified, and the enthusiasts of the nation—who had not gotten the word that driving for fun was gone forever—puzzled over why everybody had acted with such maniacal haste. They responded in a variety of ways: Some kept their old Pony cars in loving repair; others turned to the few sporty vehicles that remained, hence the booming sales of Corvette, Datsun Z-cars and Porsches. And still others began to buy in ever-escalating numbers the only legitimate Pony cars that, in some bizarre role as an automotive Ceolanth, had defied evolution and had remained in production. Those cars were the F-bodied sisters from Pontiac

and Chevrolet, the Firebird and Camaro, which remained in the marketplace as rather wispy reminders of the old days. Each year, with the exception of the modestly sporty Camaro Rallye Sport and the Firebird Formula, the cars became increasingly aimed at an audience of secretaries and suburban housewives. Only one car of the lot, the Firebird Trans-Am, sustained an unvarnished position as a pure, all-out-hell-for-leather performance automobile. Why Pontiac chose to keep the Trans-Am around in the face of the retreating competition is of little interest here, other than to note the irony that of all the machines of the species there is little debating the fact that the best of the lot was preserved. (Automotive Darwinism is alive and well)!

The Pontiac Trans-Am turned into a hellishly successful car in the face of all the gloomy sales forecasts. As the years passed it lost some of the brutal acceleration it enjoyed during its 455 Super Duty era, but that lapse in power was more than offset by steady improvements in suspension and running gear that created a delightful American 2+2 Grand Touring automobile. Pontiac stylists were not totally immune to the temptations of littering its splendid contours with increasing acreages of cornball decals, but in general the Trans-Am remained what it was when introduced in its most recent form during the middle of the 1969–70 model year: the sportiest, most roadable four-place automobile built by an American manufacturer.

Then a strange thing happened. In 1976, Trans-Ams began accounting for half of all Firebird sales. The surprise mini-boom did not escape the Motor City sales analysts and prompted attempts to cash in on what was considered a ren-

ED SPERKO

aissance of the performance market. Perhaps the most spectacular—and superficial—effort came from Ford, where the Mustang II was decked out in garish paint and tape combinations to become the Cobra II. Chrysler has made a similarly feeble gesture with its Plymouth Volaré Road Runner, while a more legitimate try was undertaken by American Motors and its Hornet AMX. But these are all stopgaps, designed to plug holes in the model lineup until proper performance machines can be created. Therefore the field was left to Trans-Am in terms of anybody manufacturing a really honest sporting coupe in the mold of the old Pony cars. Until now, that is, when Chevrolet unloads its all-new Z/28 Camaro on an unsuspecting industry and a delighted public.

The Z/28 was last seen in 1974 when the power and speed that emanated from its light, high-revving small-block engine was in a state of seemingly terminal decline. Rather than let the proud name become just another plastic appli-

que on the flanks of various ordinary cars—as happened to the Pontiac GTO and Plymouth Road Runner—Chevrolet yanked the car off the market. Now it returns in a fashion that is sure to blow

The Z/28 and Trans-Am
may look alike,
but the resemblance
is only
F-body skin deep.

the lid off the entire world of fast automobiles and end, once and for all, the notion that Detroit and the American public have forgotten performance.

We first encountered the automobile on the flat terrain of General Motors' Mesa Arizona Proving Ground, where it appeared in the proud possession of Jack Turner, the Chevrolet engineer who headed the design team for the Z/28

project. It was hardly a dazzling visual sight, mainly because we were so familiar with the liquid lines of the Camaro after so many years, but the presence of spoilers fore and aft, relatively discreet decal treatment and custom wheels indicated that this was no ordinary machine. A few moments in the car, with Turner lashing furiously around a small test loop, removed all doubt. "We think this is a pretty special machine," said Turner, a confident, square-shouldered guy who learned to drive—and dig cars—on the convoluted mountain roads around Old Forge, New York. "I wanted a *road* car, one that was fun to drive, like the Porsche 924. We had a Porsche during the initial stages of this project, and we were really impressed with its handling. But frankly, I think this machine will run right with it." And then he accelerated to 105 mph on a long straight and flung the Z/28 sideways. The car yawed to the left, its body rolling slightly, its steel-belted tires screeching angrily, then snapped back on course. Turner yanked

the wheel hard right, and the car responded with the same precision. "I wanted a car with a lot of linear stability, one that would make really good transitions, both in lane-changing and in hard cornering." After the car had returned to straight-line travel, we noticed that Turner had negotiated both brutal slides with one hand. Perhaps he had something here. But proving-ground running can be deceiving. The surfaces are often billiard-table-smooth or unnaturally rough. Both can give invalid impressions of an automobile, so we fled the compound and headed for a stretch of bumpy, twisting mountain road running northeast away from the ragged collection of gas stations and fast-food joints known as Apache Junction. There the Camaro revealed itself as a road machine of the first rank. Its 350 V-8 (operating through a catalyst and two small resonators but no mufflers) sang that

---

Even with the Batmobile nose and screaming-chicken decals the Trans-Am has survived self-caricature.

---

special, keening song that issues only from good Chevy small-blocks, while the Z/28 blitzed up the canyons and charged over the arroyos. It was as close to being a neutral steerer as any car with a heavy iron engine tucked up front probably can be and could be easily kicked into more gentle oversteer/understeer conditions by easy application of the throttle or brake.

It was a treat for Turner to work on a machine like the Z/28. For the past four years he had been assigned to Chevrolet's new B-body intermediates, and it was he and his fellows who created the "F-41" optional suspension that makes large, solid-axle sedans handle like tiny sports cars. "There is only one way to make a suspension work, and that's out here," he said gesturing at the blurred dirt banks and cactus. "I've worked with computers, and they'll only take you so far. Then you have to get out here and drive 'em. You take a lot of cars like this with big front sway bars, and when you drive 'em really hard you get bad understeer and the feeling that the front wheels are doing all the work. I like to feel the rear wheels working too. That's

where this car really has an edge."

Did he mean the Z/28 had an *edge* on the Pontiac Trans-Am, the majordomo in this field? "We're buddies with all the guys at Pontiac," said Turner affably, "but they are our rivals too. Sure, they are interested in what we're doing with this machine, and we've shown 'em most of what we've done. But not all of it. We've got some stuff in reserve. We're not finished with this project by a long shot. Wait until you see what we do next year." (Turner's claims for improvement boggle the mind, based on this year's car, although we know the '78 Camaro will use the same basic body. The 1978 Z/28 will have a better integrated front and rear bumper, plus louvers in

the front fenders, *a la* the new T-Birds and Continentals.)

Before climbing aboard the Z/28, we had spent some time in Los Angeles with a 1977 Trans-Am. The City of Vapors was in the midst of one of its rare monsoons, and all of our driving was spent hissing along soaked roads and freeways with the gentle clatter of the wipers mingling with the soft exhaust note and the faint mechanical whines rising out of the engine and transmission. Trans-Ams are old friends, essentially unchanged over the past few years, save for the 1977 addition of a weird Batmobile grille treatment and the use of a somewhat tamer drivetrain. Our test machine was the Special Edition, which meant that its black body was decked out in a variety of gold stripes and decals, plus gold-anodized alloy wheels and Hurst hatch sunroofs (weighing a hefty 108 pounds). This

package costs an extra $1143, which made it the biggest contributor in boosting the base price from $5427 to $8161. Our car was what you might call "loaded" and in its own way lent emphasis to the fact that a good Trans-Am can be purchased without the effluvia for about $6500 to $7000. All of the right suspension pieces come as part of the base car, as does the striking interior and exterior styling bits. Therefore we recommend the car with simple options like air-conditioning, radio and the $50-extra 200 hp, 400-cubic inch engine. The basic Trans-Am motor is rated at 180 hp, and the extra half-a-yard produces a slightly tweaked version of the same powerplant with a better horsepower

curve, a different camshaft and higher compression ratio. Unless you are fascinated with the notion of displaying yourself publicly in the overblown Special Edition (when will car makers purge themselves of the idea that hairy decals must be present on all fast cars?), you can purchase a Trans-Am for relatively low cost.

Because the Trans-Am and the Z/28 are the same automobile in terms of the chassis and inner body panels, there is very little difference in weight or even performance. They are both highly pleasurable to drive and difficult to tell apart until really hard cornering begins. Because of its larger front sway bar, it would seem logical to assume that the Trans-Am might lapse into serious understeer more quickly than the Z/28, but skidpad calculations do not bear this out. Our Trans-Am generated 0.80 G, while our Z/28 could do no better than

0.74 G and exhibited considerably more understeer in the process. If either of the cars seemed to be neutral steering within the rather sterile precincts of the skidpad, it was the Trans-Am, regardless of the pleasant sensations generated by the Z/28 in the Arizona mountains.

If the Trans-Am can claim an advantage in terms of lateral acceleration, then the Z/28 is a winner in straight-ahead performance. It ran the quarter-mile in 16.3 seconds (83.1 mph), which was clearly superior to the Trans-Am's 16.9 seconds at 82.0 mph. Moreover, our Z/28 produced a top speed of 105

ROBIN RIGGS

The Trans-Am's edge over the Z/28 inside is its fat steering wheel: "Wait till next year," says Chevy.

---

mph (limited by the redline and the 3.73 rear axle), while the Trans-Am with a 3.23 final-drive ratio was no faster than 110 mph.

The major drawback of both these cars is usable interior space. The shape of the vehicles produces dwarf-sized rear seats with limited headroom and visibility and ludicrously tiny trunks. The instrumentation and decor of the Trans-Am is much sportier and features an excellent, small, vinyl-rimmed steering wheel in contrast to the Z/28's dull black four-spoker that first appeared on the Vega (that hopefully will soon be discarded in favor of a smaller, three-spoke sports wheel). "Don't forget, we're not finished," says Jack Turner, pledging that the 1978 version will contain all the proper components.

Both cars are superior examples of what a true American GT automobile should be. However they both need to be updated; for instance, thin-shell bucket seats with full-back adjustments and stalk controls for the headlight dimmer and windshield wiper/washer are long overdue. Both are two-hand, two-feet automobiles when driven properly and the omission of such components is inexcusable. Otherwise it is hard to find serious fault with either machine, although we eagerly await the results of Chevrolet's escalation of the rivalry in this recently moribund field, both in terms of its neighbors at Pontiac as well as the rest of the industry. ●

Pontiac's T/A 400: The Same Power in a Smaller Package

● Special performance engines are all but extinct in Detroit, but Pontiac is bucking the trend with a new powerhouse for the 1977 Trans-Am. There were two goals in developing this engine: better fuel economy and performance at least as good as last year's. The first suggested smaller displacement, so the 455-cubic inch V-8 was dropped in favor of the old standby 400. To cut the energy loss this move involved, long hours were spent in the dyno room to fatten up torque curves.

Cylinder heads from Pontiac's 350 V-8 were specified for the T/A 400. They are identical in every way to 400 heads except for combustion chamber volume. Since this dimension is smaller, compression ratio is automatically boosted from 7.6 to 8.0. The camshaft is unique to this engine, and its timing events have been chosen to improve high rpm breathing. In addition, calibration of the Rochester Quadrajet carburetor and the spark advance curve in the GM high-energy ignition are specific to the T/A 400. A low-back pressure muffler completes the package. Actually, there is so much restriction through the single catalytic converter that the Trans-Am is fairly quiet with no muffler whatsoever.

As the above curves illustrate, a significant achievement has been made. The new T/A 400 engine actually smokes its

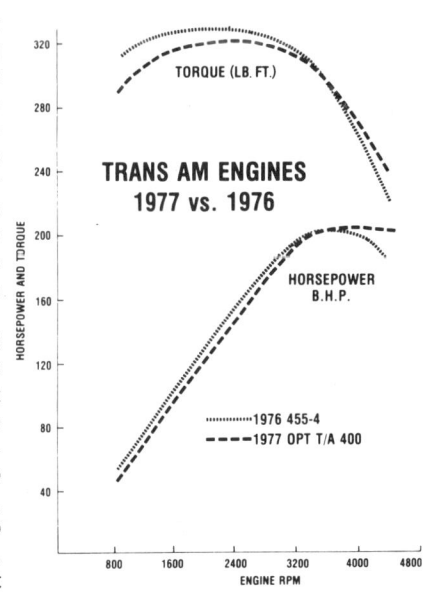

predecessor above 3600 rpm, and the gain over a standard 400 is a healthy 20 horsepower. The low rpm range is obviously softer, but Pontiac claims the better high-speed breathing makes 1977 editions quicker. In any case, it's the thought that counts. And when Pontiac thinks horsepower, we all get there a little quicker.

—Don Sherman

What "Z/28" Really Gets You, Besides Home Quicker

It gets you everything above, except Camaro Chief Engineer Tom Zimmer.

• The Z/28 is a special automobile. While it bears close physical resemblance to other Camaros, its suspension is available only within the Z/28 package and cannot be ordered as an option on tamer Camaros or other Chevrolets. The original Z/28 was introduced in late 1967 as an option symbol for the high-performance 302-cubic inch engine that was available in the Camaro of that era. Now it stands for a suspension system, rather than an engine (which is a stock LM-1, 350-cu. in.) four-barrel V-8 with an increased diameter air-conditioning pulley). It is expected to produce about 180 hp, and that typifies the change in thinking in Detroit, where nimble roadholding has replaced raw, eyeball-rupturing acceleration as the central theme of performance automobiles.

The Z/28's suspension has been totally and originally revised front and rear. The front end carries a larger sway bar, increased spring rates, specially-valved shocks and revised jounce travel. At the rear is a new, larger sway bar, stiffer springs, different shocks and higher-durometer shackle bushings with new shackles. These components, coupled with Goodyear GR70-15 steel-belted radial tires (also used on the Corvette) on 7.5-inch rims form the key to the Z/28's superior handling. The steering gear is a 14:1 straight-ratio unit with somewhat increased effort.

Chevrolet engineers wanted to employ a dual-catalyst exhaust system of the type being used on their Nova police cars, but cost considerations prevented such a luxury. They compromised by using a single catalyst feeding directly into a pair of resonators. This produces a relatively-free exhaust system and a healthy exhaust note.

The drivetrain is completed with a Borg-Warner T-10 four-speed gearbox of the same design used in the original Z/28 and on numerous Corvettes. It replaces the widely-employed Saginaw unit because of durability. It has been modified to carry a 2.64-to-one first-gear ratio. A larger 11-inch clutch and pressure plate are part of the package, although less ambitious enthusiasts can circumvent the entire problem by ordering an optional Corvette CBC three-speed automatic. A final drive ratio of 3.73 to one for the manual transmission and 3.42 to one for the automatic provide good mid-range performance, satisfactory acceleration and 105 to 115 mph top speed, depending on the ratio and the driver's resolve to override the 5000-rpm redline.

While Chevrolet has not announced a final price list for the Z/28, insiders believe that it will be closely aligned with the Trans-Am. This means that another superb-handling sporting vehicle will be available for $6000 to $7000, depending on the options.

—*Brock Yates*

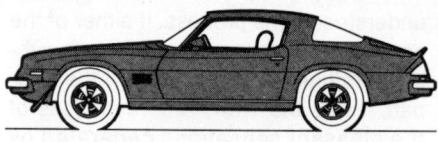

HEINZ MAURER

CAMARO Z/28

Manufacturer: Chevrolet Motor Division
General Motors Corporation
Warren, Michigan

Vehicle type: front-engine, rear-wheel-drive, 2+2-passenger coupe

Price as tested:
(Manufacturer's suggested retail price, including all options listed below, dealer preparation and delivery charges, does not include state and local taxes, license or freight charges)

Options on test car: base Camaro; Z/28 package; air-conditioning; white letter tires; AM/FM stereo radio; other comfort options.

ENGINE
Type: V-8, water-cooled, cast-iron block and heads, 5 main bearings
Bore x stroke . . . . .4.00 x 3.48 in, 101.6 x 88.4mm
Displacement . . . . .350 cu in, 5730cc
Compression ratio . . . . .8.5 to one
Carburetion . . . . .1x4-bbl Rochester Quadrajet
Valve gear . . . . . . .pushrods, overhead valves, hydraulic lifters
Torque (SAE net) . . . . .270 lbs-ft @ 2400 rpm
Max. recommended engine speed . . . . .5000 rpm

DRIVETRAIN
Transmission . . . . .4-speed, all-synchro
Final drive ratio . . . . .3.73 to one

Gear	Ratio	Mph/1000 rpm	Max. test speed
I	2.64	8.0	40 mph (5000 rpm)
II	1.75	12.1	60 mph (5000 rpm)
III	1.34	15.7	79 mph (5000 rpm)
IV	1.00	21.1	111 mph (5250 rpm)

DIMENSIONS AND CAPACITIES
Wheelbase . . . . .108.0 in
Track, F/R . . . . .61.6/60.3 in
Length . . . . .195.4 in
Width . . . . .74.4 in
Height . . . . .49.2 in
Ground clearance . . . . .4.9 in
Curb weight . . . . .3828 lbs
Weight distribution, F/R 56.1/43.9%
Fuel capacity . . . . .21.0 gal
Oil capacity . . . . .5.0 qts

SUSPENSION
F: . . . . .ind, unequal-length control arms, anti-sway bar
R: . . . . .rigid axle, semi-elliptic leaf springs, anti-sway bar

STEERING
Type . . . . .recirculating ball, power-assisted
Turns lock-to-lock 2.4
Turning circle curb-to-curb . . . . .38.5 ft

BRAKES
F: . . . . .11.0-in vented disc, power-assisted
R: . . . . .9.5 x 2.0-in cast-iron drum, power-assisted

WHEELS AND TIRES
Wheel size . . . . .7.0 x 15-in
Wheel type . . . . .styled steel, 5-bolt
Tire make and size . . . .Goodyear Custom Steelgard, GR70-15
Tire type .steel-belted radial ply, tubeless
Test inflation pressures, F/R .26/26 psi
Tire load rating . . . . .1620 lbs per tire @ 32 psi

PERFORMANCE
Zero to	Seconds
30 mph	2.8
40 mph	4.4
50 mph	6.3
60 mph	8.6
70 mph	11.6
80 mph	15.4
90 mph	20.1
100 mph	25.8

Standing ¼-mile . . . . .16.3 sec @ 83.1 mph
Top speed (at redline) . . . . .105 mph
70-0 mph . . . . .208 ft (0.79 G)
Fuel economy, *C/D* mileage cycle . . . .14.5 mpg, urban driving
17.0 mpg, highway driving

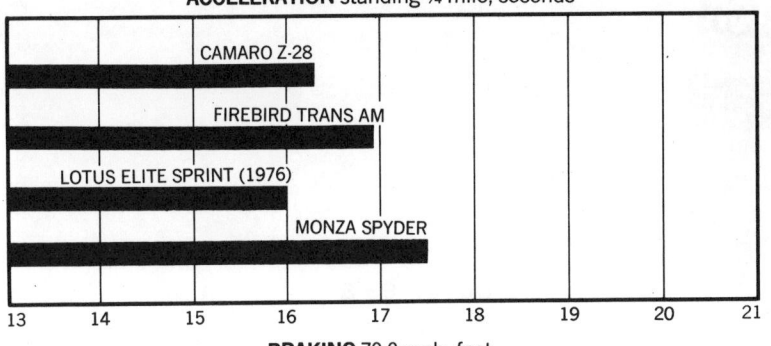

ACCELERATION standing ¼ mile, seconds

- CAMARO Z-28
- FIREBIRD TRANS AM
- LOTUS ELITE SPRINT (1976)
- MONZA SPYDER

13 14 15 16 17 18 19 20 21

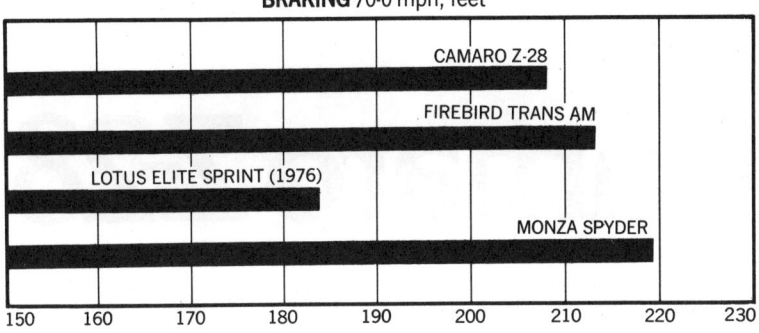

BRAKING 70-0 mph, feet

- CAMARO Z-28
- FIREBIRD TRANS AM
- LOTUS ELITE SPRINT (1976)
- MONZA SPYDER

150 160 170 180 190 200 210 220 230

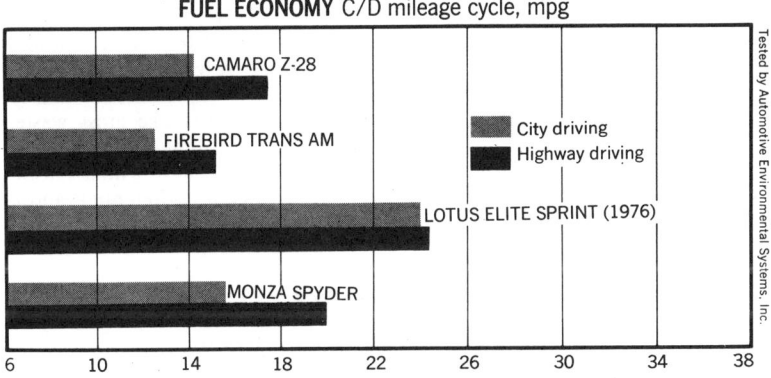

FUEL ECONOMY C/D mileage cycle, mpg

- CAMARO Z-28
- FIREBIRD TRANS AM
- LOTUS ELITE SPRINT (1976)
- MONZA SPYDER

City driving
Highway driving

6 10 14 18 22 26 30 34 38

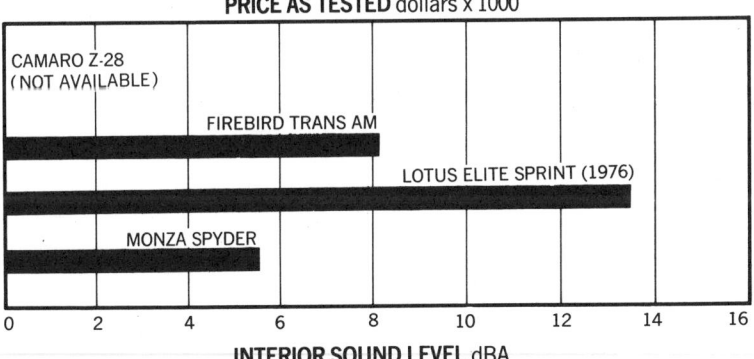

PRICE AS TESTED dollars x 1000

- CAMARO Z-28 (NOT AVAILABLE)
- FIREBIRD TRANS AM
- LOTUS ELITE SPRINT (1976)
- MONZA SPYDER

0 2 4 6 8 10 12 14 16

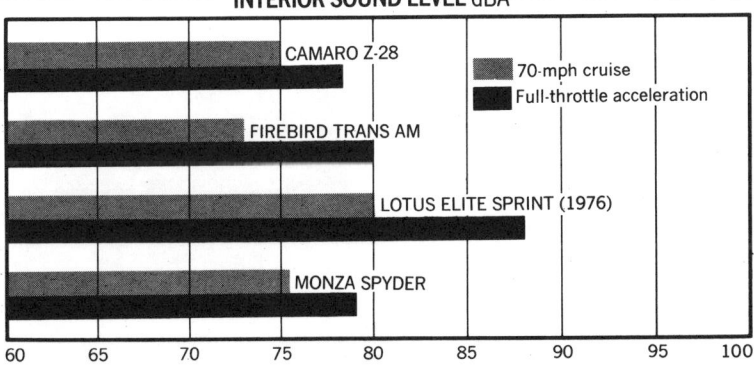

INTERIOR SOUND LEVEL dBA

- CAMARO Z-28
- FIREBIRD TRANS AM
- LOTUS ELITE SPRINT (1976)
- MONZA SPYDER

70-mph cruise
Full-throttle acceleration

60 65 70 75 80 85 90 95 100

Tested by Automotive Environmental Systems, Inc.

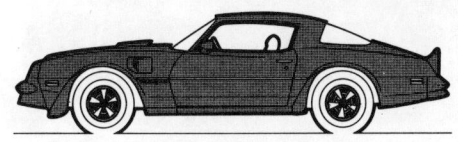

FIREBIRD TRANS-AM

Manufacturer: Pontiac Motor Division
General Motors Corporation
Pontiac, Michigan

Vehicle type: front-engine, rear-wheel-drive, 2+2-passenger coupe

Price as tested: $8161
(Manufacturer's suggested retail price, including all options listed below, dealer preparation and delivery charges, does not include state and local taxes, license or freight charges)

Options on test car: base Firebird Trans-Am, $5456; T/A 400 engine, $50; Special Edition package, $1143; air-conditioning, $478; AM/FM stereo, $233; white-letter tires, $46; power windows, $108; custom-trim group, $118; other options, $579.

ENGINE
Type: V-8 water-cooled, cast-iron block and heads, 5 main bearings
Bore x stroke ....4.12 x 3.75 in, 104.7 x 95.2mm
Displacement ....…...................400 cu in, 6550cc
Compression ratio ....8.0 to one
Carburetion ....1x4-bbl Rochester Quadrajet
Valve gear ....pushrods, overhead valves, hydraulic lifters
Power (SAE net) ....200 bhp @ 3600 rpm
Torque (SAE net) ....325 lbs-ft @ 2400 rpm
Specific power output ....0.50 bhp/cu in, 30.5 bhp/liter
Max. recommended engine speed ....5000 rpm

DRIVETRAIN
Transmission........................4-speed, all-synchro
Final drive ratio ....3.23 to one

Gear	Ratio	Mph/1000 rpm	Max. test speed
I	2.43	10.0	50 mph (5000 rpm)
II	1.61	15.1	76 mph (5000 rpm)
III	1.23	19.8	99 mph (5000 rpm)
IV	1.00	24.3	110 mph (4550 rpm)

DIMENSIONS AND CAPACITIES
Wheelbase ....108.1 in
Track, F/R ....61.2/60.3 in
Length ....196.8 in
Width...73.0 in
Height ....49.6 in
Ground clearance ....5.3 in
Curb weight ....3830 lbs
Weight distribution, F/R 58.2/41.8%
Fuel capacity...................................21.0 gal
Oil capacity ....6.0 qts

SUSPENSION
F: .ind, unequal-length control arms, coil springs, anti-sway bar
R: ....rigid axle, semi-elliptic leaf springs, anti-sway bar

STEERING
Type ....recirculating ball, power-assisted
Turns lock-to-lock....................................2.4
Turning circle curb-to-curb ....38.9 ft

BRAKES
F: ....11.0-in dia vented disc, power-assisted
R: ....9.5 x 2.0-in cast-iron drum, power-assisted

WHEELS AND TIRES
Wheel size...................................7.0 x 15-in
Wheel type ....cast aluminum, 5-bolt
Tire make and size .....Uniroyal Steel Belted Radial, GR70-15
Tire type ....steel-belted, radial ply, tubeless

PERFORMANCE

Zero to	Seconds
30 mph 3.1	
40 mph 4.5	
50 mph 6.6	
60 mph 9.3	
70 mph 12.4	
80 mph 16.4	
90 mph 22.2	
100 mph 29.3	

Standing ¼-mile ....16.9 sec @ 82.0 mph
Top speed (observed) ....110 mph
70-0 mph ....213 ft (0.77 G)
Fuel economy, C/D mileage cycle ....12.5 mpg, urban driving
15.0 mpg, highway driving

SuperNova becomes a
streetable IROC racer.

PHOTOGRAPHY: LARRY GRIFFIN

Chevrolet Camaro Z-28

ROAD TEST

It's apparent right away that our usual environment is no place to begin getting the full measure of just what Chevrolet's reincarnated Z-28 is about. The freeways and surface streets of Los Angeles are fine for the legions of faceless, bland little commutercars that most of us run—some of those are pretty fully taxed just keeping up with the normal flow of traffic, and getting around the typical freeway on-ramp without becoming four-wheeled road-blocks holding up the lines of cars behind them. It doesn't take a whole lot of room to get to know a car with such low limits.

And then there's the Z-28, the limits of which are anything but low, and which clearly is not in its element dodging through traffic on the San Diego freeway, over the Sepulveda Pass. Understand, it does that very well; it's directional stability is very good, it's got super brakes, it answers the helm *right* now, and it has more than enough torque for quick lane changes. But really, that's not the sort of driving this car was built for. It was built for lonely roads, endless series of winding, twisting corners, and large throttle openings. Sound a little antisocial? A little unpractical? Well maybe, but so be it. The thing is, the Camaro, in Z-28 form or in any other, has never been what you'd call a completely practical car. There's front seat comfort in spades, to be sure, especially with the tilt steering wheel, but the rear seat? Forget it; it was never made for hauling real people. And the trunk? Ah, probably at 6.4 cubic feet it's big enough to stomp a nice, limber duffel bag down into, but if you figure on hauling too much more than that, you'd better try to fit it into the back seats. And it's heavy, tipping the scales at just over 3700 pounds. Since it takes energy to move weight, your average Camaro owner can figure on running copious amounts of fuel through his car. So much for practicality. But the Camaro does have a few things going for it, not the least of which is the most beautiful shape to emerge from Detroit in a decade, and with its front and rear spoilers it looks every bit as svelte and purposeful as a One Ton racing sloop. It's also got General Motor's engineering background behind it, and the widest possible assortment of drivetrain and suspension components for Chevrolet's product planners and engineers to tinker with. With that much variety on tap, some amazing extremes are possible; you can order up a Camaro that runs like a six-cylinder Nova—after all, it's all Nova underneath—or you can dial one up that thinks it's an IROC racer. Which is exactly the point of the 1977 Z-28. The first suspicion that such might be the case occurred at Riverside International Raceway this past summer during the second and third IROC races. Chevrolet had not produced a Z-28 for two full model years, not since 1974 and the gasoline shortage, yet the IROC Camaros bore great, obvious

Z-28 identification. Hmmm. Obviously something was afoot at Chevrolet. Thus it was that nobody was terribly surprised when Chevrolet announced that introduction of the 1977 Z-28 would take place at this year's IROC finale in Daytona Beach. After all, the whole setup is a natural. Because of the television exposure given IROC, the Camaro has become *very* well known in its racing clothes, and for Chevrolet not to capitalize on that by building streetable quasi-IROC cars seemed like gross waste. Hence the 1977 Z-28. But is it really a streetable IROC car? Of course not. Instead it's just your standard Camaro with a 350 cid V-8, a four-speed trans, an optional locking differential, and a few pieces of trick suspension. A lot of cars have rolled out of

Detroit with the same kinds of bits tacked on them and a lot more undoubtedly will follow. What sets the Z-28 apart from all the rest, however, is that it flat *works*. Somehow, you know it will from the moment you insert the key in the ignition and fire the car up. It's unmuffled, and what greets your ear is a beautiful, throaty gurgle from that big Chevy V-8. That exhaust system is a little strange—the dump tubes from the headers join just ahead of a single catalytic converter, and split again downstream of it, their cry quietened slightly by a pair of small resonators just ahead of the rear axle. So while the Z-28 doesn't really have a dual exhaust system in the purest sense, it also has but one converter, a sure boon come replacement time.

Ah, the sound of the exhaust note—not really obtrusive, but not to be ignored, either. At steady-state cruising it's a velvet-smooth murmur, under hard acceleration it's an earthy, commanding roar and under compression deceleration, there's just enough subtle popping and backfiring to keep the strokes in their Impalas awake and quivering.

Happily, the Z is not all bark and no bite; while it carries a typically desmogged 350 V-8 engine, it also carries a four-speed transmission and a 3.73:1 rear axle ratio. So at highway speeds it turns considerable revolutions; that's one big reason why the fuel numbers are no better than they are. But that rear axle number also allows a great deal of torque multiplication to the rear

wheels. As you accelerate hard the revs stay up—and you go fast. Well, maybe not as fast as a pre-smog factory hot rod, but these days any piece of Detroit iron that'll get to 60 mph in eight seconds flat, or do the quarter-mile in 16.3 seconds at 85.1 mph is no slouch. The Z-28 will do all of that.

It also goes around corners so hard it'll make your ears bleed, pulling an honest-to-god .78g on our skidpad, a number very few other cars can duplicate. And many of the ones that can cost at least double the Z-28's approximately $5200 base price. The nice

part about all that handling power is that given the proper situation and occasion it's all usable. The suspension setup is such that you can hang the car right out, and no matter what you do, there'll be no surprises. It's totally predictable, even down to it's ultimate cornering attitude, understeer, which a bit of throttle will instantly change to power oversteer. That understeer is there because of a relatively small rear anti-roll bar and some cleverly placed bumpstops which greatly increase the car's front roll resistance when it gets heeled over all the way. We removed them for one try at the skidpad; the understeer was not as noticeable and the lateral acceleration number went up. We'll tell you all about that, about some other tricks bound to improve the Z's handling, and about a possible fix for the car's poor fuel economy in a special Z-28 update. So stay tuned.

The car's springs are so stiff—stiffer even than those on its sister, the Pontiac Firebird TransAm—that the ride is very firm indeed. The shock valving also has been biased towards use by the sporting driver so you get none of the float at speed normally associated with American iron. But while the ride is firm, it isn't so hard that your dental work is jarred out every time you cross a freeway expansion joint. Chevrolet's chassis guys are to be congratulated; they've done their jobs very well, and a good old fashioned flog through the curvey stuff will show you just *how* well.

First, you'll notice that the car's cornering attitude is very flat, with very little body lean. That's because of those stiff springs. It's

How the one Red Rocket eludes the Highway Patrol in a dozen states, and collects the world's largest pile of Mobil receipts, Coke bottles and cracker wrappers.

Chevrolet has chosen to preview its 1977 Z-28 Camaros on the morning of the IROC finale at Daytona in mid-February. After a casual breakfast, Chevrolet General Manager Robert D. Lund introduces the '77 Z-28 to the press by saying, "We firmly believe the Z-28 may well prove to be the best handling production vehicle ever built and that it will set a new standard for production cars of the future." Then they tell us we can try the cars on the infield road course, but we shouldn't go fast. Everybody looks at everybody else, shrugs, and commences to haul ass.

Anticipating the drive back to California in the Z-28, I'm already worried about The Law. I mean, we asked for a fairly bright color so our pictures would look good, but this car is done up in what should be listed in Chevy's color chart as *Arrest Me Red*. This car has a Visibility Factor of about 48 on a scale of 10. It's a good thing I have a suitcase full of CB equipment and assorted radar detectors, sort of a one-man swap meet.

Out of the speedway gates and onto the roads, it's soon apparent that the Z-28 is an excellent GT car. It eats up the miles effortlessly, swallowing great gulps of landscape at a single sitting, a sitting which is also effortless because the seats are such an improvement over previous Camaro designs.

Along with great gulps of landscape the Red Rocket also consumes great gulps of unleaded gas, the penalty you pay for 350 cubic inches and a four-barrel carb under the hood, all to pull around 3700 pounds of automotive sculpture. The overall fuel average for the eight-day trip will work out to an unrepentant 12.4 mpg.

Up through Lake City and Tallahassee, then across the southwestern corner of Georgia, we head into the two-lanes of Alabama and Mississippi, encountering more car-to-car moving radar than all the rest of the country must have added together. On one

stretch we intercept The Evil Beam five times, at two-mile intervals. The detectors are screaming their glorious little beepers off and I smile real pretty as I flash by at Double Nickles.

I angle on to the northwest, passing through Tupelo, New Albany and Holly Springs, then hole up for the night at the West Memphis Holiday Inn, on the Arkansas side of the Mississippi River.

The next morning the sky opens between West Memphis and Little Rock. Interstate 40 is deluged in a downpour that has the truckers fighting against the dreaded jack-knife. The wind blows ever harder. I take the Red Rocket off the interstate at Little Rock as the rain passes on through and we hurtle into the great driving roads of the Ozarks, over to the gathering of houses called Ola, then north on Arkansas Highway 7 to Harrison. *National Geo-*

graphic once named Highway 7 as one of the ten most beautiful roads in the country and I can't disagree.

By the time we're into Missouri the atmosphere is orange with blowing dust. It's being carried all the way from the Red River Valley. A strange monochromatic glow filters the light and I'd like to shoot pictures of the red car against the golden winter grass of rolling hills, but the wind is blowing so hard it will force the red grit into my Nikon's inner workings. I pass it up and hustle through the remarkable whoop-de-doos of Missouri Highway 90, a miniature Nurburgring.

We make our way through the familiar maze of roads into Kansas and stop for two days in the town of Independence where I grew up, and my mother fixes the best meals I've had in months.

On the morning I am to leave, I wake up in the wee small hours and peer outside. There's a light drizzle. When the alarm goes off at 5:30, two inches of snow have collected and more is falling. We listen to the weather reports, say our good-byes, and I leave not knowing whether I'll be going through Amarillo and Albuquerque or cutting south. By the time we pull into Oklahoma City the CB is carrying word of worsening weather in the Texas panhandle and New Mexico. I change my night's reservations and head south to Dallas, another old stomping ground, then westward through Midland and Odessa toward El Paso. Once again the CB has saved a lot of trouble. The unit Pioneer has loaned me for the trip is a 40-channel/AM/FM pushbutton stereo unit, and it works beautifully. Between the CB and the battery of three radar detectors, we're almost bulletproof.

By the end of the day the Red Rocket has swallowed 1050 miles and spewed them out the back. El Paso looks mighty good, but I'm tired only from the long hours and the constant Bearwatch, not from driving the car, which is as comfortable and secure as I could wish.

I sleep late in El Paso and leave town on the deserted interchanges of a sunny Sunday morning. Shortly after entering New Mexico I begin hearing reports of a westbound Cadillac containing three of the most de-luscious young ladies ever to pass beneath the window of a Peterbilt. We hold a steady pace on the assumption we'll catch them or they'll catch us, and the CB fairly hums for miles until it's almost afire with the truckers' running commentary on the sweet young contents of the Cadillac. "I be fall in love with

the one in the red bandana. Hacksaw, they be comin' up on your elbow, but don't you be get in a state of activation with my Beaver. She be fall in love with *me!*"

"What'chew mean, your Beaver?"

"She smile and wave and she got that one gleam in her eye be only for me alone, don'tcha know."

Pretty soon they've passed an eighteen-wheeler under the steady hand of the Cherokee and a co-driver by the name of Leroy. I don't know what Leroy's handle is and couldn't care less by this time. When the Cherokee allows that Leroy was so excited he took a sponge bath in preparation for the arriving girls, I can't stand it anymore.

"Cherokee, you got a copy on this Red Rocket?"

"You got the Cherokee."

"What be the 20 on those Cadillac Beavers?" I have to ask.

"They be followin' a little red Camaro, don'tcha know. It be havin' Florida plates."

Assorted gasping and choking noises.

"That Camaro almost run off the road up there, Red Rocket."

"This *is* the Red Rocket, the red Camaro. I'm in it!"

"Oooeee! You be their front door!"

The "Cadillac" I've spent 40 miles looking for is a Continental and there are *five* people in it. The extra two are Momma and Daddy. Right away the word spreads that the girls are right behind the Red Rocket and the truckers plead with me to slow down so they can enjoy extended "farfetched fits of fanciful flusterbation." Then the Continental slips away during a gas stop in Lordsburg and it's over.

It's a perfect day as the Red Rocket slips into Arizona. The run to Blythe, on the California line, is unattended, but crossing the Colorado River is like entering a combat zone. The word is out that the California Highway Patrol is up in force. They may not have radar, but they do have a lot of manpower and it seems to stretch endlessly between the state's border with Arizona and Los Angeles. Crossing an otherwise empty desert at little more than 55 mph is a ridiculous way to end a journey of almost 4000 miles but, enclosed in the Red Rocket's softly rumbling interior, I find myself thinking how nice it is to take a really long trip in a comfortable, responsive car, a car you can become friends with, especially when you've got a company credit card.—*Larry Griffin*

anti-roll bars aren't as heavy as those used on the TransAm, but they're there. Thus there is very little oddball behavior when the car is in a transient maneuver—that is, initiating or ending a turn. You turn the wheel and it just goes where it's pointed, thanks in no small degree to what has to be one of the best power steering units available anywhere today. Nope, the steering isn't rack and pinion, it's just good ol' Amurikin recirculating ball, but hooked to GM's staight-ratio power steering it's as fast (at 2.6 turns lock-to-lock) and as precise as any of them and provides just the right amount of feedback to the driver.

We've driven some Camaros, rental cars for the most part, that were real dogs; none of the parts seemed to work in concert with any of the others. This definitely is not the case with the 1977 Z-28. It's a total car, obviously very well designed to work as a package, a unit. It does just that, providing its driver with more satisfaction than we would have thought possible. American cars flat aren't supposed to be this much fun; at least, they never have been before. We suspect that with a few minor changes, the current edition of the Camaro Z-28 could set handling and drivability standards for the entire industry. We always suspected General Motors could do it, if it just would. ■

SPECIFICATIONS

ENGINE

Type	OHV V-8
Displacement, cu in	350
Displacement, cc	5733
Bore x stroke, in	4.00 x 3.48
Bore x stroke, mm	101.6 x 88.4
Compression ratio	8.5:1
Hp at rpm, net	170@3800
Torque at rpm, lb/ft, net	260@2400
Carburetion	1 4-V

DRIVELINE

Transmission	4-spd manual

Gear ratios:

1st	2.64:1
2nd	1.75:1
3rd	1.34:1
4th	1.00:1
Final drive ratio	3.73:1
Driving wheels	rear

GENERAL

Wheelbase, ins	108.0
Overall length, ins	195.4
Width, ins	74.4
Height, ins	49.2
Front track, ins	61.6
Rear track, ins	60.3
Trunk capacity, cu ft	6.4
Curb weight, lbs	3730
Distribution, % front/rear	58/42
Power-to-weight ratio, lbs/hp	23.3

BODY AND CHASSIS

Body/frame construction	unit w/subframe
Brakes, front/rear	ventilated disc/drum
Swept area, sq in	326.4
Swept area, sq in/1000 lb	87.5
Steering	recirc. ball
Ratio	13.0:1
Turns, lock-to-lock	2.6
Turning circle, ft	38.5

Front suspension: Independent, upper and lower control arms, coil springs, tubular shocks, anti-roll bar

Rear suspension: Live axle, leaf springs, tubular shocks, anti-roll bar

WHEELS AND TIRES

Wheels	15 x 7.0
Tires	GR70x15
	Goodyear Steelgard

INSTRUMENTATION

Instruments: 0-130 mph speedo, 0-7000 rpm tach, fuel level, temp, volts, clock

Warning lights: directionals, high beam, oil press, brake, seat belts

PRICE

Factory list, as tested: $6406.06

Options included in price: Air cond—$478; AM/FM stereo—$226; power windows—$108; floor mats—$16; tilt wheel—$57; console—$75; power door locks—$68; rear defog—$48; tinted glass—$50; Positraction—$54; intermittent wipers—$30; deluxe belts—$19; auxiliary lighting—$27

TEST RESULTS

ACCELERATION, SEC.

0-30 mph	3.0
0-40 mph	4.4
0-50 mph	6.2
0-60 mph	8.0
0-70 mph	10.9
0-80 mph	13.9
Standing start, ¼ mile	16.3
Speed at end ¼ mile, mph	85.1
Avg accel over ¼ mile, g	0.24

SPEEDS IN GEARS, MPH

1st (5000 rpm)	40
2nd (5000 rpm)	60
3rd (5000 rpm)	81
4th (5400 rpm) (observed)	115
Engine revs at 70 mph	3300

SPEEDOMETER ERROR

Indicated speed	True speed
40 mph	41 mph
50 mph	51 mph
60 mph	61 mph
70 mph	71 mph
80 mph	81 mph

INTERIOR NOISE, dBA

Idle	59
Max 1st gear	79
Steady 40 mph	70
50 mph	69
60 mph	74
70 mph	75

BRAKES

Average stopping distance from 60 mph, ft	157
Avg deceleration rate, g	0.77

FUEL ECONOMY

Overall avg range	12-17 mpg
Range on 21.0 gal tank	357 miles
Fuel required	unleaded

HANDLING

Avg speed on 100-ft rad, mph	34.2
Lateral acceleration, g	0.78
Transient response, avg speed, mph	24.2

RATING

PERFORMANCE/ECONOMY

*Acceleration	4
*Fuel Economy	2

RIDE/HANDLING

*Lateral Acceleration	5
Subjective handling	4
Predictability	4
Ride	3
Steering	4

ENGINE/DRIVETRAIN

Starting	4
Throttle Response	4
Noise/Vibration	3
Shifting Action	3

BRAKES

*Stopping Distance	4
Fade Resistance	3
Subjective Feel	2

COMFORT/ERGONOMICS

*Interior Noise	3
Controls/Instruments	3
Visibility	2
Entry/Exit	2
Front Seat Comfort	4
Rear Seat Comfort	2
Space Utilization	1
Interior Environment	4

QUALITY

Assembly	4
Finish	3
Hardware/Trim	3

TOTAL	**80**
Percentile rating	**64**

*Denotes recorded data

5=Excellent, 4=Above Average, 3=Average, 2=Below Average, 1=Poor, 0=Unacceptable.

Test Equipment Used: Testron Fifth Wheel and Pulse Totalizer, Lamar Data Recording System, Esterline-Angus Recorder, Sun Tachometer, EDL Pocket-Probe Pyrometer, General Radio Sound Level Meter.

Suddenly it's 1970   _by BOB HALL_

1977½ Chevrolet Camaro Z-28

Road Test

One of my first assignments as a _Motor Trend_ staffer, some three years ago, was to assist the engineering editor in a road test of the Challenger, Javelin, Firebird and Camaro. Up until that time, I had thought that Detroit was incapable of building a sporty GT car which looked good, went quickly and handled well. The 1974 Camaro we tested proved me quite wrong. It was a Z-28.

Well, the Z-28 was missing from the 1975 Chevrolet lineup, so it was assumed by yours truly that the Z-car had become another fatality of the ever-tightening noose of the "clean-air" standards. The real reason for the demise of the sportiest Camaro was (as I later discovered) the car's inability to meet some of the new-

for-1975 _noise_ standards. To convert the Z to meet these regs would have required the use of a new floor pan (too expensive at the time) or converting the Z-28 into little more than a trim package. Chevrolet wisely decided to let the Z rest in peace... temporarily.

As of spring 1977 the Z-28 is back. At first glance, one is tempted to think that Chevrolet's product planners are out of their collective minds. Gasoline certainly won't be getting cheaper in the months and years ahead, and '77 emission standards are the toughest to date, so why bother with a performance car like the Z-28? Perhaps the biggest reason can be summed up in two words: Firebird Trans Am. The Trans Am is the best-selling Firebird by a large margin, and it stands to reason that the Chevrolet people felt it was a bit

unfair for Pontiac to walk away with the performance pie. Ergo, return of the Z-car.

Like earlier Zs, the 1977 car is offered with only one engine, which in this case is a 350cid hydraulic-lifter unit similar to the one used in the 1974 Z-28. Standard transmission is a heavy-duty Borg-Warner 4-speed manual, and 3-speed automatic (fitted to our test car) is offered as an option. The only other item of the driveline different from the standard Camaro is the use of an "open" exhaust system using dual resonators in place of mufflers. According to Chevrolet engineers, this reduces exhaust back pressure by 40% at 4000 rpm.

To say these modifications alter the performance of the Camaro would be an understatement. With a 0-60 time of 8.15 sec and the ability

sorbers are just the start. Since GR70-15 radial tires are used (in place of the FR78-14s offered as the biggest tire on the regular Camaro), alterations were made to the front and rear stabilizer bars, spring rates and rear spring shackles. The larger tires are mounted on 15x7 styled steel wheels.

The end result of these various modifications is nothing short of incredible. The Z-28 is the best-handling American production car I have even driven. It is essentially a neutral

car, with no understeer or oversteer at hand unless one makes a deliberate attempt to coax one of these peculiarities to the surface. Tromping on the loud pedal in mid-corner will bring the tail around in short order (not advisable if the road surface is the least bit damp). On dry pavement, I never encountered the slightest semblance of understeer in any but moderate-speed "U" turns, when the nose would run a tad wide. The standard power steering is geared slightly higher than that on the regu-

Chevrolet Camaro Z-28

Specifications:

GENERAL

Manufacturer	Chevrolet Motor Division, General Motors Corporation, Detroit, Michigan
Number of U.S. dealers	6030
Warranty	12 months/12,000 miles
Base list price	$5170.60
Options on test car	Air conditioning ($478), automatic transmission ($282), AM radio with stereo tape ($209), cruise control ($80), plus various comfort, convenience and trim items totaling $499
Price as tested	$6718.60

POWER UNIT

Type	Water-cooled OHV V-8
Bore & stroke	4.00 x 3.48 in.
Displacement	350cid
Maximum net HP	170 hp at 3800 rpm
Maximum net torque	270 lb-ft at 2400 rpm
Compression ratio	8.5:1
Carburetion	single 4-bbl

DRIVETRAIN

Transmission type	3-spd automatic
Final drive ratio	3.42:1

CHASSIS

Body/frame	Unitized
Suspension, front	Unequal-length A-arms, coil springs, tubular shock absorbers, stabilizer bar
rear	Live axle, semi-elliptic leaf springs, tubular shock absorbers, stabilizer bar
Brakes, front	11.0-in. vented discs
rear	9.5- x 2.0-in. drums
Steering system	Recirculating ball
Steering ratio	14.0:1
Tire make & size	Goodyear steel-belted radial, GR70 x 15

DIMENSIONS

Wheelbase	108.0 in.
Track, front	61.6 in.
rear	60.3 in.
Length	195.4 in.
Width	74.4 in.
Height	49.2 in.
Weight	3684 lb
Fuel capacity	21.0 gals.

PERFORMANCE

0-30 mph	3.1 sec
0-60 mph	8.1 sec
40-60 mph	5.0 sec
Quarter mile	15.4 sec
Speed at end of quarter mile	90.05 mph
Braking, 30-0 mph	31.0 ft
60-0 mph	130.1 ft
Fuel economy, 73-mile MT loop	14.8 mpg

to turn consistent quarter mile E.T.s in the low 15s. This seems a little on the fast side for a car meeting 1977 emissions levels, so we have a very strong suspicion that our test car had been "massaged" somewhat. It would not be too far off base to assume that the engine had been blueprinted. Even allowing for this minor "modification," the Z is no slouch (we'd expect a non-massaged Z-28 to be only 8-10% slower than our warmed-over test car). Throttle response is, as one would expect, good.

If there is any major failing attributable to the powertrain, it would have to be less-than-sparkling fuel economy. On our 73-mile test loop of city and highway driving, the Z-28 could manage no better than 14.8 mpg, but the sort of person who buys a Z-car hopefully isn't purchasing the car for reasons of economy.

As quick as the Z-28 is, its most outstanding characteristic is its handling. The suspension system has been given the most extensive reworking of any portion of the car. Stiffer springs and specific shock ab-

lar Camaro, with a 14.1:1 overall ratio rather than the normal 16.1:1. This increases the steering effort slightly, but it also quickens the steering, so it is a reasonable trade-off.

The Z-28's interior doesn't differ from that of the more mundane versions of the Camaro. Certain items from the Camaro Type LT are standard on the Z, like twin "sport" (our quotes) mirrors, full instrumentation, concealed windshield wipers and simulated leather instrument panel-surround overlay (it looks better than fake wood). Our test car had standard Camaro seats with the optional "sport cloth" fabric. The Type LT trim package with more comfortable (at least to me) bucket seats is available for those willing to spend a little more money.

There are a number of failings, or rather low points, in the Camaro interior that are carried over into the Z-28. The first of these is the laughable rear seat accommodation. Although the car seems to be a full 4-seater, it is for all intents and purposes a 2 + 2, and a marginal one at that. The ashtray is still over just to the right of the steering column, near the driver, but mounted so low that the reach is an awkward one, and a

very long one for the front seat passenger. One other point that is not in keeping with the overall interior appointments is the AN6 2-position adjustable seatback on the driver's side only. It is best described as a very inadequate and crude version of a semi-reclining seat. As good a GT car as the Z-28 is, this omission becomes an annoying fault.

The Camaro is now in its fourth year without a major restyling, but its simplicity of line belies that fact. About the only detail on the car which strikes a false note is the NASA duct-shaped decal on the hood. Looks kinda like a two-dimensional hood scoop.

Overall, it's quite easy to be enthusiastic about the new Z-28. It lives up to the name of its predecessors, and that is something that the new generation of AMXs, Road Runners and Cobras would be hard-pressed to do. Even though it isn't as fast as the last Z-car, the 1974, it can still show a clean pair of heels to most other 350s in its class. Almost every car enthusiast has had the feeling that, after the emission standards stabilized for a couple of years, the age of performance would come back. It looks as if they were right. MT

Camaro Z28

Ladies and gentlemen, let's have a big hand for the car that came back.

BY DON SHERMAN

ROAD TEST:

• The unpretentious collection of letters and numbers we all know and love as RPO Z28 has a vigor so enduring that combined forces of bad and evil have never been able to erase this option from Chevrolet order blanks. GM's own president tried to eradicate the whole Camaro/Firebird line during the craze of early Seventies deproliferation. Internal inertia overruled that mo-

tion. And the worst handiwork of the de-performance lobby effected but a two year lapse in Z28s before Chevrolet had to answer pent-up demand with a third generation. Score one for outside influence.

Last year's Mark III return engagement was met with such roaring applause that the sportiest Camaro bows into 1978 with a new costume and full-fledged star status

in the Chevrolet cast. While the 1977 Z28 look was little more than paint and tape make-up over a base Camaro, new tooling money has paid for the most thorough facelift of this old tragedian since the great redesign of 1970. Aluminum bumpers have given way to the soft look. Underneath a smooth mask of flexible urethane, this new Camaro packs front and rear aluminum

impact rams padded with molded plastic cushions. Weight savings is zero in front but almost 50 pounds in back. The execution is identical to Pontiac's Firebird and very similar to Porsche's 928, each living proof that bumper cars can be beautiful.

The Camaro is, however, unique in this elite group in having a design continuity the others can only envy. Guys who lusted after the Ferrari-snout, dive-plane tail Camaros in 1970 can still buy the look they liked way-back-when, brand new today. It's a major part of what nurtures a dedicated following for Chevrolets in general and Z28s in particular. And just to make sure no one misses this new edition, the three magic Z 2 8 characters now sparkle under a transparent plastic lens to magnify the identification badge for extra impact. There's a NACA duct big enough to feed a 747 on the hood, complemented by a sizeable set of exhaust registers on each front fender. Where other cars are chromed, the Z28 is color-coded. Trim moldings are flat-black, door handles and the new alloy wheels are keyed to body color. The really bright stuff is saved for triple-hue taillamps and the accent stripes. It all works so well that folks in California flag you down to bestow their ultimate compliment, "Bitch-in mochine!"

You get real dual exhausts, one per fender, but the NACA duct is phony.

These rave reviews only underline the fact that the Z28 is off on a flash-before-function tangent. The 1978 version is virtually devoid of mechanical alteration. There has been a little re-engineering to stiffen the front structure, which in turn makes the front anti-sway bar more effective, but the rest of the powertrain and chassis is intact. Our old friend, the LM-1, 350-cubic inch four-barrel V-8 is back, still rated at 180 hp, but there's more vitality when you put your foot down. A new cold air duct on the intake side and more efficient exhaust ports help high rpm breathing considerably, even though the dynamometer peak hasn't budged since last year. We also had the advantage of a non-airconditioned test car this time around. (There are substantial parasitic losses to the compressor drive and cooling fan with AC, even when it's switched off). This package delivered not only third gear rubber on demand, but also a neat, clean 0 to 60 time of 7.3 seconds. We found a sixteen-flat quarter-mile ET and enough energy to push it all the way up to 123 mph. You do have to twist the engine 800 rpm past the conservative 5000 rpm redline for the latter feat, but we noticed no distress whatsoever doing so.

We were frankly surprised to find new vigor in the acceleration department (1.3-seconds quicker 0 to 60 mph, 0.3-seconds quicker quarter-mile), and we were equally disappointed to find little annual progress in handling. The 1978 Z28 suffers from the same problem getting around corners we found last year: understeer at the limit. Fender contours prohibit the use of either wider wheels, or bigger tires in production, and jounce travel is, in fact, restricted in front to allow running clearance for GR70-15 tires. The fit problem has to do with fender lip contours uncomfortably close to the tire's shoulder when the wheel moves into full jounce. Why this area wasn't opened up when the front fenders were being retooled isn't immediately clear, but the Band-Aid solution is a spacer under each front suspension jounce bumper.

Camaros never were big on suspension travel, and this loss is painful. Jack Turner is the Chevrolet man responsible for the way the Z28 handles and we've spent considerable time probing his inner-most thoughts for explanation. You may remember him as the man who engineered handling into the down-sized Impala/Caprice line with the F41 suspension option.

For starters, Jack Turner has little interest in competing against either the Corvette or the Firebird T/A for king of the handling hill. His desire is real-life roadability in the Z28, which means giving up

some skidpad and slalom course gription to make both ends of the car work off-track. The Z28 is more softly sprung, has "looser" shock valving, lower steering effort and smaller anti-sway bars than the Pontiac Trans Am. The effect on driving feel is so dramatic that it's hard to believe these two cars share any parts, let alone the whole body shell, steering linkage and suspension geometries.

Jack Turner has spotted the Z28 toward the soft end of suspension tune because he wants it to be capable on rough "chatter bump" pavement as well as glass-smooth roads. Any car tends to bounce more from peak to peak in a rough turn as spring and sway-bar rates are raised. This not only wipes out lateral adhesion, but it also works the structure so much that the car ends up with what Jack Turner calls a "junky feel"—what we'd probably call terminal squeaks and rattles. Straight-line ride is also a major concern to Turner, because he feels a genuine road car should not grind down its driver with fatigue when driven hard in day-long stretches. Shocks are tuned more for ride than handling in the Camaro, and tire pressure is set at a rather soft 24 psi cold.

We took some special pains to test these theories. One of Jack Turner's favorite ride

and handling trips is the route to Mount Palomar in the southwestern corner of the country. The run up to the California Institute of Technology's observatory contains one fantastic seven-mile stretch of seven percent grade. It is a road racer's paradise, the perfect way to flog a suspension, have fun and escape the LA basin.

Most of the turns are second gear, 35–40 mph switchbacks that frequently tighten halfway through. Since most of the corner is usually blind, there are few guard rails and the opposite lane is frequently full of pickup truck, good speed adjustability *after* entry is a must. The Camaro's bias towards understeer is ideal for this, because even if you boil in ten mph too fast and wrench the wheel, the back end always stays put on the right side of the road. And when all the front cornering adhesion is used up, there are two techniques that work to cut back unwanted velocity: You can steer in more and let the additional understeer scrub off speed, or you can step into the brakes without upsetting stability. If you get halfway into the turn and find out your entry speed erred on the conservative side, it's just as simple to stay hard on the throttle, unwind the steering as necessary and about one time out of four, the tail will calmly drift out just like Bob Bon-

durant said it would. With the Camaro's quick 2.8 turn lock-to-lock steering, the three and nine o'clock hand position works all the way up the mountain. All the moves are slow and predictable in the Z28, so almost anybody can have handling fun on their own private hill, with no need for a USAC driver's license.

Advanced speed freaks, however, might like a little less understeer and this was particularly evident on the way *down* Mount Palomar. Here you're more likely in third gear than second, and more time is spent on the brakes than on the throttle. The effective understeer is heavier and more a hindrance because at times it can plow you right off the road. We also noticed that the combination of power and handling was enough to drive the Z28 well into the intermediate stages of brake fade. We never had to slow the pace substantially, but stopping ability was obviously melting away with heat build up.

My personal conclusion about the Camaro's handling is that it's perfect for novice Nuvolaris. You can pitch it around and hunt for the apex with ham-hands and club-feet and the worst this car will do is understeer. The best it will do is get you around smoothly and quickly within an 0.77 g limit. As a learner's GT, the Z28 is

63

ideal. The base car goes out the door for less than a Scirocco, which makes it THE bargain basement handler.

Chevrolet may not be trying for one-g cornering in the Z28, but it is more serious in its intentions on other fronts. The combination of radial tires and Jack Turner's resistance to selling a road racer has made the smooth pavement ride a joy to behold. Rough pavement, however, is another matter, and when the bumps start crashing through the limited suspension travel, a Scirocco seems not so expensive after all. The bombed out streets of New York City are enough to drive the Z28 well past that "junky" creaking structure feeling that Jack Turner was avoiding, but the same applies to supposedly "bullet-proof" pick-up trucks we've endured here. Worse still, any Camaro or Firebird jumps from lane to lane in the Big Apple, crippled by the niggardly suspension travel.

Compensation comes in the form of a soothing interior. Sumptuous Type LT trimmings are now available in the Z28, a real boon to those who prefer their Chevy 2+2 with the best of everything. Our test car came through with a taxicab yellow outside screaming performance from every pore, a real contrast to the interior. Inside,

knob, or more correctly the shifter it's connected to. There are those who fondly reminisce of vaguely remembered "good old days", when muscle car levers were stamped with "Hurst", every shift made Zorro look arthritic and molten blobs of rubber trailed out the back of the car. In replacement, we have today's Z28, third gear will produce weak chirps at best and the shifter is by Inland. Chevrolet claims this design works better than the Hursts it's tried, but we have mixed emotions. The one we used in California worked perfectly, the one we drove in New York inspired a few complaints. Our resident ex-quarter-miler experienced embarassing one-two hangups on power shifts and others felt the gear-to-gear travel was on the long side. There was, however, general appreciation for one of the few surviving four-speeders in all the land. The ratios are spot-on, there is sparkle to the torque curve and a throaty rumble from the pipes is well worth the loss of power-shiftability.

The next bone of contention is the Z28's string-wrapped steering wheel. We'll give the stylists one point for creativity—no other car has such a wheel—but from this point on, we have no staff agreement on the scoring. I was appalled at first sight,

but grew to appreciate this test-tube touch. The large diameter is perfect for leverage and the nobbly surface gives plenty of grip without gloves. The Palomar run did leave me with sandpapered hands—at least on the palm side—but the wheel's aggressive tread did avoid a sweaty grip.

Others here are less impressed. String-wrapping works on badminton rackets, they say, but this is a car. Low class, they say, particularly when there has been so little attempt to disguise the molding of the fake-string rim, the spokes and the hub all in one homogeneous squirt.

We'd be a whole lot less likely to unravel such loose ends if the Z28 were just a run of the mill car. But it isn't. Most of us have grown up lusting after, owning, or in our case, testing Z28s year after year for a decade. It is practically *the* charter member of America's performance hall of fame. We can all rest assured. The Jack Turners of Warren, Michigan have served the fan club well. Nineteen seventy eight brings the best rounded Z28 ever. The knife edge of acceleration and handling is blunted, but ride, styling and interior comfort are all honed to a new brilliance. In ten years, when we look back to 1978, we'll remember the Z28 fondly. ●

Sign here for handling fun. You need no prerequisites to apply.

the decor was as reserved as a Brooks Brothers' fitting room. A whole autumnal palette of earth tones swept over walls, ceiling and floor. The seats were a particularly natty selection of designer's wovens, and the same fabric was also stitched and padded into each door panel's centerpiece.

With the walls draped in primo cloth, squishy vinyl, color-keyed carpet and one elegantly molded armrest/grab handle per outboard elbow, it's very easy to lapse into momentary over-comfort in a highly optioned Z28. Fortunately, there are two reminders carefully positioned by Chevrolet to snap you back into the banzai mode: A black shift knob the size of an eight ball and a Porsche-style steering wheel wrapped in pseudo-string. Both items remind you the Z28 is more GT than LT, and if the office poll is any indication, they also inspire long arguments about the net desirability of Camaros old and new.

On the right hand, we have the big

ACCELERATION standing ¼ mile, seconds

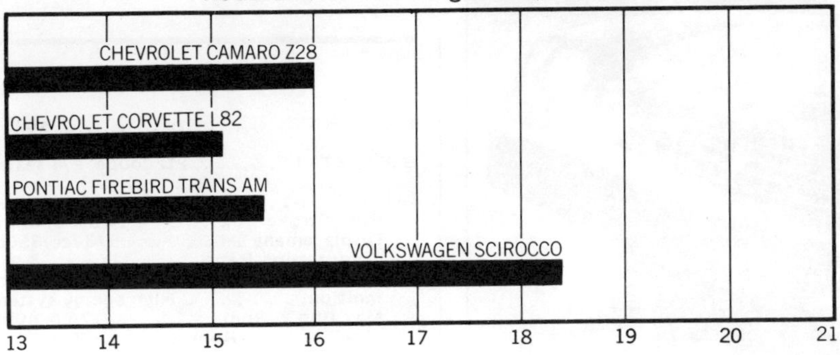

- CHEVROLET CAMARO Z28
- CHEVROLET CORVETTE L82
- PONTIAC FIREBIRD TRANS AM
- VOLKSWAGEN SCIROCCO

13 14 15 16 17 18 19 20 21

BRAKING 70-0 mph, feet

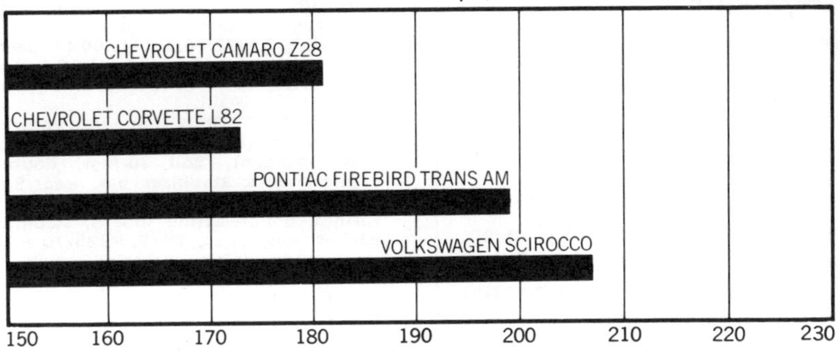

- CHEVROLET CAMARO Z28
- CHEVROLET CORVETTE L82
- PONTIAC FIREBIRD TRANS AM
- VOLKSWAGEN SCIROCCO

150 160 170 180 190 200 210 220 230

FUEL ECONOMY C/D mileage cycle, mpg

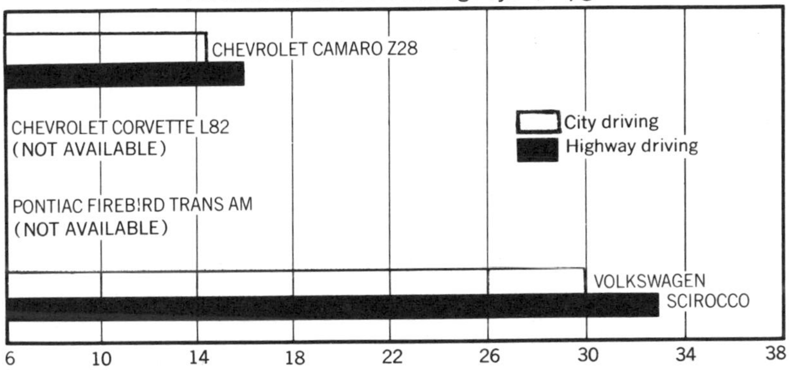

- CHEVROLET CAMARO Z28
- CHEVROLET CORVETTE L82 (NOT AVAILABLE)
- PONTIAC FIREBIRD TRANS AM (NOT AVAILABLE)
- VOLKSWAGEN SCIROCCO

☐ City driving
■ Highway driving

6 10 14 18 22 26 30 34 38

PRICE AS TESTED dollars x 1000

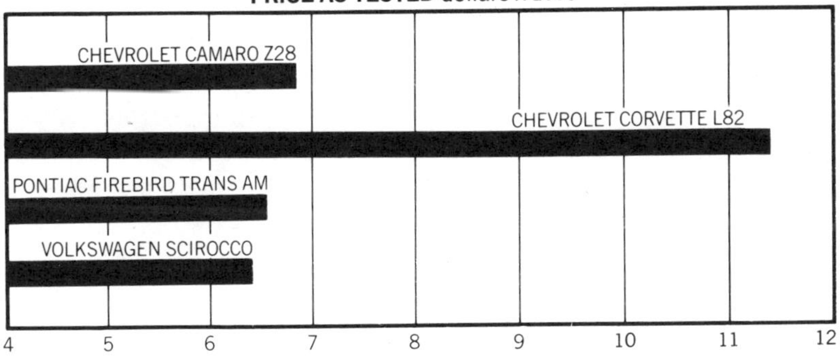

- CHEVROLET CAMARO Z28
- CHEVROLET CORVETTE L82
- PONTIAC FIREBIRD TRANS AM
- VOLKSWAGEN SCIROCCO

4 5 6 7 8 9 10 11 12

INTERIOR SOUND LEVEL dBA

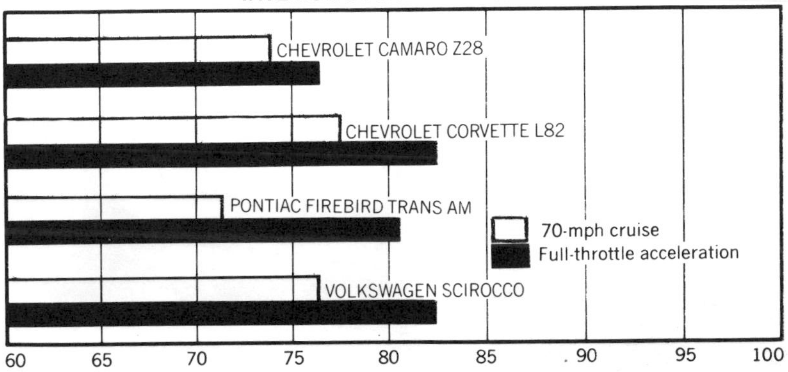

- CHEVROLET CAMARO Z28
- CHEVROLET CORVETTE L82
- PONTIAC FIREBIRD TRANS AM
- VOLKSWAGEN SCIROCCO

☐ 70-mph cruise
■ Full-throttle acceleration

60 65 70 75 80 85 90 95 100

CHEVROLET CAMARO Z28

Manufacturer: Chevrolet Motor Division
General Motors Corporation
Milford, Michigan 48090

Vehicle type: front-engine, rear-wheel-drive, 2 + 2-passenger coupe

Price as tested: $6818.85
(Manufacturer's suggested retail price, including all options listed below, dealer preparation and delivery charges, does not include state and local taxes, license or freight charges)

Options on test car: base Camaro Z28, $5603.85; alloy wheels, $195; positraction differential, $59; heavy duty radiator, $31; custom sport cloth bucket seats, $315; adjustable driver's seatback, $21; console, $80; tilt wheel, $69; AM/FM radio, $149; style trim group, $70; tinted glass, $56; rear defogger, $51; intermittent wipers, $32; auxiliary lighting, $28; deluxe seatbelts, $21; floor mats, $20; door edge guards, $11; dual horns, $7.

ENGINE
Type: V-8, water-cooled, cast-iron block and heads, 5 main bearings
Bore x stroke . . . . 4.00 x 3.78 in, 101.6 x 96.0mm
Displacement . . . . 350 cu in, 5730cc
Compression ratio . . . . 8.2 to one
Carburetion . . . . 1x4-bbl Rochester Quadrajet
Power (SAE net) . . . . 185 bhp @ 4000 rpm
Torque (SAE net) . . . . 280 lbs-ft @ 2400 rpm
Max. recommended engine speed . . . . 5000 rpm

DRIVETRAIN
Transmission . . . . 4-speed, all-synchro
Final drive ratio . . . . 3.73 to one

Gear	Ratio	Mph/1000 rpm	Max. test speed
I	2.64	8.0	40 mph (5000 rpm)
II	1.75	12.0	60 mph (5000 rpm)
III	1.34	15.7	79 mph (5000 rpm)
IV	1.00	21.1	123 mph (5800 rpm)

DIMENSIONS AND CAPACITIES
Wheelbase . . . . 108.0 in
Track, F/R . . . . 61.3/60.0 in
Length . . . . 197.6 in
Width . . . . 74.5 in
Height . . . . 49.2 in
Curb weight . . . . 3560 lbs
Weight distribution, F/R 56.2/43.8%
Fuel capacity . . . . 21.0 gal
Oil capacity . . . . 5.0 qts

SUSPENSION
F: .ind, unequal-length control arms, coil springs, anti-sway bar
R: . . . . rigid axle, semi-elliptic leaf springs, anti-sway bar

STEERING
Type . . . . recirculating ball, variable ratio, power-assisted
Turns lock-to-lock 2.6
Turning circle curb-to-curb . . . . 38.5 ft

BRAKES
F: . . . . 11.0-in dia vented disc, power-assisted
R: . . . . 9.5x2.0-in cast iron drum, power-assisted

WHEELS AND TIRES
Wheel size . . . . 7.0 x 15-in
Wheel type . . . . cast aluminum, 5-bolt
Tire make and size . . . . . . Firestone Steel Radial 500, GR70-15
Test inflation pressures, F/R . . . . 24/24 psi

PERFORMANCE

Zero to	Seconds
30 mph	2.7
40 mph	3.9
50 mph	5.5
60 mph	7.3
70 mph	9.8
80 mph	12.5
90 mph	15.7
100 mph	20.4

Standing ¼-mile . . . . 16.0 sec @ 91.1 mph
Top speed (observed) . . . . 123 mph
70-0 mph . . . . 181 ft (0.91 g)
Fuel economy, C/D mileage cycle . . . . 14.5 mpg, urban driving
16.0 mpg, highway driving

Camaro

DON'T LOOK for "Berlinetta" in the dictionary. Where you will find it is on Ferraris (probably the first to use it) and now, on top-of-the-line Camaros. It's set apart from other Camaros by its "unique exterior pin striping, bright grille treatment, black painted rocker panels, body-color styled wheels and special rear lamp styling. With a "custom level" interior and a few handling/performance options, it probably qualifies as a GT car. But, it's the Z28 that really does.

Not only does the Z28 look mean, and with the standard 350cid/5.7-liter V8 and four-speed close ratio box run mean, it is mean. Standard suspension is the F-41 sport suspension, which includes larger front and rear stabilizer bars (1.125 and .625-in.) and special front and rear shock absorbers. Steel radials, P225/70 R-15, are standard on 7-in. rims.

Stylewise, the Z28 now has a three-piece air dam and front wheel opening flares to complement the rear deck spoiler. The dam is semi-flex plastic and is trimmed with tri-striping to blend with side and rear paint accents.

1979 CAMARO Z28

BASE PRICE $6115

BODY STYLE. . . . . 2D coupe, 2/4-seater

ENGINE . . . . . . OHV V8, front-mounted
  Bore/Stroke . . . . .4.0 x 3.48 ins
  Displacement 5737cc/350ci
  Compression Ratio 8.2:1
  Carburetion 4-bbl
  Ignition. . . . . . . High energy system
  Max Bhp @ Rpm . . . . . .175 @ 4000
  Max Torque @ Rpm . . . . .270 @ 2400

DRIVETRAIN 4-speed manual, with single, dry-plate clutch, or 3-speed auto torque converter with planetary gears.
  Ratios . . 2.64/1.74/1.34/1.00 (4-speed)
          2.52/1.52/1.00 (auto).
  Final Drive. . 3.73 (4-speed), 2.56 (auto)

CHASSIS & BODY Body-frame integral with separate partial frame. Front suspension is independent, coil springs, double-acting shocks, stabilizer bar. Rear Suspension, Salisbury, with multiple leaf springs, double-acting shocks, stabilizer bar. Wheels, Tires, 15x7, P225/70 R-15 steel-belted radials. Steering power, recirculating ball, tilt wheel, 2.4 turns lock-to-lock, 38.5 ft. turning diameter. Brakes, front disc, rear drums.

DIMENSIONS & CAPACITIES
  Wheelbase . . . . 108 ins
  Track, front/rear . . . . . .61.3/60.0 ins
  Length . . . . 197.6 ins
  Width. . . . . 74.5 ins
  Height . . . . 49.2 ins
  Ground Clearance. . . . . .4.9 ins
  Curb Weight . . . . .3636 lbs
  Luggage Capacity . . . . 6.4 cu. ft
  Fuel Capacity . . . . .21 gals

PERFORMANCE/FUEL ECONOMY

EPA Mpg	City	Hwy	Comb
Manual	NA	NA	NA
Auto	16	21	18

IROC CAMARO vs Z-28

One for show, both for go

FEW PEOPLE HAVE done more to bolster the sporting image of the Chevrolet Camaro than Roger Penske. Penske, Les Richter and Michael Phelps are the principals behind the International Race of Champions, an annual invitational series that pits a dozen top drivers from the three major forms of motor racing (stock, championship and sports/formula cars), against each other. The best nine finishers in the first three races go on to the finale and a chance at the $50,000 first prize awarded to the points leader who is not necessarily the race winner.

When the championship was conceived in 1973, Penske purchased 15 Porsche Carrera RSRs for his racing stable. That season the IROC was staged strictly on road courses so the Porsches were an obvious choice. Furthermore, they were almost ready-to-race as they came from the factory, so in theory only fuel was needed to put the cars on the track. Penske's alliance with the Porsche factory for which he raced 917 turbos in the Can-Am might have influenced his choice, but this is not germane to our story. What is, is that after one season of IROC

racing, the Porsches were sold (many are still being raced today) and replaced with Camaros.

According to Jay Signore, Vice President and General Manager of Penske Racing and the person who helped arrange this test, the Chevrolet Camaro was chosen because oval track races would be included in the format and the Chevys would be more suitable for such use. Also Penske Racing's "long Trans-Am experience and the engineering familiarity of its personnel" would make it easier for Penske crewmen to set up and maintain the cars. Lastly, the proven track record of Chevrolet engines and components made Penske choose the Camaro. Little or nothing was said about a few oval track drivers who disliked "those funny furrin cars." Nor was much said about the costs and the problems of maintaining cars as intricate as Porsches. So the Camaros seemed ideal (Penske being a Chevrolet dealer may have had some bearing on the decision) and under the direction of the late Mark Donohue, 15 cars were modified for racing and pressed into service in the fall of 1974. Essentially, the IROC Camaros were similar to the Chevys raced in the Sports Car Club of America's A Sedan category except for some suspension modifications and engine displacement (the Penske sedans used 350 rather than 305-cu-in. engines).

Unfortunately, it didn't take long for Penske and company to determine that even the Camaros were less than ideal for the enthusiastic driving style of many IROC racers. The cars were difficult to set up when straight, and after they'd been bent—heaven help the poor crewmen who spent a hectic night rebuilding a car between Race Two on Saturday and Race Three on Sunday. In spite of these difficulties, the production Camaros were used for three seasons of racing, then sold to enterprising Trans-Am and Camel GT racers.

The present generation IROC Camaro is quite simply an oval track racing sedan. One might call it a stock car which is correct only in United States Auto Club (USAC) parlance. In the National Association for Stock Car Auto Racing (NASCAR) terminology, the Camaro is considered a Late Model Sportsman and not a stocker per se.

All 15 IROC Camaros were constructed in the Arden, North Carolina shops of Banjo Mathews, NASCAR racing star turned race car builder. With Banjo's strong stock car grounding, it's no wonder there's a lot of NASCAR and very little Chevrolet in every IROC Camaro. The engine, bodywork, gearbox and sometimes the steering box are about the only parts that come from the General Motors parts bins.

Like most cars built today, the production Camaro uses unit-body construction, meaning that suspension and driveline components are attached directly to the body. This won't do for the racing version which must be more durable and more adjustable than its production car counterpart. The heavy-duty suspension and driveline parts need something more substantial than pressed steel for attachment. Mathews gets around the unit-body problem quite easily—he simply builds a whole new frame under the unit body using rectangular steel stock for the main rails and round tube for the auxiliary members which form subframes that strengthen the main frame and provide mounting points for various components. There's a subframe up front surrounding the engine compartment and one in the rear encircling the trunk.

Lending even more rigidity to the frame is the rollcage, made up of large tubular steel hoops that encircle the entire passenger compartment. The hoops are tied together with cross braces and further strengthened by steel intrusion barriers that bridge the door openings.

The effectiveness of the NASCAR-type rollcage was proven at the IROC V finale at Daytona. Richard Petty got sideways trying to avoid a spinning car and his Camaro was struck broadside by Johnny Rutherford's car which was traveling about 155 mph at the time. Petty was shaken up by the accident and spent one night at a medical center where he was placed under observation. But the following day he was back driving his Dodge Grand National stocker in the Daytona 500.

While the stock Camaro front suspension uses stamped steel upper and lower A-arms and coil springs, the IROC sedan relies on parts manufactured by Stock Car Products and installed by Mathews. These include a lower control arm made of steel plate, an upper A-arm made of tubular steel and a heavy-duty front spindle. A single Monroe shock absorber attached to the lower control arm and upper subframe rail damps each front wheel's vertical movements.

Although both the road car and the racer have front coil springs, the IROC Camaro's are fitted with a large screw that allows the mechanics to quickly change the loading on each wheel. This practice, called weight jacking, is the primary means of changing the handling characteristics of the car. To put things in perspective, our Riverside test car carried 920 lb on its left front wheel and 827 lb on its right front.

Depending on the track, either a Chevrolet or a Ford steering box is used. The reason for the choice is the ratio; the Chevy's is 20:1 while the Ford's is 24:1. The slower Ford box is used on oval tracks, the quicker Chevy unit on road courses.

Front hubs on the racer are Holman-Moody products and while both road and race cars use front disc brakes, the IROC Camaro's are 12-in. diameter, dual-caliper ventilated units manufactured by Hurst Airheart. Both cars use a non-adjustable front antiroll bar, 1.1-in. thick on the production car and 1.0-in. on the racer.

Production car and racer use a live axle, but the IROC car's is a Ford ¾-ton truck part modified for racing. It's standard stock car fare and includes a Holman-Moody center section with full-floating axles. These are not attached to the wheel bearings, but are independently suspended to keep the hub and wheel from falling off in case of axle failure. The IROC sedan's rear end doesn't have quick change capability and ratios are switched by replacing the center section. Ratios range from 3.00:1 for the oval at Daytona to 3.91:1 for the road course at Riverside. For oval track use the differentiating action of the rear end is retained while on road courses the rear is locked.

In the production Camaro the rear leaf springs do double duty: They locate the axle as well as provide springing. However, in the interests of easier adjustability, the IROC cars have coil springs. Chevrolet truck trailing arms provide the longitudinal positioning while a Panhard rod lends lateral location. Holman-Moody hubs and Hurst Airheart disc brakes identical to the fronts are used. A single Monroe shock is fitted to each rear wheel and unlike the production car, which has a 0.63-in. anti-roll bar, the racer has none. Both rears have a weight jacking screw running through their centers, and at Riverside, the loading was 704 lb on the left and 750 on the right.

Other running gear and driveline essentials include Norris Industries 15 x 9.5-in. steel wheels shod with Goodyear 8.00/

Front suspension (top) uses unequal length upper and lower A-arms, coil springs. Screw in center of coil adjusts loading on each wheel.

Rear suspension (bottom) also has coil springs and weight adjusting screws. Hurst-Airheart disc brakes are used on all four wheels.

IROC's wagonmaster Jay Signore after Riverside's 2-day bash.

SPECIFICATIONS COMPARISON
Production Camaro Z-28 & IROC Camaro

	Production	Racing
Price	$6819	approx $28,000
General:		
Weight, lb	3590 (curb)	3280 (race)
Weight distribution (with driver), front/rear, %	56/44	55/45
Track, front/rear, in.	61.6/60.3	65.0/65.0
Width	74.5	80.0
Height	49.2	50.0
Ground clearance	4.9	6.0
Usable trunk space, cu ft	10.7	nil
Fuel capacity, U.S. gal.	21.0	33.0
Engine:		
Bore x stroke, mm	102.0 x 88.4	101.6 x 88.9
Displacement, cc/cu in.	5735/350	5737/350
Compression ratio	8.2:1	12.0:1
Bhp @ rpm	185 @ 4000	450 @ 6500
Torque @ rpm, lb-ft	280 @ 2400	396 @ 5000
Carburetion	one Rochester (4V)	one Holley (4V)
Fuel requirement	unleaded, 91-oct	premium, 102-oct
Drivetrain:		
Gear ratios:		
4th	1.00	1.00
3rd	1.34	1.23
2nd	1.75	1.61
1st	2.64	2.64
Final drive ratio	3.73:1	3.91:1
Chassis:		
Body/frame	unit steel	unit body with separate steel frame
Brake system	11.0-in. vented discs front, 9.5 x 2.0-in. drums rear; vacuum assisted	12.0-in. Hurst-Airheart vented discs front and rear
Swept area, sq in.	326	497
Wheels	cast alloy, 15 x 7	Norris Industries steel disc, 15 x 9½
Tires	Firestone Steel Radial 500, GR70-15	Goodyear Blue Streak Stock Car Special, 8.00/8.20-15
Steering, turns, lock to lock	2.6	2.5
Front suspension	unequal-length A-arms, coil springs, tube shocks, anti-roll bar	unequal-length A-arms, coil springs, Monroe tube shocks, anti-roll bar
Rear suspension	live axle on leaf springs, tube shocks, anti-roll bar	live axle on long trailing arms & Panhard rod, coil springs, Monroe tube shocks
Instrumentation:		
Instruments	130-mph speedo, 7000-rpm tach, oil press., coolant temp, ammeter, fuel level, clock	10,000-rpm tach, oil press., oil temp, coolant temp, voltmeter
Warning lights	handbrake, brake system seatbelt, hazard, high beam, directionals	ignition
Accommodation:		
Seating capacity, persons	4	1
Seat width, in.	2 x 18.5	16.0
Head room, f/r	35.0/33.0	37.0
Seat back adjustment, deg	4	0
Calculated data:		
Lb/bhp (test weight)	19.9	7.4
Mph/1000 rpm (4th gear)	22.0	21.7
Engine revs/mi (60 mph)	2730	2760
Piston travel, ft/mi	1585	1610
R&T steering index	100.1	0.90
Brake swept area, sq in./ton	177	300

8.20-15 Grand National tires and a Borg-Warner T10X 4-speed transmission.

Road car and racer use the same basic 350-cu-in. Chevrolet engine, but except for the bore and stroke, there is little similarity. The production Z-28 engine uses a cast-iron crankshaft, forged connecting rods and cast pistons and develops 185 bhp at 4000 rpm. The racing powerplant, built by Traco Engineering, Culver City, California, has a forged crank, rods and pistons and produces 450 bhp at 6500 rpm. The ignition is a transistorized Delco unit just like the production car's, but the intake manifold is an Edelbrock Scorpion fitted with a Holley 4-barrel carburetor. Hedman 180-degree exhaust headers, a Weaver dry sump unit, a Henny oil pan and a Schiefer clutch and flywheel are a few of the other mechanical building blocks used on the racing engine.

Incidentally, Penske Racing has about two dozen engines at the ready and they can be replaced as needed. However, the Chevy's strong point is reliability and unless something drastic happens, the engines seem to survive thrashings quite well. They are freshened up by Traco periodically.

The pleasantly appointed interior of the production Z-28 is luxurious compared to the race car's. The road car has a full interior, comfortable seats and a reasonably outfitted instrument panel. The racer has nothing save a bucket seat, a full set of competition seatbelts and a panel lined with oil and water temperature gauges, an oil pressure gauge, voltmeter and that all-important tachometer.

For safety's sake the IROC Camaro uses a specially built, 33.0-gal. fuel cell instead of the 21.0-gal. tank found in the production car. The race car also has a 4.5-gal. oil reservoir located behind the driver's seat and an on-board fire extinguishing system. Very little of this is visible from the grandstand and to the casual observer an IROC Camaro looks like a production Z-28 with flared fenders, big wheels and tires and flashy paint. Never mind that it has no side glass or interior and that the fender flares and all of the front end save the hood are fiberglass.

Now maybe the IROC Camaro looks like a road-going Z-28 with big numbers on its flanks, but when that healthy engine lights off, there's no question about the car's real nature. A raspy note from the car's 180-degree headers makes the engine sound like a 6-cylinder, but let us assure you, few sixes or even V-8s perform as well as this engine once it's allowed to unwind. We mention this last fact because by normal comparative standards—standing-start acceleration runs to 60 mph and in the quarter-mile—the racing version isn't appreciably quicker than the production car. The performance chart shows the details and illustrates one very important fact; namely that the race Camaro doesn't come alive until about 90 mph. At this point the emission-control laden road car is gasping for breath while the free-breathing racer is revving happily. The performance of each engine is reflected in the respective car's 0 to 100 mph times—20.0 seconds for the production Z-28 vs 11.0 sec for the IROC sedan. Top speed also differs greatly and where the stock Camaro peaks at 107 mph at 7000 rpm, a check of the gear ratio chart and tire diameters told us that the IROC Camaro as raced at Riverside would turn 152 mph at 7000 rpm. It would be even faster with taller gearing at a track like Daytona.

It's obvious the racing Camaro is very fast. But given the parameters of normal driving, so is the production Z-28. The latter accelerates to the accursed Double Nickel (55 mph) quickly and can buzz along an interstate fast enough to rouse the smokies. What's more, the driver will be able to hear the command to "Pull over," because even at 90 mph the road car registers only 79 dBA on the noise meter. At that speed the racer is showing a pain-inducing 113 dBA reading.

As expected, the racer handles like, well, like a racer. Because this one's a circle track car, it takes some horsing to get it around quickly. Brake pedal effort is high and there is some darting when stopping. And no wonder: With different camber settings up front and biased tire pressures and wheel loads, the IROC Camaro wanted to pull to the right under braking and on the straights. For this reason our stopping distances were not particularly impressive. Around the paddock area the racer's unassisted steering combined with all that Goodyear rubber calls for strong arm tactics, but at track speeds the steering isn't overly heavy. Although these cars can be set up to handle as desired, our test car understeered mildly until more power was applied. Then the rear end would break loose, but not uncontrollably. In the long run our Engineering Editor found the IROC racer to be a "balanced, forgiving car for the most part."

The road-going Z-28 exhibited some of the same characteristics as the IROC sedan. It understeered too, especially in low-speed turns. But a quick downshift and the application of throttle would break loose the rear wheels and slide the car around the turn, just like the racer. Perhaps the technique seems crude, but it's reasonably safe and sure a lot of fun for the accomplished driver.

The IROC Camaro's ride can be described in one word—stiff. It's a racer which is all the explanation that's required. The production Z-28's ride is firm and a bit choppy over rough surfaces, a function of the live rear axle and the optional suspension which includes stiffer than normal springs and heavy-duty shocks.

The road car's power-assisted steering helps control. It allows the driver to maneuver briskly, but it also forces him to sacrifice some road feel. Most drivers are willing to pay that price and in time the experienced driver can adapt to this light-handedness.

Unlike some cars which unfortunately have changed with the times, the Camaro still has the same good looks it was born with. True, the latest version has molded plastic front and rear ends designed to withstand the impact of a 5-mph bash. But the components are tastefully integrated into the body and in some respects are more eye-catching than their all-steel counterparts of a few years ago. The 1978 version also has special wheels, side louvers, a non-functional NACA duct in the hood and various visual appliques. It sounds right, too, which undoubtedly contributes further to its sporting image. The price also sounds right and can be kept under $6500 by the judicious buyer.

A few years ago it was rumored that the Camaro would be dropped from the Chevrolet lineup. Customer demand turned the company's head around. Watching those dozen champions battling it out in the race-prepared version leads us to believe that Roger Penske and the International Race of Champions had a lot to do with it too.

SCALE: 10" DIVISIONS

PRICE
List price ....approx $28,000

MANUFACTURER
Banjo's Performancenter
Airport Rd
Arden, N.C. 28704

GENERAL
Curb weight, lb	3280
Test weight	3315
Weight distribution (with driver), front/rear, %	55/45
Wheelbase, in.	108.0
Track, front/rear	65.0/65.0
Length	197.6
Width	80.0
Height	50.0
Ground clearance	6.0
Overhang, front/rear	43.8/45.8
Usable trunk space, cu ft	nil
Fuel capacity, U.S. gal.	33.0

ENGINE
Type	ohv V-8
Bore x stroke, mm	101.6 x 88.9
Equivalent in.	4.00 x 3.50
Displacement, cc/cu in.	5737/350
Compression ratio	12.0:1
Bhp @ rpm, net	450 @ 6500
Equivalent mph	141
Torque @ rpm, lb-ft	396 @ 5000
Equivalent mph	109
Carburetion	one Holley (4V)
Fuel requirement	premium, 102-oct

DRIVETRAIN
Transmission	4-sp manual
Gear ratios: 4th (1.00)	3.91:1
3rd (1.23)	4.81:1
2nd (1.61)	6.30:1
1st (2.64)	10.32:1
Final drive ratio	3.91:1

CHASSIS & BODY
Layout	front engine/rear drive
Body/frame	unit body with separate steel frame
Brake system	12.0-in. Hurst-Airheart vented discs front and rear
Swept area, sq in.	497
Wheels	Norris Industries steel disc, 15 x 9½
Tires	Goodyear Blue Streak Stock Car Special, 8.00/8.20-15
Steering type	recirculating ball
Overall ratio	na
Turns, lock-to-lock	2.5
Turning circle, ft.	36.0

Front suspension: unequal-length A-arms, coil springs, Monroe tube shocks, anti-roll bar
Rear suspension: live axle on long trailing arms & Panhard rod, coil springs, Monroe tube shocks

INSTRUMENTATION
Instruments: 10,000-rpm tach, oil press., oil temp, coolant temp, voltmeter
Warning lights: ignition

ACCOMMODATION
Seating capacity, persons	1
Seat width, in.	16.0
Head room	39.0
Seat back adjustment, deg	0

CALCULATED DATA
Lb/bhp (test weight)	7.4
Mph/1000 rpm (4th gear)	21.7
Engine revs/mi (60 mph)	2760
Piston travel, ft/mi	1610
R&T steering index	0.90
Brake swept area, sq in./ton	300

ROAD TEST RESULTS

ACCELERATION
Time to distance, sec:
0–100 ft	3.1
0–500 ft	7.5
0–1320 ft (¼ mi)	13.3

Speed at end of ¼ mi, mph ..110.5
Time to speed, sec:
0–30 mph	2.2
0–40 mph	3.0
0–50 mph	3.9
0–60 mph	5.2
0–70 mph	6.3
0–80 mph	7.5
0–100 mph	11.0
0–110 mph	13.2

SPEEDS IN GEARS
4th gear (7000 rpm)	152
3rd (7000)	121
2nd (7000)	92
1st (7000)	56

FUEL ECONOMY
Race driving, mpg	4.5
Cruising range, mi (1-gal. res)	144

BRAKES
Minimum stopping distances, ft:
From 60 mph	na
From 80 mph	292

Control in panic stop ....fair
Pedal effort for 0.5g stop, lb 70
Fade: percent increase in pedal effort to maintain 0.5g deceleration in 6 stops from 60 mph......nil
Parking: hold 30% grade? .... na
Overall brake rating...................fair

INTERIOR NOISE
All noise readings in dBA:
Idle in neutral	103
Maximum, 1st gear	127
Constant 30 mph	na
50 mph	104
70 mph	115
90 mph	113

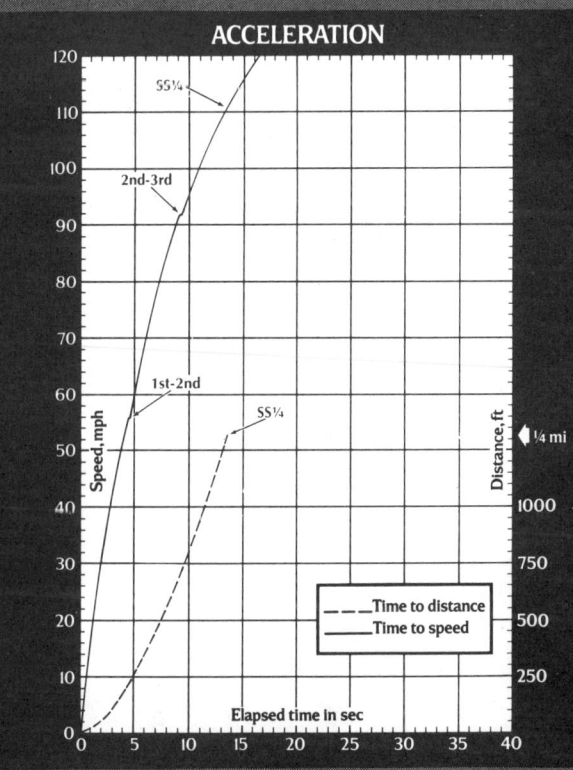

ACCELERATION

Ponycar Shootout

Once again, the Z28 Camaro takes on a performance-loaded Mustang

by Fred Stafford

Road Test

It is almost as if Detroit were caught in a time warp. Fast quarter-mile cars are supposed to be fading from the scene in light of federal mandates for fuel economy, restrictive emissions controls and the 55-mph speed limit. Yet the 1979 Camaro Z28 and Mustang Cobra (V-8) are surprisingly exciting automobiles. Dead stock from the showroom floor, these two take you back nearly 10 years in terms of performance.

Granted, they are not quite as quick as their namesakes of a decade ago, but performance is something that must be measured in relative terms, and by 1979 standards, the Z28 and Cobra are in Detroit's top-seeded ranks.

Their intent is obvious. Ford and Chevrolet have aimed them at a new generation of youthful drivers who want cars that provide more than a sporty image. They want a piece of the performance the generation before them enjoyed during the 1960s, and that is exactly what the Z28 and Cobra offer.

Ford and Chevrolet butted heads both on the track and on the street with Camaro and Mustang during the late 1960s and early '70s. Then came the oil crisis; speed was suddenly socially unacceptable, and the great dogfights between the two ponycars ended.

Chevrolet actually allowed the Z28 to die at the end of 1974, feeling the demand for high-performance specialty cars was not strong enough to continue the model. Chevrolet, however, could no longer ignore the sales trend of Pontiac's Trans Am (cast in the same mold as the Z28). Once Pontiac fought and got increased production (both cars are built on the same lines), Chevrolet began to wonder if the decision to kill the Z28 had not been premature. In February 1977, this intracorporate rivalry caused the Camaro musclecar to be reborn.

Ford was less kind to the Cobra name. It appeared sporadically on various Mustang and Torino models during the late '60s and early '70s, and faded entirely when the Mustang II was introduced in 1974. In 1977, Ford "stuck" spoilers and stripes on a Mustang II and called it a Cobra. The car wasn't even a poor imitation of what the name once stood for, and those who held a deep affection for the original Mustang Cobra were greatly offended.

So here we are in 1979 with two cars that finally do justice to their heritage.

Z28 and Cobra actually deliver what their names imply, and the stage is set for a return to the stoplight skirmishes that once were recognized as the ultimate test of a car's worth. Ford has its billion-dollar baby and Chevrolet its old yet refined workhorse that hasn't undergone a major physical change in nine years.

Physically, the cars are drastically different. And well you might expect them to be, with nearly a decade separating their design concepts. The Z28 is very sleek and low-slung in the style of a European GT, while the Mustang is tall and very angular. The detail work of the two cars reveals a great deal about their general character. For some misguided reason, Ford can't seem to market a sporty car without overdressing it. The clean basic lines of the car are distorted by add-ons that look like they came from an

automotive bargain basement. The bulbous non-functioning hood scoop is one such item that every Cobra owner will have to put up with, but fortunately, Ford had the presence of mind to make the horrendous Cobra hood decal optional. At $78, it is a worthwhile deletion from anyone's order form.

The dual rectangular headlights and sloping eggcrate grille give the Mustang a crisp, sporting appearance. Black accenting around all of the windows and black trim along the baseline of the car are included with the Cobra package. The effect is nothing new but nonetheless very effective.

The Z28 gets its point across in a much more mature manner. Its very clean, subtle accenting makes the Mustang look cluttered by comparison. The soft nose section eliminates the need for

BOB D'OLIVO

a separate bumper, thus creating a fresh image from the start.

Large front and rear spoilers blend nicely into the weathered lines of the Camaro, enhancing its overall design. In a way, they give it the bold appearance of an IROC racer without making it look like a home-built hot rod. Again, the hood scoop is strictly for show, but it does complement the car's basic image.

A sign of the Camaro's age is the use of round headlamps. At a time when rectangular lights are the rage, this retention of circular beams sets it apart in an odd yet familair fashion.

On the inside, the story line doesn't change very much. The Mustang underwhelms you with flimsy plastic appointments. The overall appearance leaves you with the impression that saving money was of greater concern than saving weight. The Z28 interior has a richer, well-made air about it.

The similarities in the basic layouts of both interiors are uncanny. This allows for an item-by-item comparison of this most critical area. There are certain things a serious driver may be willing to put up with, but lack of functionality is not one of them. Both Ford and Chevrolet have the bases covered on this point. Well-instrumented dashes provide the vital information.

Speedometer and tachometer are the dominant facets of each instrument panel. They are located side-by-side, directly over the steering column of each car, with the only major difference being that the tach is on the left in the Mustang and on the right in the Camaro. An interesting and annoying feature of the Mustang tach is its lack of redline indicator. Flanking the main dials on each side are two smaller gauges. They are alternator, engine temperature, fuel and oil pressure on the Mustang; fuel, engine temperature, oil pressure and a clock on the Z28. Mustang relies more heavily on European-style steering column controls than the Camaro, but all vital controls are well placed in both vehicles. The instrumentation of each is easy to read, when you can see it. The small-diameter wheel in the Z28 obstructs some of the outer gauges, a problem that does not exist on the Mustang.

Well, enough about the physical attri-

butes. Let us not forget that performance is the main commodity in the offing here, and the real purpose of this test is to determine exactly which is the superior machine.

For general hustling about, be it in city traffic, on the highway or a twisting country lane, the Z28 is the more desirable

vehicle. It has a surefooted feel to it and tracks confidently wherever you point it. The torquey Chevrolet 350 V-8 is much more manageable throughout its rpm range. The Cobra's 302 V-8 bucks and coughs when the revs get low, but the Camaro could be dropped all the way down to idle speed (about 900 rpm) in

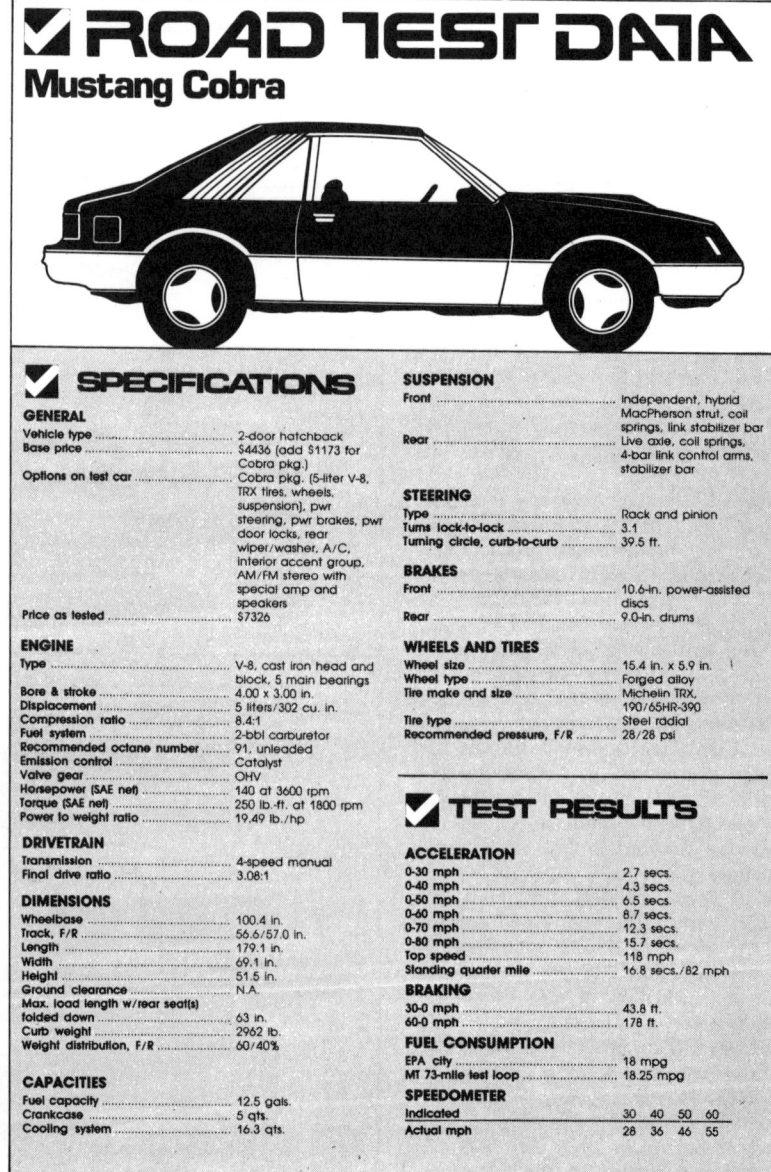

ROAD TEST DATA
Mustang Cobra

SPECIFICATIONS

GENERAL
Vehicle type	2-door hatchback
Base price	$4436 (add $1173 for Cobra pkg.)
Options on test car	Cobra pkg. (5-liter V-8, TRX tires, wheels, suspension), pwr steering, pwr brakes, pwr door locks, rear wiper/washer, A/C, interior accent group, AM/FM stereo with special amp and speakers
Price as tested	$7326

ENGINE
Type	V-8, cast iron head and block, 5 main bearings
Bore & stroke	4.00 x 3.00 in.
Displacement	5 liters/302 cu. in.
Compression ratio	8.4:1
Fuel system	2-bbl carburetor
Recommended octane number	91, unleaded
Emission control	Catalyst
Valve gear	OHV
Horsepower (SAE net)	140 at 3600 rpm
Torque (SAE net)	250 lb.-ft. at 1800 rpm
Power to weight ratio	19.49 lb./hp

DRIVETRAIN
Transmission	4-speed manual
Final drive ratio	3.08:1

DIMENSIONS
Wheelbase	100.4 in.
Track, F/R	56.6/57.0 in.
Length	179.1 in.
Width	69.1 in.
Height	51.5 in.
Ground clearance	N.A.
Max. load length w/rear seat(s) folded down	63 in.
Curb weight	2962 lb.
Weight distribution, F/R	60/40%

CAPACITIES
Fuel capacity	12.5 gals.
Crankcase	5 qts.
Cooling system	16.3 qts.

SUSPENSION
Front	Independent, hybrid MacPherson strut, coil springs, link stabilizer bar
Rear	Live axle, coil springs, 4-bar link control arms, stabilizer bar

STEERING
Type	Rack and pinion
Turns lock-to-lock	3.1
Turning circle, curb-to-curb	39.5 ft.

BRAKES
Front	10.6-in. power-assisted discs
Rear	9.0-in. drums

WHEELS AND TIRES
Wheel size	15.4 in. x 5.9 in.
Wheel type	Forged alloy
Tire make and size	Michelin TRX, 190/65HR-390
Tire type	Steel radial
Recommended pressure, F/R	28/28 psi

TEST RESULTS

ACCELERATION
0-30 mph	2.7 secs.
0-40 mph	4.3 secs.
0-50 mph	6.5 secs.
0-60 mph	8.7 secs.
0-70 mph	12.3 secs.
0-80 mph	15.7 secs.
Top speed	118 mph
Standing quarter mile	16.8 secs./82 mph

BRAKING
30-0 mph	43.8 ft.
60-0 mph	178 ft.

FUEL CONSUMPTION
EPA city	18 mpg
MT 73-mile test loop	18.25 mpg

SPEEDOMETER
Indicated	30	40	50	60
Actual mph	28	36	46	55

4th and still be placed under full throttle without the slightest complaint.

The Mustang has a much lighter feel about it, and well it should, weighing nearly 600 pounds less (2962 vs. 3560) than the Camaro. The Cobra reacts like a small sedan that has been overstuffed with horsepower. It can be twitchy when making abrupt changes in direction and has a very light feel in the rear end. The latter is a result of the heavy V-8 up front and is very noticeable during braking and high-speed cornering. The Z28 comes off as more of a true GT, while the Cobra is more of a hybrid.

In tight, level situations, the Mustang is the more maneuverable of the two. This was demonstrated clearly when we subjected both vehicles to a timed lane-change exercise. The smaller, more agile Mustang slipped through the 712-foot pylon course in only 10.3 seconds. The longer, heavier Camaro proved less willing to make pinpoint direction changes and could do no better than 10.8 seconds.

As heavy as it is, the Z28 was the faster car through the quarter mile. It knocked off the 1320 feet in 16.4 seconds at 84.8 mph. The Cobra's best was 16.8 seconds at 82.2 mph.

Offsetting the weight disadvantage for the Camaro was its larger (350cid vs. 302cid), more powerful (175 vs. 140 horsepower) engine and lower rearend ratio (3.73 vs. 3.08). The taller gearing of the Mustang was very apparent during the quarter mile runs. The shift to 3rd gear couldn't be made until the very last moment.

A combination of discs in the front and drums in the rear is used on both cars. Pedal response was excellent on both, and positioning of the pedals was good. From 30 mph, the braking distances were almost identical at an even 43 foot for the Z28 and 43.8 feet for the Cobra. As the speeds went up, however, the Cobra's brakes lost their effectiveness. Lots of nose dive tended to cause the rear wheels to float and lose traction. The best distance achieved from 60 mph to a full stop was 178 feet. By comparison, the Z28 stopped very well from high speeds. It was stable and consistent. Sixty to a full stop required only 157 feet.

For all the time and money Ford spent developing the new Cobra, it is quite apparent that it still doesn't match the older Z28 in many respects. But there is a considerable difference in cost, with the Mustang going for $7326 and the Z28 selling for $8814. The extra bucks for the Camaro, however, are well spent if comfortable, fast cruising is what you are after.

With some more fine tuning and some general cleaning up of detail, the Mustang could eventually change this situation. At any rate, performance once again has become available, and that's the most important story of all—only this time it's total performance.

✓ ROAD TEST DATA
Camaro Z28

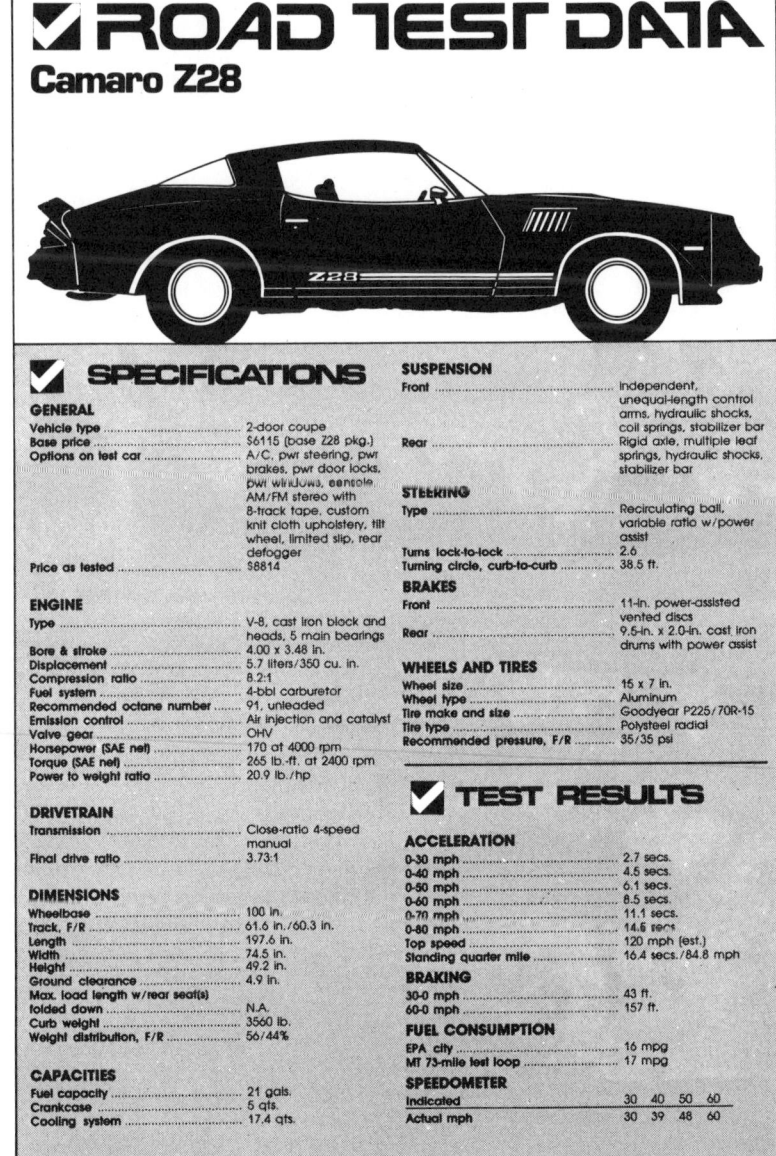

✓ SPECIFICATIONS

GENERAL

Vehicle type	2-door coupe
Base price	$6115 (base Z28 pkg.)
Options on test car	A/C, pwr steering, pwr brakes, pwr door locks, pwr windows, console AM/FM stereo with 8-track tape, custom knit cloth upholstery, tilt wheel, limited slip, rear defogger
Price as tested	$8814

ENGINE

Type	V-8, cast iron block and heads, 5 main bearings
Bore & stroke	4.00 x 3.48 in.
Displacement	5.7 liters/350 cu. in.
Compression ratio	8.2:1
Fuel system	4-bbl carburetor
Recommended octane number	91, unleaded
Emission control	Air injection and catalyst
Valve gear	OHV
Horsepower (SAE net)	170 at 4000 rpm
Torque (SAE net)	265 lb.-ft. at 2400 rpm
Power to weight ratio	20.9 lb./hp

DRIVETRAIN

Transmission	Close-ratio 4-speed manual
Final drive ratio	3.73:1

DIMENSIONS

Wheelbase	100 in.
Track, F/R	61.6 in./60.3 in.
Length	197.6 in.
Width	74.5 in.
Height	49.2 in.
Ground clearance	4.9 in.
Max. load length w/rear seat(s) folded down	N.A.
Curb weight	3560 lb.
Weight distribution, F/R	56/44%

CAPACITIES

Fuel capacity	21 gals.
Crankcase	5 qts.
Cooling system	17.4 qts.

SUSPENSION

Front	Independent, unequal-length control arms, hydraulic shocks, coil springs, stabilizer bar
Rear	Rigid axle, multiple leaf springs, hydraulic shocks, stabilizer bar

STEERING

Type	Recirculating ball, variable ratio w/power assist
Turns lock-to-lock	2.6
Turning circle, curb-to-curb	38.5 ft.

BRAKES

Front	11-in. power-assisted vented discs
Rear	9.5-in. x 2.0-in. cast iron drums with power assist

WHEELS AND TIRES

Wheel size	15 x 7 in.
Wheel type	Aluminum
Tire make and size	Goodyear P225/70R-15
Tire type	Polysteel radial
Recommended pressure, F/R	35/35 psi

✓ TEST RESULTS

ACCELERATION

0-30 mph	2.7 secs.
0-40 mph	4.5 secs.
0-50 mph	6.1 secs.
0-60 mph	8.5 secs.
0-70 mph	11.1 secs.
0-80 mph	14.6 secs.
Top speed	120 mph (est.)
Standing quarter mile	16.4 secs./84.8 mph

BRAKING

30-0 mph	43 ft.
60-0 mph	157 ft.

FUEL CONSUMPTION

EPA city	16 mpg
MT 73-mile test loop	17 mpg

SPEEDOMETER

Indicated	30	40	50	60
Actual mph	30	39	48	60

CLONING CAMAROS

Z28 VS. FACTORY IMPOSTER: GUESS WHICH CAR HAS
THE ALUMINUM ENGINE?

By Dave Wallace

By a stroke of sheer, happy coincidence, two brand-new Z28 Camaros, both black, have fallen into our hot little hands at once. We've come to think of them as sisters, as fraternal twins: born of the same mother in the same year and virtually identical in most ways, but vastly dissimilar in others. And both desirable.

One sister got the manners, is friendly and fashionable and predictable; no surprises here. She's a solid, accepted member of the community, if a bit shy and unsure of herself in certain situations. The quiet one.

Her sister is noisy and impulsive, a little rough around the edges for some tastes. She's stronger and louder and sexier. The wild one. The one with the aluminum motor and cylinder heads, tube headers, free-flowing exhaust, Holley double-pump carburetor, forged pistons, solid-lifter camshaft and cowl induction, among other things. Unfortunately, this lady is not a real

lady at all, and she's definitely not for sale.

In truth the wild child is a test-tube Camaro, a supernatural clone of the Z28 they're actually selling in the Chevy stores this year. Like a couple of mad movie scientists, Camaro engineers Bill Howell and Fred Scaafsman, among others, whipped this baby up in a back room somewhere as a rolling engineering exercise. We first made the lady's acquaintance last summer in Detroit, where the wild one stole the new-car preview show from the '79 Camaro and Corvette. Fitted with BBS wheels and sticky tires for the occasion, she upstaged even the graceful L82 Vette in acceleration and handling drills, winning the heart of every participating journalist. And the writers' enthusiasm was not lost on Chevy's L.A. press rep, Wayne Thoms, who subsequently arranged to have the mystery car trucked west for a few exclusive weeks with Petersen Publishing Company personnel. We fought bitterly and openly, brother against brother, for the opportunity to court this lady. Said HOT ROD Associate Editor

Marlan Davis, whose 16th birthday occurred too late for the Supercar Sixties: "If it wasn't for the government, they'd be selling cars like this by now." We'll never know for sure.

Instead, they're building and selling cars more like the production Z-car, the quiet one: a real-world, government-approved version that comes with a comparatively sluggish, conventional iron small-block. Ours came as well within a $400 optional accessory of a (gulp!) five-digit suggested retail price tag, but the fact that Chevy sells out its Z-cars every season says that lots of folks are still set on owning a genuine Z28 Camaro, window stickers be damned. Then again this contemporary version, heir to a marque carved into country roads and drag strips by solid-lifter 302 small-blocks a decade ago, is not everyone's idea of a $10,000 Z-car.

For one thing, the '79 model is relatively slow. Even by today's embarrassing standards, a 16.12-second quarter-mile is nothing to write home about. (The wild child's 14.0s at 103 mph, with street tires yet, is more like it.)

The bark is still there, thanks to a two-into-one-into-two "dual" exhaust route interrupted only by resonators, not mufflers, but not enough bite to run alongside new L82 Corvettes or WS6 Trans Am Firebirds. And that goes double for the corners, where the 4-barrel iron 350 just can't muster enough power quickly enough to keep things interesting. Too bad; the Z28 suspension treatment (stiffer shocks and springs, front and rear sway bars, front subframe braces) and disc/drum brakes seemed ready and willing and hungry for more horsepower; and our tour with the quicker, lighter experimental Camaro, which was essentially stock beyond its exotic alloy powerplant, proved it: The power never did run away from the handling or the stopping.

We stress these facts up front because the prospective Z28 buyer deserves to be warned: This car has "race me" written all over itself, from the reflective trim tape to the plastic air dam, wheel flares, fender louvers, deck-lid spoiler and dummy hood duct. And as any Z-car driver can attest, the car is frequently invited to back up the splashy graphics. It goes with the territory. *(continued overleaf)*

Cockpit is solid, spacious and comfortable (for front-seat passengers). Z28 instrument package brings nifty 130-mph speedo and 7000-rpm tach, only lacks oil pressure gauge.

Chevrolet's ninth annual update of the F-body Camaro is another visual winner. Top-of-the-line Z28 option further includes two-tone stripe job, new front wheel flares and air dam, blacked-out body moldings. Z-car identification graces the nose, tail, doors and (optional) aluminum wheel centers. Red circular Z28 emblems also appear on inside door panels and steering wheel.

CLONING CAMAROS

Experimental aluminum-motored Z-car came equipped with a functional, one-off, rear-opening hood scoop and compatible air cleaner in place of the sealed NACA duct found on production hoods. Electrically operated plastic "doors" open under wide-open throttle situations. Sealed air cleaner serves a spread-bore, 650-cfm Holley double-pumper, one of the few non-factory items selected by the Chevy engineers. (Another is the set of small-tube Blackjack exhaust headers.) Electric choke was

added to No. 4165 carb to assist with cold-starting. Alloy engine block was stuffed with L82 bottom-end components, comes up with a final compression ratio of 9.9:1. Solid-lifter camshaft was last seen on early Z-cars, features 307º/319º duration and .432-/.452-inch valve lift. L82 distributor retained stock '78 Corvette advance curve, sees full advance at 2500 rpm. Intake manifold is late-model GM aluminum model for Q-jet carb.

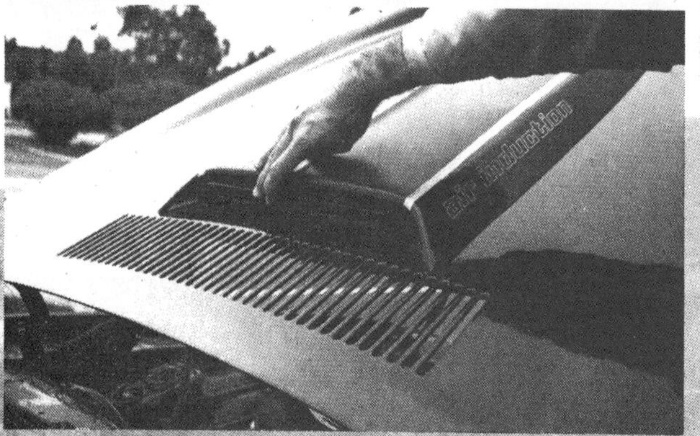

Inside his new Camaro, the Z28 owner won't have to make excuses for much of anything. Between the exterior graphics and the well-appointed interior, it would seem that somebody at Chevrolet has a direct pipeline into the heart of every high-school cheerleader in America. Heck, even their mothers would approve of the smoked T-top, automatic transmission, air conditioning, tilt steering wheel, rear-window defogger, shifter console, FM-stereo radio and power everything. Plush but bulky, and slow to respond. For a better idea of what the Z28 is really designed to do, we highly recommend a test ride with a 4-speed version (not available in California) without the hatch roof.

Besides robbing the operator of a couple of miles per gallon of unleaded fuel, and up to .4-second and 5 mph in the quarter-mile, the Hydramatic gearbox brings an idiotproof selector that makes downshifting difficult; we'd go with the 4-speed. And some engineers insist that cutting away half of a unibody's roof negatively affects a car's structural integrity, and therefore its handling characteristics. Having both a hatched and a nonhatched model in our possession simultaneously, we reached a similar conclusion. The glass panels also rattle like crazy on broken pavement, but your lady friends and their mothers won't likely care about stuff like that; for viewing cloud formations, rainbows and the underbellies of jet aircraft, a T-top is still pretty hard to beat.

For these reasons and others, how well any new Z28 actually performs has an awful lot to do with what the original owner adds and subtracts in the first place. In the second place, the automotive aftermarket and Chevrolet itself can help you duplicate the performance characteristics of the aluminum-block experimental Z28 assembled last year by the factory engineers.

For instance, the wild child's 130-pound frontal weight advantage results, in this case, from Chevy's production alloy engine block and a priceless set of Jim Hall's old Chaparral cylinder heads, also aluminum. But any Camaro owner can redistribute a similar percentage of his car's bulk by sending his battery to the trunk and his hood right out the door, replacing same in fiberglass. As for the difference in power output, we don't have to tell you that coming up with another 100 ponies or so is no big deal with any small-block Chevy motor. The handling and brakes come free with every new Z28, not to mention some of the snappiest paint and bodywork ever to spring from an American auto factory. Get it all together in a tire-spinning, corner-burning, head-turning, no-hassle street package and you'd have some late-model Camaro, all right. Maybe even the next-best thing to an aluminum-block Z-car!

HR

CONTINUED FROM PAGE 45

three drivers, idling off the line and punching it from there, shifting right at 5000 rpm. We netted a best run of 15.35 seconds at exactly 91 miles per hour flat. The automatic car, idled out of the gate and shifted automatically, scored a best performance after seven runs of 16.17 at 84.19 mph and suffering fuel starvation and/or vapor pressure problems during the course of the running. The total combined aggregate average mileage for the two cars for the entire testing period worked out to 13.95 miles per gallon, and that particular figure is a lot lower than it could be were the car placed in the hands of saner folk who possibly didn't appreciate it as much as we did and who could light-foot it occasionally.

We hasten to add that absolutely nothing was done to the cars during the drag strip session, and we point out that, with a super 4-speed handler and a handful of ordinary tricks for better bite and free horsepower, we could have worried the car down into the high-14-second bracket in a couple of hours or less. The 15.35/91-mph clocking was merely indicative of showroom-stock performance levels from one particular car that had been whipped unmercifully before it ever saw the drag strip, by us and by Chevrolet engineers at the GM Desert Proving Grounds in Mesa, Arizona, where we picked up the cars.

The group of engineers and designers that brought the Z/28 out of the ashes stronger than it has been in years is to be congratulated. They have done a terrific job with the Z/28 package, to build a car that is neutral and linear, eminently predictable, and one hell of a lot of fun to drive, fast or slow, in traffic or all alone. Perhaps the best part is that, unlike some special models, the Z/28 package can be added to the absolute bottom-of-the-line Camaro, putting the car within reach of anyone who has about $5000 to spend. Now it is up to the Camaro engineers and designers to bring the rest of the car up to the level of the Z/28 package, by offering driver-appeal items like readable instrumentation, infinitely adjustable seatbacks for the bucket seats, adjustable floor pedals, and a telescoping steering column to add to the tilt feature. The new Z is so neat that it seems a shame to deny complete driving comfort to as many different-sized drivers as possible. With additional features such as these, a little higher level of overall finish, and the availability of a "delete option" for the Z/28 cosmetics, the car would be nearly perfect as a Q-ship or a Cannonball Baker coast-to-coast racer for the masses. The Z is dead. Long live the Z. **HR**

HOT ROD MAGAZINE'S ROAD TEST SPECIFICATIONS
1979 Chevrolet Camaro Z28

Engine Type	V8
Cubic Inches/Liters	350/5.7
Bore & Stroke	4.00x3.48 inches
Carburetion/Injection	Single 4-barrel
Compression Ratio	8.2:1
Net Horsepower/RPM	175/4000
Net Torque/RPM	270/2400
Fuel Type	Unleaded gas
Wheelbase	108.0 inches
Weight	3752 pounds
Transmission	3-speed automatic
Final-Drive Ratio	3.42:1
Brakes, Front/Rear	Disc/Drum
Wheel Size	15x7 inches
Tires, Make & Size	Goodyear P225/70R
Performance, ¼-mile	16.12 seconds, 85.95 mph
Fuel Economy (average)	12.2 mpg
Base Price	$6115
Optional Equipment	Air conditioning (includes heavy duty radiator), power steering, power brakes, limited-slip differential, console, electric rear-window defogger, power door locks, color-keyed floor mats, tinted glass, lighting group, AM/FM stereo radio w/8-track cassette, rear speaker, power antenna, removable glass roof panels, speed control, Comfortilt steering wheel, automatic transmission, sport cloth interior, aluminum wheels, power windows, intermittent windshield wipers
Price As Tested	$9600

80 Vette

by Peter Frey

Of the massive arsenal that Chevrolet has assembled to do battle in the new-car wars, there are two remaining survivors of a less inhibited age. The "F" car, otherwise known at the Camaro, was first introduced in 1966, with the single major body change taking place in 1970. The top of the Camaro line is the justly famous Z28, which has established a tradition of performance not confined just to the drivetrain, but also extended to the brakes and suspension. It shares basic mechanical and chassis components with its fraternal twin, Pontiac's Trans Am Firebird, but is markedly different in appearance. The second survivor is the "Y" car, the legendary Corvette, which for 22 years has been America's only 2-seat sports car, since the demise of the 2-seat Thunderbirds. It has undergone three major body changes since its introduction in 1953, with its present basic shape making its maiden appearance in 1971.

In recent years both cars have, like all the rest, fallen prey to the degenerative effects of federal meddling. Chevrolet has expended much money and effort, in engineering and advertising, to insure that the performance image of the cars remains intact, a task at which they have been relatively successful. The side effect of this program of "image maintenance" has been that the

evolution of the cars has slowed to a crawl. Federal emissions and fuel economy regulations effectively dictate what combinations of engines, transmissions, and rear axle ratios can be offered. Chevrolet has been forced to keep both the Corvette and Z28 in a holding pattern, confining the yearly changes to aesthetic fiddling and engineering refinements of hardware that are getting decidedly long in the tooth.

The key descriptive word about the 1980 versions of the cars appears at the beginning of a company press release. "The 1980 Chevrolet... no magic, no miracles, just solid engineering... provides fuel economy the times demand... *preserves* appearance, comfort, performance...." The entire statement is a blueprint of the philosophy behind the cars, but the key word is "preserves." It is a word that implies maintenance of the status quo rather than progress, and that is essentially how it is for 1980. To be fair, they have made a couple of changes which, though scarcely dramatic, will serve to distinguish these cars from last year's.

Z28 Camaro

The changes they have made to the Z28 include a new grille, which is now exclusive to the Z28; different striping graphics and interior trim; an optional

set of aluminum alloy wheels rather like those of the Datsun 280ZX; and the leading edge of the rear wheelwells has sprouted a set of Trans Am-like air deflectors that nicely complete the muscular look of the car.

They have also equipped the car with a pair of doors in the trailing edge of the hood scoop that was previously strictly decorative. They flip open, sucking cooler outside air into the carburetor and producing, we were told, an additional 5 horsepower. The doors are solenoid operated and controlled by a switch on the accelerator pedal. They open only during brisk acceleration, remaining closed when the car is cruising. A further functional change is that the fender vents now serve to exhaust hot engine compartment air, helping to keep underhood temperatures down. One of the engineers we spoke to said he was surprised that the fresh-air package had made it into production. Not only did they have to do battle with the accountants over the cost of the program, but the moan of inrushing air had to be sound-engineered down to acceptable levels, and there was some effect on the emissions figures—all of which had to be coped with before they could put the program into production. It was an interesting lesson in how complicated a process it is these days to make what seems a minor change in a car.

& Z28

Sampling the fruits of survival

In 49 states, the standard engine will be the 350cid LM-1 V-8, with either a 4-speed manual transmission and a 3.08 axle, or a 3-speed automatic with an axle ratio of 3.42.

Transmission Ratios (Z28)

4-speed manual

1st	3.42
2nd	2.28
3rd	1.45
4th	1.0

3-speed automatic

1st	2.52
2nd	1.52
3rd	1.0

California will have to struggle along with a single available drivetrain, consisting of the less potent 305cid V-8, called the LG4, an automatic trans, and a 3.42 axle. Emission control is air injection, with California cars also equipped with the C-4 (Computer Controlled Catalytic Converter) system.

Suspension changes that differentiate the Z28 from other Camaros includes larger diameter front and rear anti-roll bars, stiffer front springs, special valving for the double-acting shock absorbers, and different rear spring shackles and bushings.

Stabilizer Bar Diameters/ Spring Rates (Z28)

Stabilizer Bar	Camaro	Z28
Front	0.9375 in.	1.125 in.
Rear	0.5625 in.	0.625 in.

Spring Rates

Front Coil	300 lb.	365 lb.
Rear Leaf	98 lb.	130 lb.

A special low-back-pressure, dual-outlet exhaust system is standard equipment, with California engines getting special laminated stainless steel tubing exhaust manifolds. The tires are P225/70R-15 steel-belted radials on 15x7-inch rims. All other Camaros have 14-inch wheels, and even the Z28's spare tire is on a 14x6-inch rim. The brakes are self-adjusting 11.0-inch ventilated discs in front and 9.5-inch finned rear drums, with power assist optional on Camaros with the base V-6 engine but mandatory at extra cost on V-8-engined cars such as the Z28. The Saginaw power steering is of the recirculating ball type, with 2.61 turns lock-to-lock as opposed to 2.41 turns for other Camaros.

Some of the service-oriented technical features include audible wear sensors in the front disc brake pads, visible wear indicators on the front suspension ball joints, a sealed battery, generator with built-in voltage regulator, high-energy electronic ignition, and a coolant recovery system for the radiator. Extensive anti-corrosion measures include drain holes located in the doors and trunk lid to allow trapped water to escape, electronically deposited dip primer for the entire body structure, zinc-plated metals used to form critical structural panels, and special wax coatings sprayed in every crevice and seam. Interior noise control measures are extensive and include an asphalt-saturated felt roof pad.

For the interior, standard equipment includes front bucket seats, a full set of gauges, and remote-control rearview mirrors. The options list goes on with such things as air conditioning, power door locks, rear window defogger, a variety of stereo radios combined with tape players and CBs, and glass T-tops. The list of minor items, from convenience groups to color-coordinated seat belts, is endless.

Our test vehicle was a particularly mean-looking orange color and managed to turn in better performance figures with an automatic trans than a 4-speed 1979 model we tested earlier in the year. Though there was a perceptible hesitation, both off the line and in the 1-2 upshift, the Z28 managed a quarter mile time of 16.09 seconds at 84.6 mph. This compares to a run of 17.37 seconds at 78.6 mph for the 1979 car. Apparently, the fresh-air package makes a distinct difference, especially considering the test conditions, which were exceptionally hot and humid, a combination that usually hinders performance. Apart from the stumble, which we were assured is an adjustment problem rather than something inherent in the system, the engine pulls strongly to its 5500-rpm redline, and the transmission shifts are very positive but smooth.

Braking performance was not quite as good as the 1979 car, taking 50 feet to stop from 30 mph, and 190 feet from 60 mph, as opposed to 42 feet and 173 feet, respectively. Since the brakes are unchanged from last year, we assume this poorer performance is due to some differences in the track surfaces and test conditions. All the stops were straight, and there was no apparent fade.

The ride and handling characteristics of the Z28 have become two of its strongest points, ever since Detroit engineers discovered that a streetable ride and good handling were not mutually exclusive. With suspension unchanged from last year, the Z28 continues to be a muscular and competent car that assures the driver it will follow his lead in any sort of high-velocity maneuver he initiates. The ride is an excellent blend of comfort and road feel, with just a bit of rear axle jounce on particularly rough surfaces. High-speed cornering produces an easily controllable understeer that can be corrected by slightly backing off the throttle, or magnified into an exceptional bit of driving by aiming for an early apex and staying on the throttle. The car responds smartly to steering and throttle inputs but much prefers smoothness to being pitched around.

With yet another year of refinement under its belt, the Z28 can be judged a worthy successor to its own tradition. Performance is better, fuel economy (though not yet officially announced) will be better, and it looks downright mean. It is a decidedly masculine car, though with its lengthy list of options, it can be luxurious too. Checking a lot of those little boxes on the order form could turn the Z28 into a very expensive piece of machinery indeed, but it would still be the best performance bargain in the world.

Corvette

The evolutionary progress of the Corvette has been so slow in recent years that Chevrolet's press releases are describing the 1980 changes as "major surgery." The most apparent changes are to the nose and tail, which now have molded-in spoilers, the front one serving to improve the aerodynamics and scoop up air to cool the engine.

The hood has a lower, more aerodynamic profile, and the front fender vents are functional. The turn-signal-activated cornering lamps, parking lamps integrated into the grille, and new flag and L82 emblems are the only other visual changes.

Under the bodywork, the bumper systems have been redesigned with the front incorporating a honeycomb and fiberglass bumper bar "energy management system." The bumper covers themselves are molded of a higher-modulus RIM material which has more "spring-back."

They still haven't bowed to the logic of making the rear window into an opening cargo hatch, but they have come up with a device that will allow you to remove and store the T-tops without compromising the limited luggage space behind the seats. Set into the fiberglass of the rear deck area are four black plastic grommets into which plugs a folding, molded plastic rack equipped with tie-down straps. This allows the driver to stow the panels externally. Practical, but a bit primitive.

The other change, the one to which the term "surgery" might apply, is the shedding of approximately 250 pounds. This was certainly a more expensive program than the visual changes and reaches into every area of the car. Engine-related weight reductions include an aluminum intake manifold and stainless steel tubing instead of cast iron for the exhaust headers. The chassis was lightened by fabricating the differential housing and support brackets from aluminum, and lightening selected chassis members and the transmission crossmember. Body weight was trimmed by using thinner windshield and door glass, lighter hood and door panels, and by making the T-top panels from a special lightweight low-density fiberglass that reduced weight by 20%. The front bumper structure was lightened by using a fiberglass face bar and corner braces. These changes dropped the Corvette's curb weight to 3519 pounds, thereby lowering it two notches in the EPA's inertia weight classification scale, to the 3625-pound category.

As the weight reduction and aerodynamic changes Chevrolet has made to the car will help toward meeting the CAFE standard, so will the alterations made to the transmissions. The manual 4-speed has higher 1st and 2nd gear ratios, which allowed installation of an economy-minded 3.07:1 rear axle, the only one available. The end result is that, at the same speed, the engine is turning fewer rpm, thereby improving fuel economy.

The 3-speed automatic now has a torque converter clutch that automatically engages above 30 mph in high gear and transfers power directly to the clutch disc and output shaft. This effectively bypasses the torque converter and its power-consumptive tendencies and helps improve mileage. When the speed drops below 30 mph, or the brakes are

ROAD TEST DATA

Camaro Z28

GENERAL	
Vehicle type	2-door coupe
Base price	N.A.
Options on test car	AM/FM stereo radio, alloy wheels, cloth interior trim
Price as tested	N.A.

ENGINE	
Type	V-8, cast iron block and heads, 5 main bearings
Bore & stroke	4.00 x 3.48 in.
Displacement	5.7 liters/350 cu. in.
Compression ratio	8.2:1
Fuel system	4-bbl carburetor
Recommended octane number	91, unleaded
Emission control	Air injection, catalytic converter
Valve gear	OHV
Horsepower (SAE net)	N.A.
Torque (SAE net)	N.A.
Power to weight ratio	N.A.

DRIVETRAIN	
Transmission	3-speed automatic
Final drive ratio	3.42:1

DIMENSIONS	
Wheelbase	108.0 in.
Track, F/R	61.3/60.0 in.
Length	197.6 in.
Width	74.5 in.
Height	49.2 in.
Ground clearance	4.9 in.
Curb weight	3636 lb.
Weight distribution, F/R	56/44%

CAPACITIES	
Fuel capacity	21 gals.
Crankcase	5 qts.
Cooling system	17.4 qts.
Trunk capacity	7.1 cu. ft.

SUSPENSION	
Front	Independent, unequal length A-arms, telescopic shocks, coil springs, stabilizer bar
Rear	Rigid axle, multiple leaf springs, telescopic shocks, stabilizer bar

STEERING	
Type	Recirculating ball, variable ratio w/power assist
Turns lock-to-lock	2.6
Turning circle, curb-to-curb	38.5 ft.

BRAKES	
Front	11-in. power-assisted vented discs
Rear	9.5-in. x 2.0-in. drums w/power assist

WHEELS AND TIRES	
Wheel size	15 x 7 in.
Wheel type	Forged aluminum
Tire make and size	Goodyear P225/70R-15
Tire type	Steel radial
Recommended pressure, F/R	26/26 psi

ACCELERATION	
0-30 mph	2.7 secs.
0-40 mph	4.0 secs.
0-50 mph	5.7 secs.
0-60 mph	8.1 secs.
0-70 mph	10.4 secs.
0-80 mph	13.8 secs.
Top speed	N.A.
Standing quarter mile	16.09 secs./84.6 mph

BRAKING	
30-0 mph	50 ft.
60-0 mph	190 ft.

FUEL CONSUMPTION	
EPA city	N.A.
SCG 73-mile test loop	N.A.

SPEEDOMETER				
Indicated	30	40	50	60
Actual mph	32	42	53	64

applied, the clutch automatically disengages. This particular feature will not be available in California.

Transmission Ratios (Corvette)

4-speed Manual

	1980	1979
1st	2.88	2.64
2nd	1.91	1.75
3rd	1.33	1.34
4th	1.0	1.0

3-speed Automatic

1st	2.52	2.52
2nd	1.52	1.52
3rd	1.0	1.0

Three separate engines are available, with 49 states being offered the choice of two Chevrolet-built 4-bbl 350cid V-8s, the L48 and the higher-performance L82. The California engine is a 305cid V-8 designated the LG4. All engines are fitted with air injection emissions controls, and California cars additionally get the Computer Controlled Catalytic Converter (C-4) system. The exhaust system has been changed by making some of the heat shields from aluminum instead of steel, and the pipes now join at the rear of the engine instead of the cross-under design.

In the interior, changes have been minor. An electric choke warning light has been added to the face of the tach, and a "check engine" warning light is added to California cars. Seven trim colors are now available, with the addition of Claret, and there is a new ribbed-pattern cloth upholstery. Leather is available for the bucket seats, and the aluminum alloy wheels can be had with polished faces. The rather short list of options includes four sound systems, glass T-top panels, and a special gymkhana suspension consisting of a .440-inch-diameter rear stabilizer bar with special bushings, stiffer springs, and special shock absorbers. The tires are P225/70R-15 steel radials, with lower-profile P225/60R-15s optional.

We actually tested two 1980 Corvettes, one an L82-engined 4-speed, the other with the L48 engine and a 3-speed automatic. We managed two acceleration runs in the 4-speed car, which produced a quarter mile time of 16.52 seconds at 84.6 mph. This is markedly poorer performance than the 1979 version generated, 15.74 seconds at 89.4 mph. The conditions of the test were very hot and humid, and we ran the 1979 car on a cooler, drier day, so the difference in performance may have been due to that. We only got in two runs because, at the start of the third, the right-side halfshaft snapped a U-joint, which produced a tremendous banging noise, demolished the shock absorber, and damaged the suspension. We were later told that a set of lighter-duty U-joints intended for an automatic-transmission car had mistak-

enly been installed in our 4-speed test vehicle.

Chevrolet showed considerable courage by giving us the sole remaining car they had available, the L48 automatic, to complete our testing. It turned a quarter mile time just fractionally slower than the L82 at 16.77 seconds and 83.9 mph. Both engines showed a dislike for higher rpm. Though they will wind to their 5500-rpm redline, they make the noises of mechanical torture in the process, and much of it is transmitted to the cockpit.

The braking performance was both better and worse than the figures for the 1979 car, taking 44 feet to stop from 30 mph, as opposed to 39 feet, and 157 feet against 176 feet from 60 mph. The brakes are unchanged, so we must assume some variance in the test conditions.

For a car with such a high-performance image, the handling has always been, and continues to be, a bit of a handful. The rear end seems to squat suddenly to the outside as the car enters a turn and the transverse leaf spring compresses, causing the weight to transfer rather suddenly. This is unsettling, both to the driver and the balance of the car, and can turn into severe oversteer if the driver backs out of the throttle in the middle of the turn. As the car exits the turn, the compression of the spring suddenly releases, causing another sudden weight transfer and a sideways lurch. The Corvette can be driven quickly, but it takes a smooth technique and a driver with quick reactions and a feeling for the timing of

steering inputs to correct for the weight transfer. The ride is smooth over good surfaces but becomes jouncy over bumps. Straight-line stability is only fair, a result of over-assisted steering, which, besides being much too sensitive, has absolutely no feel.

In 1980, the Corvette is as it has been, with a couple of minor changes that affect the car's looks and performance but not its personality. Whether the Corvette still deserves its reputation depends on what you compare it to. Its capabilities, in terms of acceleration, have been on the decline for years; so if you compare it to its previous performance, it may not look good. It is, however, still the only 2-seat sports car made by an American manufacturer, and in comparison to other machinery currently available, it is indeed stellar.

Conclusions

Despite the lack of any dramatic evolutionary progress in either the Corvette or Z28, Chevrolet has done an excellent job of maintaining the image and performance level of both cars in the face of a desperate need to improve fuel economy. They are not the snorting beasts they once were, but they are still the twin peaks in Chevrolet's mountain of high-performance tradition. The early part of the Eighties is supposed to bring a complete rebirth of both cars— new shapes, new suspensions, new engines—and we, the enthusiast faithful, wait in eager anticipation. We know they will be truly splendid machines. They'll have to be, because they have a tough act to follow.   SCg

ROAD TEST DATA

Corvette L82

GENERAL

Vehicle type	Front-engine, rear-drive, 2-pass. coupe
Base price	N.A.
Options on test car	L-82 engine, 4-speed manual trans., AM/FM stereo tape player, external T-top panel stowage rack
Price as tested	N.A.

ENGINE

Type	OHV V-8, water cooled, cast iron block & heads, 5 main bearings
Bore & stroke	4.00 x 3.48 in.
Displacement	350 cu. in.
Compression ratio	8.9:1
Fuel system	4-bbl carburetor
Recommended octane number	Unleaded
Emission control	Federal
Valve gear	Overhead valves
Horsepower (SAE net)	N.A.
Torque (SAE net)	N.A.
Power to weight ratio	N.A.

DRIVETRAIN

Transmission	4-speed manual
Final drive ratio	3.07:1

DIMENSIONS

Wheelbase	98.0 in.
Track, F/R	58.7/59.5 in.
Length	185.3 in.
Width	69.0 in.
Height	48.0 in.
Ground clearance	4.3 in.
Curb weight	3519 lb.
Weight distribution, F/R	N.A.

CAPACITIES

Fuel capacity	24 gals.
Crankcase	4.0 qts.
Cooling system	21.6 qts.
Trunk capacity	8/4 cu. ft.

SUSPENSION

Front	Independent, unequal-length A-arms, coil springs, stabilizer bar, telescopic shock absorbers
Rear	Independent, transverse leaf spring, lateral struts, control arms, telescopic shock absorbers

STEERING

Type	Recirculating ball, power assist
Turns lock-to-lock	2.9
Turning circle, curb-to-curb	37.0 ft.

BRAKES

Front	11.75-in. discs, power assist
Rear	11.75-in. discs, power assist

WHEELS AND TIRES

Wheel size	15 x 8 in.
Wheel type	Aluminum alloy
Tire make and size	Goodyear P225/70R-15B
Tire type	Steel radials
Recommended pressure, F/R	35/35 psi

ACCELERATION

0-30 mph	2.7 secs.
0-40 mph	4.1 secs.
0-50 mph	5.7 secs.
0-60 mph	8.1 secs.
0-70 mph	10.3 secs.
0-80 mph	13.7 secs.
Top speed	N.A.
Standing quarter mile	16.18 secs./85.6 mph

BRAKING

30-0 mph	43 ft.
60-0 mph	182 ft.

FUEL CONSUMPTION

EPA city	N.A.
MT 73-mile test loop	N.A.

SPEEDOMETER

Indicated	30	40	50	60
Actual mph	30	40	50	60

CAMARO Z28

BATHURST
BEAST OR
MOUNTAIN
MULE?

Some racers believe the Chevrolet's "image" car could be just the thing
for this year's Bathurst. After checking out the street version,
recalling the IROC race cars and investigating local tuning potential we
still don't know if they're on the right track!

IT WAS A NATURAL reaction to back off as I heard the "thwack-thwack-thwack" of the "Copper Chopper" overhead. Sure enough, within a couple of minutes there was a patrol car slinking past to see what was going on.

It must have been quite a disappointment for the boys in blue because absolutely nothing was "going on". We were just taking a few action photographs of Bill Patterson's Chevrolet Camaro Z 28.

That a chopper would spot the white machine with its rather lairish stripes, cruising up and down the Yarra Boulevard, proved beyond all doubt that you need a big bank balance and a steely cool nerve if you want to hang onto your licence in such a car. History has proved that Bill Patterson has those qualities!

It was the thought of similar Z 28 Camaros thundering around Mount Panorama in a few weeks time that lead us to sampling this "Last of the Pony Cars", versions of which appear to have performed very well in the International Race of Champions or IROC races held over the past couple of years in the USA.

At last count there were to be five of them running in the Hardie Ferodo 1000 on September 30th, although the usual lack of decisiveness by the Confederation of Australian Motor Sports certainly was making things difficult for those intending to be so equipped for the "Big One".

It was after CAMS and the HF organisers altered the Australian touring car regulations that the feasibility of running rare overseas cars came into focus.

The old regulations stated that such cars could only be eligible for local racing so long as there were 25 examples of the type imported into Australia. What with import quota restrictions, not to mention heavy import duties, it was really not a practical proposition for companies such as BMW or Porsche to use up a valuable import licence on a racing car. Besides, both concerns were more troubled by finding sufficient licences to meet the demands of their customers, needing race victory advertising like a hole in the head.

The new rules stated simply that, so long as an overseas car was recognised as a production tourer by the world motor sport governing body, a single race version could be brought here and be eligible. Mind you, it had to be made to comply with local rules regarding preparation and modification, but that didn't appear to be much of a problem.

Following all this, rather than a rash of Schnitzer BMWs or fancy Ford Capris, only the Chevrolet Camaro came under consideration to test the new rules. Actually, in standard form the car is not really much of a fireball. Top speed is around 190 km/h, but the standing 400 metres takes around 16 seconds — less with an inspired driver!

In the USA it costs USS$6819, which is almost USA$1000 more than the ordinary Camaro. Here is Australia though, you're going to be asked to pay around A$24,000 for one, even though you could probably buy it in the US, import it and have it converted to right hand drive for well under A$20,000!

What do you get for your money? Well there are quite a few comfort bits and pieces that wouldn't be of any great interest to someone with racing in mind. Mostly

though, its the looks that you're paying for.

There's the distinctive nose with its blacked out centre grille, and a farily deep spoiler beneath. Then at the rear there's another spoiler. Add to these features a "looks only" bonnet scoop and Z 28 striping along either side, around the hood scoop and across the rear deck.

Underneath there's the 5736cc (350) V8 engine, complete with all the American anti — emmission gear, including the under floor catalytic converter. A few hundred miles on leaded fuel soon fixed that lot up, although it doesn't add a great deal to the 129 kW of power at 4000 rpm!

As you might expect, torque is pretty good at 365 Nm from a low 2400 rpm. Standard transmission is a four speed gearbox, but Patto's car, as driven, featured the Turbo-Hydramatic three speed auto.

Chassis-wise, there's not a great deal that's different from a normal Camaro, and that hasn't changed a great deal over the

remote control exterior rear view mirrors on both sides, stereo cassette and radio, plus a neat little CB radio set-up. Oddly enough, the bucket seats don't have reclining back rests, while the rear seat space is, from my experience of Camaros in the US, for legless dwarfs only!

Also optioned onto this car is the removable roof. A pair of perspex panels can easily be removed to provide a measure of open air motoring, but still retaining the central roof strength in the event of an accident because of the "Targa" type design.

Practicality is not the real strength of any Camaro as I found during a three week touring holiday a couple of years ago. Boot space is minimal because of the bulk of the spare wheel in an already pint sized hole. Bill Patterson's car had a space saver spare however, and this helps a little. For anything more than a normal suitcase though, the occasional rear seat has to brought into use for baggage. Incredible lack of space efficiency in such a large car.

". . . We rather liked the small steering wheel, its rim moulded to simulate the cord binding that those '-Good ol' boys' down south in NASCAR territory use."

years. Front suspension is by double wishbones and coil springs, using uprated telescopic shock absorbers. At the rear there's a live axle suspended on semi eliptical leaf springs, again with a sway bar and uprated shockers.

Although disc brakes are featured up front, drums are standard on the rear. There's a whole list of performance options to chose from in this respect however, this being one of the reasons why the Camaro should be attractive as a Bathurst racer.

Patto's car has Goodyear Steelgard 7 inch wide radials fitted to Z 28 spoked alloy wheels of 15 inch diameter. Really they are very attractive wheels, and the large amount of dishing on them makes them look considerably wider than they are.

This particular model also has a full range of comfort items of the sort you'd expect for a very successful man who still retains a lot of interest in performance cars. There's air conditioning, electric window winders,

With Bill Patterson away on business, we managed to persuade his team to let us take the Camaro off for a while just to see how it felt.

Surprisingly, it was by no means a barnstorming performer, especially in automatic form, but we could well imagine that a manual might be something else again. A very low first gear saw the engine spinning up to the 5000 rpm red mark very quickly indeed. The tacho runs round to 7000 rpm, but we reckon that's a comfort to the optimist rather than the realist! Similarly, the speedometer goes to 130 mph.

At low speeds the power steering was very good indeed, and we rather liked the small steering wheel, its rim moulded to simulate the cord binding that those "Good ol' boys" down south in NASCAR territory use to bind their wheels. At higher speeds the steering was rather sensitive, but there was still good response for quick correction where necessary.

LEFT: Removable smoked perspex panels over both front seats provide comfortable open air motoring.

BELOW: US anti emmission gear fills the underhood area, hiding the 350 inch engine. BELOW LEFT: Although access to the rear seats is good, they're not too comfortable for taller people. Besides they're more than likely to be occupied by luggage!

Of course the one thing that makes a Z28 feel good is the exhaust note from those twin chrome pipes. Even at a low speed cruise they burble away beautifully, Give it a bit more gas and the note gets increasingly insistent, more or less challenging the driver to go for the lot. Certainly the engine revs out easily, despite all the emmission gear, top and second ratios appearing to be well thought out for their respective duties.

With the sort of torque available, steering at speed is more a matter of right foot than steering wheel. It's all understeer if left to its' own devices, but it does respond well to a bit of purposeful action!

Perhaps the biggest disappointment with this car, as with most cars built in the USA over the past few years, is the rapid appearance of rattles and squeaks everywhere. True some of the scuttle noises would have been a direct result of the conversion from left to right hand drive, but door mountings, and some flexing of the body sidewalls had their own noises to add to the total. It wouldn't be normal to suffer such things in a 10,000 kilometre Holden or Ford!

Still, for better or for worse, the Z28 has a fair reputation, which is certainly strong enough for local racers to consider making a Bathurst contender out of the type.

How are they going about it?

David Segal takes up the story.

Z28 RACING AUSTRALIAN STYLE

TWO MONTHS AGO the American challenge to Bathurst looked strong. At least four, and possibly five Z28 Camaros were to challenge the might of the long time victorious Toranas and Falcons.

But then came the problems. Victorian Warren Cullen decided that his Torana was too quick to abandon in favour of the American iron; fellow Victorian ace and five time Bathurst victor Bob Jane, had trouble getting his car into the country on time, deciding instead to bring it out for the 1980 season. Then Sydneysider Ron Dickson found he didn't have the time nor money to prepare his original two cars, dropping his entry down to one. It was three down, two to go.

The beginning of August and the two remaining cars for Dickson and former Australian champion Kevin Bartlett, were due to arrive. There were just two very short months before the big race, already time was against the Z28s.

But the dramas hadn't ended yet. The wharfies had a beef over something and decided a strike was called for. That left our two remaining cars sitting nicely packed on boats, in the middle of Sydney harbour. The old line about 'so near, yet so far', has never been more apt.

At the time of writing, that was the situation. Stalemate. Would the Z28s, any Z28s, get to the Mount? It was starting to look worryingly unlikely.

There was of course another factor in the saga. The old homologation problem!

The Confederation of Australian Motor Sport announced several months ago, that you were now able to race a model of which there was just one (presumably yours) in the country.

That CAMS announcement started the whole Z28 Camaro Bathurst ball rolling.

And with it came homologation problems of a different kind. The car in general was okay, but two areas were in shades of grey; engine and brakes.

GM builds several different engines in the Z28 to cope with different rules and environments. For example California gets a very smogged up 'super-clean' engine, and some mountainous states get 'high altitude' engines. The majority though, get the LM1 engine, a slightly emissioned 350 V8.

That's where the trouble began. In 1979 racers are allowed to run non-emissioned engines here, but for 1980 the rules change and emissioned engines must be used.

The locals claimed that whilst the Camaro would be at a disadvantage by running their emission engines in 1979, they would be at an advantage in 1980 with their less strangled units.

At the same time we had the potential Camaro racers telling us that they could get non-emissioned engines (from a source still undisclosed), and could therefore run them at Bathurst this year. Confused? Join the club.

CAMS, in one of its more sensible moves, finally resolved the issue by saying simply that the car must use the engine (or an identically similar unit) fitted on delivery.

Thus, predictably, none of the racers have sourced their cars from California!

That problem may have been solved, but the brake issue isn't. In the States the Z28 comes with a disc front/drum rear system. But GM has developed and claims to be making, a four wheel disc set up. In accordance with requests from Australian drivers, GM has presented four wheel disc brake homologation papers to the FIA (the world motor sport controlling body) in Paris, for their approval.

This is the fourth such time the GM has done so since 1971; on the three previous occasions, approval was not forthcoming (for a variety of reasons).

On the latest occasion (at the time of going to press), the FIA has requested more production details from the General, before saying yea or nay.

Until that is resolved, and until CAMS gets an answer one way or the other, the Z28s will have to race on the disc/drum system.

You've got to say that if anyone gets a Camaro to Bathurst after all that, they deserve some sort of award!

According to one of the two remaining Z28 entrants Ron Dickson, his AWA backed car "will be there", no matter what.

The Dickson car is being prepared by ex-Ford works team driver Fred Gibson, who originally was to drive the second Dickson car.

The Z28, as we mentioned was still on the water as we went to press, but is a brand new '79 model with the 350 V8 and Muncie four speed manual. Freddie has a long list of things to do to it, and expects it to turn a wheel for the first time on the Wednesday before the big race, maybe later if the wharfies strike lasts much longer.

Already an engine is being prepared for the car. The regulations don't allow for many mods, and Fred intends staying with known quantities wherever possible. A steel crank and rods, a special camshaft, lifters, valve springs, roller rockers and so on will be featured, the types and variations of which will depend on dyno testing results.

A Holley carb and Mallory twin point ignition wil be used, the engine wil run a 10.5:1 compression ratio, will be dry sumped and should push out in the region of 340 bhp. That's 10 bhp more than the Falcons, and 50m bhp more than the Toranas, but 100 bhp LESS than the IROC Camaros raced Stateside!

The racing Z28 will use a standard radiator for cooling, but an oil cooler will be positioned just behind it.

The gearbox will have the usual ratio changes, and will be thoroughly checked out, but will otherwise remain standard.

Z28 RACING
AMERICAN STYLE

Ride height will be lowered all round, re-rated, Selbys springs and anti-roll bars will be fitted, as will Koni double acting shock absorbers. Wheels will be composite racing items of a 10 in wide by 15 in diameter size.

The boot will house a huge 130 litre fuel tank, filled by the new dry-break fuelling system. This new system has just been introduced to touring car racing, as safeguard against spillage and possible fuel fires, and has been in use in American NASCAR racing for almost 10 years.

The Camaro tank will be filled through a trap door cut into the bootlid.

Also in the boot, sitting next to the fuel tank, will be the oil catch tank for the dry-sump system.

Touring car regs stipulate that the car's body must remain stock, as must a good portion of the interior. What they can do however, is add special racing seats, harnesses, instruments and so on to the interior. The Dickson car will use a Schiell racing seat, a six point harness, a full roll cage, a small Momo steering wheel, a full fire extinguisher system, and extra instruments for oil pressure and temperature, water temperature, and of course, engine revolutions.

That, very briefly, will complete the Z28 Camaro Bathurst car. Of course the question now is, will the two cars that are going to

run, make it? That's up to the wharfies initially, and later to the teams themselves.

The question of whether the cars will be competitive against the favoured Toranas (and the less favoured Falcons), with all those years of local racing behind them, will remain unanswered until the big day.

At least we can thank the Z28 Camaro for adding some new interest to the quick end of the field.

Ron Dickson (far left) is the only confirmed driver of the AWA Chevrolet Camaro Z 28 at Bathurst so far. The car is being built by Fred Gibson, a past Ford ace!

OVER THE YEARS, Chevrolet's Camaro has attained a surprising aura, despite its fairly humble beginnings. That Australian teams might consider it as the basis for a Bathurst car is not really too surprising under the circumstances. However, there are plenty of drawbacks.

In the old days Trans Am racing, on which the car's reputation was built, wasn't too far divorced from the sort of racing and regulations existing here. Of late though, the use of the latest Z 28 Camaros in International Race Of Champions events has resulted in them getting a long way from the production roots.

If you've ever tried driving a street car around a banked oval speedway you'd understand a few of the difficulties. Then trying to run the same car on a road course such as Riverside in California would quickly underline its drawbacks. Besides, even Roger Penske, the "proprietor" of IROC, could never persuade top pro drivers to get into street machines without full safety and dynamic preparation.

Because of all this, the fifteen or so Camaros that were regularly used in IROC events were specially built by Banjo Mathews as his North Carolina stock car production factory.

Consider the choice of either Chevrolet or Ford steering gear depending on the sort of course, and the use of a Ford truck back axles suspended on coil springs rather than the standard leaf sprung Chevrolet part!

But it starts long before all that. Firstly Mathews fits each car out with a complete tubular chassis throughout, this taking all the loads fed in by sus-

pension and transmission, while at the same time providing enough driver protection for safety in 220 km plus accidents. If you haven't noticed, there are plenty of accidents in IROC racing!

The pressed steel front suspension wishbones are thrown out the door to be replaced by steel plate lower wishbones and tubular steel upper units all complete with a heavy duty stub axle. Ford's three quarter ton truck back axle is used a great deal in all makes of stock car "down south" so it easily replaces the standard Chevrolet item, its centre section being from Hollman Moody, the drive shafts being fully floating.

These rear axles don't have quick change gear for ratios, but the Hollman Moody centre section can be changed completely to attain the correct ratio for the track.

Chevrolet truck radius rods locate the coil sprung axle and a lateral Panhard rod is added to the set-up. Norris STEEL wheels are used rather than the fancy alloy type fitted to most Z 28s, and these are 9.5 inches wide. They use Goodyear Grand National tyres.

We mentioned the fact that the steering is considerably altered on IROC Camaros. The choice of either Ford or Chevrolet depends on the track, the former's lower ratio suiting it better for oval speedways.

All four corners of these special Z 28s have weight jacking facilities so that they can be accurately set up for a wide variety of tracks.

Naturally enough, brakes are pretty important in racing, so the 11 inch ventilated discs of the standard car are replaced by 12 inch type from Hurst Airheart. Out go the standard rear drums

to be replaced by the same discs as fitted up front.

Tuning Chevrolet's 350 inch V8 engine is left to good old Traco engineering. Forged crank, connecting rods and pistons replace the standard parts; helping to raise power from a little over 180 bhp at 4000 rpm to a resounding 450 bhp at 6500 rpm. Induction is by a big Holley carb feeding through Edelbrock's famed Scorpion intake manifold. Hedman 180 degree exhaust manifold replaces the normal castings.

With all that happening inside the engine, there's a great need for extra lubrication and a good strong transmission. The former is looked after by a Weaver dry sump set-up in a specially designed anti-surge sump. The latter is the province of Schiefer whose clutch and flywheel assembly ensures that the power is transmitted through to the Borg Warner T 10X four speed manual gearbox.

There's a great deal more that goes into these weapons, but by now you must be getting the feeling that our own CAMS would be just a little put-out if such a dastardly thing ever appeared at Bathurst, even if Harry Firth might rub his hands with glee!

It achieves almost 50% cuts in acceleration times compared with the street car though, as well as a top speed, depending on gearing, approaching 250 km/h.

And by the way, the IROC car costs a little more too at almost US $30,000!

So, when you come to think about it, that might not be the way our local racers would ready a car for the Hardie Ferodo 1000!

ROAD TEST

Chevrolet Camaro Z28

A medieval warrior on the path to a rocking chair.

• The Z28, before our very eyes, has become a museum piece. The transformation required only a few years, but it is complete. Henceforth, you will find the Z28 cataloged under the heading "Warfare, Medieval." Its subheading is "Armor, Personal."

The armor is rusting in place, not yet literally, but it is surely creaking and groaning with the effort of mobilization. The reason for this progressively worsening hitch in its gait is simple: there is insufficient oil to ease its machinations. And, just as medieval jousting was phased out in the face of more modern

methods of aggression, cars like the Z28 are folding beneath the pressure of more modern methods of combining excitement and transportation. The time has come when it is only right that cars such as the Z28 should metamorphose. Eventually, we may rake and suck so much from the earth that it will collapse in on itself or perhaps erupt its cauldron innards through the gaps we continue to make in its crust. Irrational machines like Z28s have provided us with wonderful entertainment many times over, but their excesses have only served to hasten their end.

But, still, the Z28 is available. It stands on its last legs, surprisingly strong in its final battle, its fading eyes hidden behind the slits and slots and appendages of its antediluvian high-performance façade. Similar appurtenances on more up-to-date machinery tell us that the future is not without hope for good times at the wheel. On the Z28, the trim seems a sad, mailed fist, shaking forlornly at the passage of time.

You can hear the clanking of armor. It comes at full throttle and it is real. The hood is topped with a low-rise bulge that swells over the air cleaner and

90

opens to the rear. Bang the throttle fully open and then closed on the four-barrel carburetor, and two solenoid-operated horizontal doors at the back of the bulge clink-clank open and shut; a gulp of fresh air from the high-pressure area at the base of the windshield has been admitted to the 5.7-liter V-8. Its reactions to your dance on the pedals are crisp and husky. The engine feels unfettered by emissions controls even though it passes every EPA test. Its dual pipes pump exhaust through a pair of resonators tuned to win over ladies normally unimpressed by outbursts of *sturm und drang.* But for all its flat-out ferocity, the exhaust note is somehow refined and appropriate.

The V-8 is impressive in the way it manhandles its 3660-pound load. Rated at 190 horsepower and 280 pounds-feet of torque, the motor will whomp up low-speed wheelspin for effect, or reel out easy revving for high-speed imperturbability. On the tachometer, 4000 rpm corresponds almost exactly with a loping 100 miles per hour, although it is confirmable only by stopwatch and plunging fuel gauge, since the speedometer punches out for lunch at 85 mph. All this is true assuming you're dealing with a four-speed, 49-state Z28 (Californians are straitjacketed with a lackadaisical automatic transmission and a bobby-soxer 5.0-liter, two-barrel engine). The four-speed linkage is sure and light for a big gearbox, but almost superfluous considering the engine's healthy output and minimal need for shifting. For passing, the car simply

picks itself up and goes *whhoOOM!*

Essaying all this heavy breathing through the gas pedal guarantees time lost in gas lines, but getting there is sure fun! While the engine is most impressive in third and fourth gears, the chassis is impressive almost anywhere the road is smooth. But assault some bumps and the car seems to be playing footsies with a bed of hot coals. Look, it's Disco Highway! Bumps and heaves are the Z28's nemeses. For the preservation of tranquillity, they should be steered clear of. The car changes direction posthaste. Almost with too much haste. The variable-ratio power steering is so quick, it tends to snap the front end from one attitude to another.

The seats are no consolation. They are raked too far back to brace your shoulders and to balance your head properly on your spine. This is an important shortcoming because you already sit low with your legs stretched out straight, hardly the best position for leverage, and you're shrouded by the mass of the car, the length of the hood, the thickness of the rear pillars, and vertical shortness of the rear window. As a result, you may feel you're not entirely on top of what's happening outside. That's unfortunate, because the Z28 likes strong inputs dealt with a deft hand. Pussyfooting is to be avoided except in the initiation of steering movements, which call for careful calculation. Chevrolet has tried to build in some lateral support for the torso, but along the base of the seats it's simply inadequate unless you're a great big fat guy. Even

the heavy clutch effort is emphasized by the flaky seats. Chevrolet has missed the boat in a big way here. Shoot, even home-grown Mustangs can be equipped with Recaros.

In spite of these functional failures, the Z28 can be impressive once you discover its strengths and withhold its muscle flexings until the right times. The car is at its best on long, sweeping corners, although the nose gets a little light over 100 mph. Trailing-throttle oversteer never enters the picture, one of the good things to be said for front-heavy weight distribution and a live-axle rear suspension. Semi-elliptic leaves hold up the back, and coils hold up the front. Roll resistance is provided by burly anti-sway bars, 1.125-inch for the front (meaning basic understeer) and 0.625-inch for the rear. The shock absorbers are specially valved and the springs are wound of heavier wire than those in milquetoast Camaros. Alas, suspension travel remains inadequate, and the shock valving is equally disappointing. Stumble across a challenging set of whoop-de-doos and the car sets up a great leaping and bounding; really bad pavement could buck you off altogether. The brakes, too, create subjective doubts. Stopping distances are acceptably short, yet you wonder, will the binders get the job done? They require a reasonable amount of pressure, and dive has been engineered out for the most part, but there is something worrisome in their feel, and pedal heights are wrong for heel-and-toeing.

Once you force yourself to stop

COUNTERPOINT

• Try to talk about a Z28 without comparing it to a Trans Am. Can't be done, and that's this car's cross to bear (its albatross?). Especially around here. Mention Trans Am and the eyes of fully 50 percent of the staff glaze over, hands clutch spasmodically for invisible steering wheels and shifters, and internal organs start involuntarily gearing up for incredible g-loadings. What doesn't become affected, unfortunately, is that part of the brain that has to do with good taste, something in which the Trans Am isn't and never has been. That's why I like the Z28 so much. It's Ben Vereen to the T/A's Disco Danny, Chick Corea to the B-52s, Tom Wolfe to Harold Robbins. I've always thought it a shame you have to wrap yourself in all that embarrassing flash and dash to enjoy the Trans Am's mechanicals. That's why I'm more than willing to give up a *little* handling, a *little* steering response, a *little* braking to avoid such close association with all that bad taste. If a car says something about its owner, I can be very comfortable with what a Z28 says about me.

—*Mike Knepper*

The Z28 is like the fabled boy with the curl in the middle of his forehead. When it's good, it's very, very good. And when it's bad, it's horrid.

The best thing about the Z28 is the way it makes you feel. Driving this car is like taking a trip back through a time warp to the halcyon pony-car era. The Z28 still tingles with excitement. It looks sexy, makes nice rumbling noises, and goes *real good* too. It was enough to make me throw a few foot-to-the-floor speed shifts just for old times' sake.

Between such blasts into the past, you can't help but notice that the Z is really showing its age. It's egregiously overweight and embarrassingly thirsty. It's a Mexican jumping bean on rough roads. And the body creaks and groans and flexes so much it makes you glad they don't build 'em like they used to. Everything about the Z28 screams "Amurrican iron." And for that I'm really taken with it, and a little nostalgic over it. But then again, I can't wait for its replacement.

—*Rich Ceppos*

I'm sure there are a bunch of muscle-minded buyers out there licking their chops in anticipation of the arrival of 1980 Z28s down at the local Chevy deal. But haven't they heard? You can buy cars with five-speed transmissions now. Fuel injection has come down to the masses. Back seats are in. You don't have to throw away trunk space or gas mileage to get handling these days. Mail-slot hood scoops are passé, and so are Z28s. But Chevrolet is grudgingly trying to squeeze a few more off the line just to keep the name alive until a new car is ready for the 1982 model year. I, for one, am not quite that patient. My *obsolete!* alarm went off a couple years back when I noticed Chevrolet planners busily swapping paint stripes while the engineers frittered their development budgets on taller axle ratios year after year. It's true that the strategists have managed to finagle a car from the Sixties all the way into the Eighties, but how will they ever gloss over 14-mpg gas mileage? Nineteen eighty-two must seem like an eternity away to those poor souls.

—*Don Sherman*

grumping about the seats and suspension, you'll find the interior quite up to date. The no-nos in ours were limited to a partially wacko (read, nonfunctioning) set of rear-defogger wires that left bands of glass either completely cleared or completely opaque with moisture; to a teeny-tiny glove box impinged upon by the ventilation system; and to a back seat almost as teeny-tiny. Also, the interior was done up in various tones of light gray (not shown). They're fine for the sake of variety, but those tones, to a shade, were light enough to show a multitude of stains, which our upholstery and carpeting did. Easier, at least, to remedy with an order blank than the almost nonexistent trunk, for which there is no known cure.

That's mostly the end of the bad news. The dash layout is very good, although the tilt-adjustable, four-spoke, heavily corded wheel sometimes plays peekaboo with the gauges (volts, tach, speedo, and temp, all in white on slate gray, with orange needles). The ventilation, heating, and air conditioning are exceptionally good, which makes them about average for GM. The heater is quick to respond with unflagging warmth on the coldest days, and the air conditioning, given half a chance, will fairly encase your elbows in icicles. Six vents take care of air distribution. There are electric controls for windows and door locks, and a power antenna for a digital-display AM/FM-stereo, which doubles as a clock.

The windshield washer-and-wiper switch can be set for intermittent operation, but oh, for controls on a stalk instead of the dash. Likewise, the push/pull button for the headlights, which, by the way, are suitable for nothing faster than a moped on a brightly lit street.

The poor headlights, at least, are not the fault of Chevrolet. We have, however, criticized many things about the Z28 that are the fault of Chevrolet. The car's lack of efficiency is no longer excusable in the civic sense. That does not mean the Z28 isn't an absolute wingdinger to rassle with when you're feeling feisty. Run the thing over the right kinds of roads and you'll make the countryside behind you retract from your path like a slingshot. There is real value to be found in entertainment of this sort. It clears your head and keeps you from seeking a rocking chair too soon. But nowadays, there are better cars for postponing rocking chairs, and the Z28 is ready for one of its own. —*Larry Griffin*

ACCELERATION standing ¼ mile, seconds

CHEVROLET CAMARO Z28
PONTIAC FIREBIRD TURBO TRANS AM
FORD MUSTANG COBRA
DATSUN 200-SX

13 14 15 16 17 18 19 20 21

BRAKING 70-0 mph, feet

PONTIAC FIREBIRD TURBO TRANS AM
CHEVROLET CAMARO Z28
FORD MUSTANG COBRA
DATSUN 200-SX

150 160 170 180 190 200 210 220 230

FUEL ECONOMY EPA estimated mpg

DATSUN 200-SX
FORD MUSTANG COBRA
CHEVROLET CAMARO Z28
PONTIAC FIREBIRD TURBO TRANS AM

0 4 8 12 16 20 24 28 32

CURRENT BASE PRICE dollars x 1000

DATSUN 200-SX
FORD MUSTANG COBRA
CHEVROLET CAMARO Z28
PONTIAC FIREBIRD TURBO TRANS AM

1 2 3 4 5 6 7 8 9

INTERIOR SOUND LEVEL dBA

PONTIAC FIREBIRD TURBO TRANS AM
DATSUN 200-SX
CHEVROLET CAMARO Z28
FORD MUSTANG COBRA

■ 70-mph cruise
■ Full-throttle acceleration

60 65 70 75 80 85 90 95 100

CHEVROLET CAMARO Z28

Manufacturer: Chevrolet Motor Division
General Motors Corporation
30003 Van Dyke
Warren, Michigan 48090

Vehicle type: front-engine, rear-wheel-drive, 4-passenger, 2-door sedan

Price as tested: $9319

Options on test car: base Chevrolet Camaro Z28, $7189; air conditioning, $566; deluxe interior, $353; AM/FM-stereo radio, $328; aluminum wheels, $257; power windows, $143; heated rear window, $107; power door locks, $93; tilt steering wheel, $81; limited-slip differential, $68; tinted glass, $68; intermittent wipers, $41; driver's adjustable seatback, $25.

ENGINE
Type: V-8, water-cooled, cast-iron block and heads, 5 main
 bearings
Bore x stroke . . . . 4.00 x 3.48 in, 102 x 88mm
Displacement . . . . 350 cu in, 5730cc
Compression ratio 8.2:1
Carburetion . . . . 1x4-bbl Rochester Quadrajet
Valve gear . . . . . . pushrods, overhead valves, hydraulic lifters
Power (SAE net) . . . . 190 bhp @ 4200 rpm
Torque (SAE net) . . . . 280 lbs-ft @ 2400 rpm
Redline . . . . 5000 rpm

DRIVETRAIN
Transmission 4-speed
Final-drive ratio 3.08:1

Gear	Ratio	Mph/1000 rpm	Max. test speed
I	3.42	7.5	37 mph (5000 rpm)
II	2.28	11.2	56 mph (5000 rpm)
III	1.45	17.7	88 mph (5000 rpm)
IV	1.00	25.6	120 mph (4700 rpm)

DIMENSIONS AND CAPACITIES
Wheelbase . . . . 108.0 in
Track, F/R . . . . 61.6/60.3 in
Length . . . . 197.6 in
Width . . . . 74.5 in
Height . . . . 49.2 in
Curb weight . . . . 3660 lbs
Weight distribution, F/R 57.4/42.6%
Fuel capacity . . . . 21.0 gal

SUSPENSION
F: . . . . ind, unequal-length control arms, coil springs,
 anti-sway bar
R: . . . . rigid axle, semi-elliptic leaf springs, anti-sway bar

STEERING
Type . . . . recirculating ball, power-assisted
Turns lock-to-lock 2.7
Turning circle curb-to-curb . . . . 38.5 ft

BRAKES
F: . . . . 11.0-in dia vented disc
R: . . . . 9.5 x 1.9-in dia finned drum
Power assist . . . . vacuum

WHEELS AND TIRES
Wheel size . . . . 15 x 7.0 in
Tire make and size . Goodyear Polysteel Radial, 225/70R-15

INTERIOR SOUND LEVEL
Idle . . . . 57 dBA
Full-throttle acceleration . . . . 87 dBA
70-mph cruising . . . . 74 dBA
70-mph coasting . . . . 72 dBA

PERFORMANCE

Zero to	Seconds
30 mph	2.9
40 mph	4.4
50 mph	6.1
60 mph	8.5
70 mph	11.0
80 mph	14.2
90 mph	18.4
100 mph	23.1

Standing ¼-mile . . . . 16.4 sec @ 86 mph
Top speed . . . . 120 mph
Braking, 70–0 mph . . . . 196 ft
EPA estimated fuel economy . . . . 14 mpg

THE GREAT CAMARO

The Guldstrand/ Adams rivalry takes to the race track to bridge the gap between theory and fact

I hate shootouts! The trouble with them is twofold: First, most people forget the primary objective of the comparison and secondly, they cop-out on the end result. So let's set the record straight about what we had hoped to accomplish when we issued the challenge to both Dick Guldstrand and Herb Adams to pit their suspension theories and parts for F-bodies (Camaros and

Firebirds) against each other in a two-day contest to see which is better.

A little background is in order to understand the "real" nature of the challenge. Dick and Herb have been hard racers and arch rivals for a number of years. They have very different ideas on preparing suspension systems for improved street cornering. Basically, Dick has maintained that you should increase the spring rate to improve stability and remove the stock rubber bushings and replace them with polyurethane to eliminate unnecessary deflection that causes a car to be less responsive. Sway bars are used only to fine tune the chassis, not control it.

Herb, on the other hand, feels that stock rate springs and moderate shock absorber valving is a better approach and that high-

speed cornering can be controlled with larger sway bars. He claims that a more softly sprung wheel and tire can follow the road surface better, providing greater tire contact and more cornering traction. A more complete explanation of their theories appears elsewhere in this article (see pages 34 and 38).

Who is right? That remains to be seen, but the basis of the controversy is that Dick claims that Herb's car will not work as well as his own setup and Herb maintains that a more severe (riding) suspension like Dick's is unnecessary for the street and even the race track.

The schedule for the two-day evaluation was as follows: Tuesday, March 17th—skidpad comparison in Long Beach, CA; Wednesday the 18th—road course comparison at Willow Springs International Raceway, Rosamond, CA. The rules were sim-

tage to some extent. Two-thirds of this section of the course was uphill, so Dick's extra power would give him a slight edge.

Tuesday morning rolled around and we showed up at a large unoccupied parking lot in Long Beach. We had brought three cars, Herb's, Dick's and a stone stock '81 4-speed Z28 Camaro for comparison to the two modified cars. We were all pretty excited and anxious to begin. A skidpad test is nothing more than driving a car around a large circle as fast as it will go without sliding outside the circumference of the circle. The circle painted here was 200 feet in diameter. Some skidpads use larger diameter circles, but 200 feet seems to be the standard. The cornering force (in Gs) is computed by taking the elapsed time that the car takes to complete one lap and plugging it into a mathematical formula:

$$\text{G force} = \frac{122.5}{\text{lap time}^2 \text{ (in seconds)}}$$

We timed the laps of both cars with

SHOOTOUT

ple: maximum wheel width—8 inches, tires—Goodyear P255 Wingfoots with ¾ tread shaved off (tires provided by Goodyear), street-package suspension kits and, finally, streetable engines. The above rules were rather liberal, but both Dick and Herb complied to the "spirit" of the rules (see "Editorially Speaking" in this issue) and it made for a good comparison of their suspension systems.

Herb showed up with his well-worn '79 Camaro that was decked out with his Stage I & II VSE suspension equipment. The engine was a stocker except for headers (with dual catalytic converters) and some carb and ignition tuning to the stock pieces. Dick's entry was a '71 Z28 (belonging to a very understanding customer). It was outfitted with Dick's street suspension mods including 30 percent higher rate front springs, polyurethane A-frame and sway bar bushings, Bilstein shocks and Corvette front disc/TA rear disc brakes. The

engine was a very nice Traco-blueprinted, low-compression 350 that produced about 330 actual horsepower and had one of the broadest powerbands we have ever encountered. The drivelines of both cars were fairly similar with 3.08 positraction rearends and manual transmissions. Herb relied on a Muncie 4-speed and Dick's car was already equipped with a Doug Nash street 5-speed.

Going in, it seemed like Guldstrand had a slight advantage with the stronger engine, closer ratio transmission and superior brakes. But our individual tests were designed to play down the horsepower differential and in the end they did just that. For instance, the skidpad requires only about a 45-mph steady cruise so hp would be no advantage, and at Willow Springs we timed the cars through the first six turns (from the end of the front straight to the beginning of the back straight), which limited any straight-away speed advan-

ordinary stopwatches, and with a 200-foot circle you can be very accurate.

The driving technique is very easy. You just straddle the line and slowly accelerate to the maximum speed that you can hold the car on the circle. If you go too fast, the car will usually push the front end out, wide of the circle (understeer), or the back end will try to slide around—a condition normally called oversteer. In either case, slightly lift off of the throttle, get back on line and try to accelerate to the point just before the car starts sliding off.

Herb took me out on the skidpad first in the stock Z28. The object was to show me the driving technique and also to blow the loose sand and gravel off the parking lot. With the tires at stock inflation levels, Herb recorded a 13.06. Then Dick took over and wheeled the stock Z28 to a 13.33. Finally it was my turn and I clicked off a 13.14 while making myself car sick. It was obvious that Herb's driving technique was well honed and Dick and I needed some practice.

THE GREAT CAMARO SHOOTOUT

Herb was the first "real" competitor out with his black Cheverra. After five laps in both directions, his times averaged 12.06 with a low of 11.93 and a high of 12.29. Then Dick took to the pad with a total of seven laps for both directions (clockwise and counterclockwise) with an average of 12.68 and a low of 12.50 and a high of 12.98. Dick's Camaro was obviously understeering, with the outside front tire smoking heavily. Another factor was present. Dick, being the hard competitor he is, was just trying to drive the car too hard. To bear this out we put Herb in Dick's car and he averaged a 12.41 for five laps. I tried my hand and averaged a 12.45 for three laps.

After spinning many laps around the 200-foot circle and playing with tire pressures, we had enough information to compile the following—Herb's Cheverra, best .86 Gs; average .84 Gs. Dick's Camaro, best .79 Gs (Herb driving), average .76 Gs.

When the sun rose on Wednesday, I was already on the road for Willow Springs Raceway and our 8:00 a.m. rendezvous. The weather was perfect. Herb and HOT ROD Associate Edi-

tors Cam Benty and Marlan Davis were already there and ready to get some track time in. While waiting for Dick to arrive, we took the stock Z28 out for a few laps and Herb showed me where the correct "line" was through the corners. Then we readied the Decateur Electronics K-1 radar gun (see sidebar) in the middle of Turn 2, a large, slightly banked sweeper that would be the fastest corner we would negotiate. We didn't know for sure which would be the most effective method of evaluating the cars—to use the radar for cornering speeds or the stopwatch for elapsed time through the eight turns.

When Dick showed up we all took turns limbering up with the stock Z28. For a showroom stock car it does an excellent job of getting around the race track. It understeers quite heavily and if we had run the car completely around the course, down the fast straights and the extremely high-speed Turn 9 (over 100 mph), both

Dick and Herb said that the car would have experienced brake fade and oil starvation in that long Turn 9.

The times for the stocker were as follows: Dick—63.08, Herb—64.16 and

The most thrilling part of the shootout was, of course, the actual track test at Willow Springs Raceway. Here Herb hooks the Cheverra through Turn 3, a tight, uphill left-hander.

The skidpad was nothing more than a 200-foot-diameter circle painted in a deserted parking lot. Here Dick Guldstrand "drives" the circle. We timed him with a stopwatch, plugged the time into a formula and came up with a G-force reading.

Stock '81 Z28 with 32 psi tire pressure recorded a best of .73 Gs and an average of .72 Gs.

Herb's Cheverra had won phase I hands down. Dick and the Guldstrand crew conceded the win. Dick was unhappy with the understeer condition that his Camaro exhibited but quipped "that's what happens when you compete with an untested car." He wasn't making excuses, just stating fact. Both Dick and his crew were also doubtful that the skidpad test would have any bearing on the actual road course test the next day. Herb, on the other hand, was feeling relieved and a little more confident. He felt that there would be many similarities between the skidpad results and the road course from previous experience . . . . "If I can only test a car for a short time, I do it on the skidpad. If I can gain a full second there it will mean at least two full seconds off my lap time at the track." Only time would tell.

myself—64.10. Dick's familiarity with the Willow Springs course and his driving ability were hard to beat. The cornering speeds clocked by the radar gun averaged 75 mph and at that we were pushing it to the limit.

Then both Herb and Dick took their respective mounts out on the course for the real shootout. It was soon evident that road racing requires a car that does everything well: cornering, braking, shifting and throttle response. If any one of those factors is deficient, it doesn't matter how good the rest of the package is, the performance will suffer. Both cars were well prepared, but each had a minor problem. Dick's car was experiencing downshifting problems and Herb's rear brakes tended to lock up if they were not kept warm. Still, each driver got off more than three clean runs with no problems. Dick logged a total of 11 timed laps and Herb responded with nine laps. The best for Dick was a 58.40. Herb's best time was a 58.32, both times so close that you couldn't

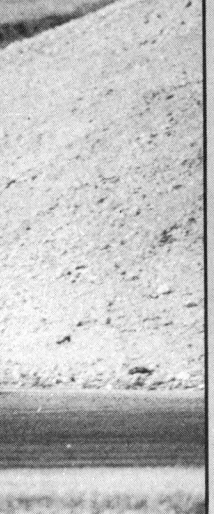

The tires used on both cars were Goodyear P255/R60-15 Wingfoots with 3/4 tread depth shaved off for racing purposes. These street tires provide amazing results, even on the race course.

Both cars were taken to Dick Guldstrand's shop in Culver City, California, and put up on the lift for inspection. It was here that we had each driver evaluate his opponent's car. Some of that information is presented in the following Guldstrand/Adams sections.

WILLOW SPRINGS RACEWAY

NUMERALS INDICATE TURNS

END TIME

START TIME

PIT AREA

call a decisive winner by the hand-held stopwatches. (Don't discount the accuracy that can be obtained with a stopwatch, however. With two people timing the same laps, the difference was never more than .1 second and usually closer to .05 second. All that it takes is practice.)

From the elapsed times it would appear that the track contest was a stalemate. To get a truer picture of what was happening, we went to the radar gun in Turn 2. On the average, Herb's Cheverra was consistently 3 mph faster in this turn at 84 mph than Dick's average 81 mph.

So who's the winner? Let's reflect on what we set out to prove. Do Herb's stock rate springing and factory rubber bushings perform as well as Dick's high rate springs and polyurethane bushings? The answer is a resounding yes. Herb's car pulled more Gs, had higher cornering speeds and identical lap times. Who can argue with that?

But there is more to handling than those criteria. Dick points out that a car should be set up to each driver's style and liking. Dick prefers a stiff, highly responsive car that understeers and can be induced into power oversteer. Herb prefers a more neutral car that can be driven to either understeer or oversteer by driver technique. These are two different schools of thought. They were put to the test and the results are here. You be the judge....

One of the most notable differences between the two Camaros was the front to rear weight distribution. Dick's Camaro weighed in with 57 percent on the front wheels, 43 percent on the rear, while Herb's recorded 53 front, 47 rear. The difference is the result of the battery being relocated to the trunk, plus the removal of the front bumper on Herb's car. This is one of the primary reasons Dick recommends higher rate front springs. Dick also feels that removing the front bumper and relocating the battery to the trunk are not suitable street modifications.

Radar Rod

You can't let the cops have all the fun, right? The new HR staff pastime is setting up radar traps on Sunset Boulevard. Favorite targets include unsuspecting LAPD motorcycle cops and a CHP sedan or two. Actually,

we procured the Decateur Electronics K-1 radar gun from Richard Hamlett of Central Police Equipment (3220 Windsor Lane, Janesville, Wisconsin 53546) to clock cornering speeds at the race track. It is an extremely valuable aid in calculating cornering speeds and straightaway speeds. In fact, it allows you to diagnose the problem areas of the race track (by relative speeds in that particular section) which cannot be determined by differences in lap time alone.

The Decateur Electronics K-1 has many features that adapt it well to many sports besides racing. It has a quick speed display time, is extremely directional (narrow beam angle), has a two-mile range and is very portable with a battery pack and carrying case. The price is approximately $1740 and should be standard equipment in any racer's arsenal of support equipment.

For more information contact Dick Hamlett at the Central Police Equipment address listed here or call (608) 754-6737.

Dick Guldstrand

> "Sway bars are not really a major part of the suspension. The sway bar is basically a tuning device to alter or improve handling characteristics such as eliminating unwanted under or oversteer."

By Marlan Davis

Dick Guldstrand has been actively involved in auto racing since 1947, when he drove a sprint car to victory while still in high school. Since then, he has driven on nearly every major race course in the world. Dick's many racing accomplishments include the first-ever Camaro Trans-Am series win and victory at the 24 Hours of Daytona driving a GT class Corvette. Today he continues to assist Chevrolet Engineering in developing the next generation Corvette, as well as serving as a consultant to four other major companies. Through all this, he still manages to find the time to personally work on customers' cars in his shop at 11924 W. Jefferson Blvd., Culver City, CA 90230, 213/391-7108.

Dick Guldstrand's handling philosophy is simple and direct: "If a car will do what you want it to do, when you want it to, the car is handling well. And that means going around a corner, or stopping, or being under control during all adverse conditions. The minute the car does something other than what you want, it is an ill-handling car. A race car is the most responsive thing you can possibly drive," but unfortunately "a race suspension is so positive you probably couldn't hiccup without changing direction. And I think that requires too much concentration and control for

the average person. Consequently, we have to isolate the driver from the absolutes."

On the other hand, a street car has too many rubber parts that eliminate response and most road feel, consequently letting the suspension move around. As a compromise, Guldstrand has developed polyurethane and nylon parts "that will allow you to do probably 75 percent of what the metal will do." And unlike race-only parts, such as metal bushings and heim-jointed strut rods, "which wouldn't last long enough to go from here to New York" and "would probably jar your teeth out," polyurethane and nylon parts will last about as long as the stock rubber pieces without being unduly harsh.

Getting down to specifics, every car—from an Impala to a Z28—comes out of Detroit with varying amounts of understeer. That's not to fault Detroit, which is only building what 90 percent of the customers want—"A cushy, soft, easy riding car that is totally unresponsive. There are very, very few people in the United States who can really drive a car well, or are even interested enough in the vehicle to drive it properly, so you must make the car totally forgiving, or you're going to hurt a lot of people."

The other 10 percent are the market Guldstrand caters to. How he "rights" Detroit's "wrongs" is influenced by his theory on the way a suspension works. According to Dick, the most important handling component is "undoubtedly the tires." Modern high-performance rubber repre-

sents "the biggest single suspension development that has occurred in the last 20 years." The best of the new breed is Goodyear's Wingfoot, which to Dick feels even "better than a P7 Pirelli. They're better in the wet, they last longer, they're a third of the price." Race tires are to be avoided. "There is very little rubber on a race tire and if you run over any little ob-

struction or anything, chances are that it'll blow out. A race tire has to run at a temperature of over 150 degrees to work"—a temperature seldom reached in street driving.

The tires must be mounted on the proper size and offset wheel. Suspension and brake clearance dictate the amount of offset required. Ideally, the offset should be kept at 0 or ½ inch positive at most. "You don't want to push the tire out from under the wheelwell; it'll destroy wheel bearings and ruin all kinds of suspension functions." The wheel's maximum width and diameter are determined by fender clearance, which on

Dick Guldstrand
Basic Suspension Package/Kit Price

Bilstein Shocks	220.00
Front Upper and Lower Control Arm Bushing Kit	90.00
Rear Spring Eye Bushings	45.00
Sway Bar Bushings and Links	30.00
Front Slalom Springs	90.00
Heavy-Duty Idler	35.00
Rear Leaf Spring Lowering Kit	65.00

Options On Test Car — $575.00

Modified Front Spindles (for Vette brakes)	380.00
Mecca Accusump	230.00
Corvette Front Rotors (used)	70.00
Corvette Front Calipers (used)	100.00
Trans Am Rear Calipers (used)	140.00
Trans Am Rear Backing Plate (new)	50.00
Trans Am Rear Rotors	250.00
Chrome Rollbar	275.00
Front Spoiler	115.00
	$1610.00

a Camaro allows for a 15x8 wheel. The wheel size in turn determines maximum tire size. With an 8-inch-wide wheel, "the tire that is required shouldn't have more than 8 or 8½ inches of tread pattern on the ground because the wheel must vertically support that tire." Putting too large a tire on too small a wheel can result in the tire coming off the wheel un-

der hard cornering. Additionally, "the wider the tire, the greater the heat buildup required" for the rubber to reach its maximum adhesion potential. Dick usually recommends the P255/R60-15 size for the Camaro.

While it's desirable to keep the rubber warm, ideally air temperature and pressure buildup inside the tire should be kept down. This is accomplished by running relatively high inflation pressures. This gives the tire better compliance, thereby resulting in less temperature and pressure buildup. For most street driving, 30 to 32 psi is the norm, with up to 40 psi being run on street tires used in competition. Front and rear tire pressures can be varied by approximately 2 to 4 pounds as a fine tuning device—more air up front tends to make the front end stick better, additional air in the rear will reduce oversteer.

Of course, the wheel and tire com-

bination must be properly aligned. Dick puts particular stress on achieving the correct caster. "You've got to look at caster as alignment torque. The more caster, the straighter the car goes and the slower it steers, so what we like is to put enough caster into the front end so that the steering wheel will return and there isn't too much caster to where it'll steer too

Polyurethane and nylon bushings firm up the suspension without the bad wear and ride characteristics of race-oriented metal bushings. They'll work up to 150 mph. Beyond that you must go to metal—but that'll be the least of your problems! Parts on shootout car included upper (1) and lower (with spacer) (2) control arm bushings, rear spring eye bushings (3), front sway bar mount bushings and brackets (4) and nylon sway bar link bushings (5).

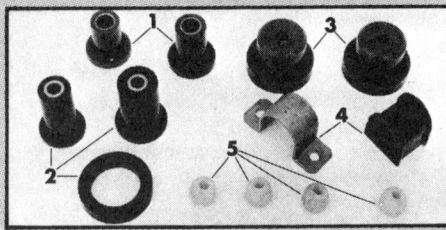

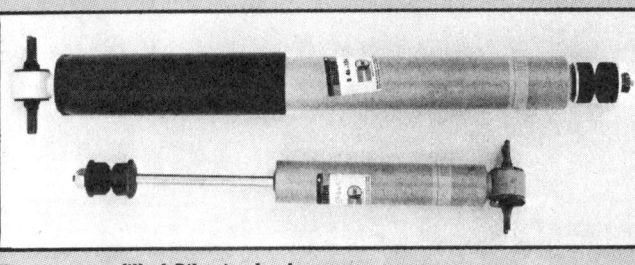

Nitrogen gas-filled Bilstein shocks are preferred for most street applications. The gas automatically lets them adjust their firmness according to the actual driving conditions encountered. The test car had Slalom valving, which is slightly firmer than the standard street shock's.

Slalom 8-coil front spring (right) is shorter than stock Camaro spring, yet its thicker coils give it a 740 lbs./in. rating, compared to stock springs' 350 lbs./in. figure.

slowly." Also, "with additional caster, turning the corner overcomes kingpin inclination, which means you keep the tire flatter on the ground." Otherwise, the tire will "turn over on the letters." In general, for GM's F-bodied cars Dick recommends 2 to 2½ degrees positive caster and 0 camber with between ⅛ to 3/16-inch toe-in.

After getting the tread in the proper relationship to the pavement, the next step is to keep "all four wheels firmly planted on the ground." That's where the suspension itself comes into play. Remembering that the biggest problem of U.S. cars is understeer, Dick's solution is to "increase the front spring rate or roll coupling (the amount of energy it takes to make the car lean over)." Roll coupling can be increased one of two ways: with springs or a combination of springs and swaybars. Dick relies on springs. "If you don't want the car

to be a go-kart and attach it directly to the frame and to the driver, you would probably want to put springs on it. That would isolate some of the shock, vibration and terror out of Mulholland Drive. Considering that the '71 Camaro (used in the shootout) has about 57 percent of its 3552-pound weight on the front nose, the biggest problem of course is going to be on the front end." To compensate, Dick installed a set of his heavy-duty slalom springs up front; the rear leaf springs were adequate and were left unchanged.

"The springs generally hold the car up, but you'll find out that it'll start bouncing up and down to where the wheels will come off the ground and you will ultimately die. So then you have to dampen that with shock absorbers, which don't hold up the car, they damp oscillations, the bouncing up and down of the vehicle."

Where then do sway bars come in? Says Dick, "They're not really a major part of the suspension. Remember we spent all this money to individually suspend all four wheels. Why on earth do you want to tie them all back together again and make it ride and handle like a Model A front end? The sway bar is basically a tuning device to alter or improve handling characteristics such as eliminating unwanted under or oversteer." They should be used to fine-tune the chassis after the spring rates are determined by what's necessary to support the car and prevent nose-dive under hard braking.

Why then the over-emphasis some people put on sway bars? "Sway bars are a real cheap, simple, straightforward fix. It takes 10 minutes to bolt a sway bar on. It takes a lot of time to design a spring and stick it on a car." Adding a sway bar is like taking a cold capsule—it relieves the symptoms, but doesn't really "cure" the patient. With a sway bar, "when you roll a car into a corner, you will be applying the weight of that particular car to the hard side of the car, and you'll be trying physically to pull the other wheel off the ground." All the load will be transferred to just two tires, which possibly could exceed their load limit and cause them to fail.

There are several additional chassis mods recommended by Dick. One is lowering the car, which improves vehicle stability and cornering ability by lowering both the center of gravity and the vehicle's rollover moment. Of course, there are limits to how low a street car can be taken down and still remain suitable to drive on the public highways; the test car used for the shootout was 1.5-inches down in the front and 1-inch in the rear,

Guldstrand

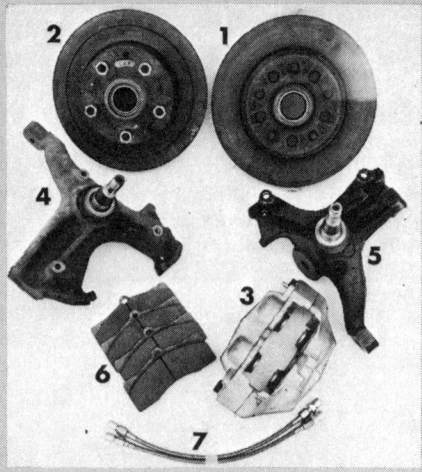

Stock Camaro front disc brakes were replaced with superior Corvette brakes. Vette rotor (1) is about 30 percent larger in area than replaced Camaro part (2), while Vette caliper assembly (3) has four pistons compared to stock unit's one. Stock Camaro spindle (4) was replaced with Guldstrand-modified part (5) to accept them. Vette brakes offer such vastly improved braking that organic pads (6) could be used. Teflon braided steel brake line (7) improves pedal feel and response.

accomplished by cutting coils from the front springs and using Dick's rear leaf spring lowering kit.

The other mod is replacement of the rubber subframe bushings by either an aluminum or polyurethane bushing to prevent unwarranted front suspension geometry changes. Aluminum bushings are considered unduly harsh for the street and subject to rapid wear. Polyurethane subframe bushings are under development and should be available by this summer. The test car ran with stock rubber subframe bushings.

The rest of the car must keep up with the suspension. For one, you've got to stop. The stock brake pads and shoes can't do the job. "If you've ever tried to stop three times on a freeway from 60 mph, you'd better do a lot of praying, because about that third stop you're going to be in trouble." To cure this brake fade, Dick sells three different pads—the inexpensive Thiocol semi-metallic pad, the more expensive Bendix semi-metallic and the full metallic pad. The latter isn't recommended for the street because of its poor cold stop characteristics. "The first stop in the morning, you've got both feet on the pedal and you're

saying your rosary." Once you've got the metallics heated up, they do "stop better than any other" and "will last five times longer than any organic pad." The stock front disc/rear drum brake system will perform satisfactorily with the stock pads in most street applications. For more severe use, the late Trans Am rear discs can be added by either swapping an entire rearend or bolting the brakes onto an earlier rear. For the ultimate in braking, high-performance Corvette calipers can be installed. They offer such an increase in brake area that you can get by with organic linings, as was the case with the test car.

The drivetrain also interacts with the suspension. A posi rearend is highly recommended for cornering consistency. Manual transmissions are preferred over automatics because "there's much more control

Stock, weak idler arm (rear) has rubber grommet under dust cover (arrow) which often wears under hard cornering loads, causing loss of steering response. Dick replaces them with Moog heavy-duty idler that includes steel grommet under dust cover and zerk fitting to lube it.

Accusump pressurized oiling system was installed to prevent oil starvation in hard corners.

Stock rear leaf springs are retained, but are dropped by Guldstrand lowering blocks and heavy-duty U-bolts. Trans Am rear disc brakes are a bolt-on swap. (Vette rear calipers aren't recommended for street use since there's no provision for emergency brake.) Note absence of rear sway bar—Dick believes that using one would induce power oversteer with a powerful motor such as the 300-hp Traco small-block used in test car.

with a manual transmission. The automatic transmission and its torque converter takes away some of the responsibility from the driver and it'll do what it wants to when it wants to do it." The test Camaro had perhaps the ultimate transmission (at least on paper): the Doug Nash 5-speed.

Once you're generating over .7-.8 G lateral adhesion, the chances are excellent that the engine oil pump is going to cavitate. All motors can benefit from a Mecca Accusump as sold by Guldstrand, Auto World, H-O Racing and others. This "poor man's dry-sump" contains a three-quart oil reserve under pressure that's instantly supplied to the engine when pressure is lost for any reason. Chevy big-blocks are 50 percent more susceptible to cavitation than the small Chevy or Pontiac, and absolutely must use this system. Over 1 G, all engines need a dry sump.

Last, but not least, there's aerodynamics. The rear spoiler may look good, but it doesn't really work until

75 mph. Much more important is the front air dam, which is effective from about 25 mph on up. Not only does the dam transfer additional cooling air to the radiator (and front brakes, if ducts are used), but by keeping air out from under the car it creates a negative pressure area, in effect "gluing" the car to the road surface.

Which is what Dick's cars do: stick like glue—on dry pavement or wet. If you have a GM F-body or Corvette, why not "spring" ahead with one of Dick Guldstrand's slalom setups? **HR**